CAKE DECORATING

1992 *Wilton* YEARBOOK

Credits

Creative Director	Richard Tracy
Editorial Director	Marie De Benedictis
Copywriters	Linda Skender
	Mary Enochs
	Marita Seiler
Production Coordinator	Mary Stahulak
Production	RNB Graphics
Senior Cake Decorator	Susan Matusiak
Cake Decorators	Mary Gavenda
	Steve Rocco
	Nancy Suffolk-Guerine
Cake Photography	Jeff Carter
Set Designer	Kim Kopp

D1319502

SO 1-DERFUL!

- 10 in. Round Pans, p. 171
- Tips 2, 3, 17, 65, 125, 129, p.134-137
- Pink, Lemon Yellow, Kelly Green Icing Colors, p. 124
- Cake Dividing Set, p. 128
- Big Bird Birthday Candle, p. 145
- Buttercream Icing, p. 93

- Using stiffened buttercream, make 60 tip 129 drop flowers with tip 3 dot centers.

- Ice 2-layer cake smooth. Using Cake Dividing Set, dot mark sides into 10ths. Connect marks with tip 17 zigzag garlands. Add tip 3 drop strings.

- Edge top with tip 17 rosette border. Edge base with tip 125 ruffle, trimmed with tip 17 rosettes. Randomly pipe dots on sides with tip 3.

- Mark message, then cover letters with tip 2 dots. Add flowers and trim with tip 65 leaves. Position candle. *Serves 24.*

GOING PLACES

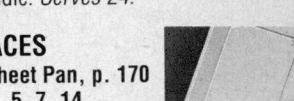

- 11x15 in. Sheet Pan, p. 170
- Tips 1, 2, 3, 5, 7, 14, p. 134-135
- Pink, Golden Yellow, Brown, Royal Blue, Sky Blue, Orange, Christmas Red, Kelly Green Icing Colors, p. 124
- '92 Pattern Book (Ground Patterns), p. 115
- Going Places Sesame Street Canister Cutter Set, p. 121
- Celebration Candles, Candleholders, p. 144
- Buttercream Icing, p. 93

- Divide cake into 3rds. With toothpick, mark Ground Patterns in sections. Ice sheet cake smooth—center white, road beige, grass green and sky areas blue.

- Print tip 3 message. Imprint Sesame Street cookie cutters. Outline with tip 1 string. Pipe in smooth details with tip 1 (flatten with finger dipped in cornstarch). Fill in remaining areas with tip 14 stars.

- Pipe tip 7 zigzag clouds. Add tip 14 star flowers and tip 2 pull-out string clumps of grass. Pipe bead borders—tip 5 on top, tip 7 at base. *Serves 20.*

BIG BANNER DAY!

- Big Bird With Banner, p. 185
- Tips 3, 4, 21, p. 134-135
- Golden Yellow, Lemon Yellow*, Royal Blue, Pink, Orange, Brown Icing Colors, p. 124
- Buttercream Icing, p. 93

* Mix Golden and Lemon Yellow together for shade shown.

- Ice sides and banner area smooth. Outline Big Bird and banner with tip 4 strings. Pipe in eyes and beak with tip 4; inside of mouth and stripes on hat with tip 3 (smooth with finger dipped in cornstarch). Add tip 3 dot pupils and eyelids.

- Cover Big Bird with tip 21 stars. Pipe tip 21 pull-out star pompon. Print tip 3 message. Trim background area and sides with tip 3 dots. Edge base with tip 21 shell border. *Serves 12.*

Favorite friends from Sesame Street are always the life of the party!

Happy Birthday Kelly

BIRTHDAYS!

Make a memory with a special first year cake!

Happy 1 Birthday JODY

BABY TALK BEAR

- Santa Bear Pan, p.186
- Tips 2, 3, 7, 16, p. 134-135
- Creamy Peach, Royal Blue, Lemon Yellow Icing Colors, p. 124
- Heart Cookie Cutter Set, p. 121
- Buttercream Icing, p. 93
- Roll-out Cookie Dough Recipe, p. 105
- Party Hat

- Cut hearts out of cookie dough. Bake and cool.
- Ice sides and background area on top peach; present yellow. Outline bear and present with tip 3 strings. Pipe in eyes, inside of ears, nose and mouth with tip 3 (flatten with finger dipped in cornstarch).
- Cover bear and bow with tip 16 stars. Print tip 2 message and tip 7 number. Add tip 2 outline eyelashes.
- Edge base with tip 16 zigzag puff border and outline with tip 3. Arrange cookies and position hat. *Serves 12.*

PONY RIDE

- Carousel Horse Pan, p.180
- Tips 3, 11, 16, 20, 46, 225, 349, p. 134-137
- Creamy Peach, Royal Blue, Lemon Yellow Icing Colors, p. 124
- Buttercream Icing, p. 93
- Multi-color candy sprinkles, 1½ in. diameter round cookie

- With stiffened buttercream, make 40 tip 225 drop flowers with tip 3 dot centers. Ice cookie smooth. Pipe tip 3 dot eyes and cheeks; outline mouth.
- Ice sides and background areas on cake top smooth. Outline horse with tip 3 strings. Pipe in eye and nostril (smooth with cornstarch).
- Cover horse's face, body, legs and carousel pole with tip 16 stars. Pipe tip 16 shell bridle and collar. Cover blanket with tip 46 basketweave. Edge with tip 16 C-motion borders.
- Pipe in mane, tail and hooves with tip 11 shell-motion (overpipe to add dimension). Pat with candy sprinkles. Position cookie face. Add tip 16 rosette curls and tip 3 dot fingers. Print tip 3 name.
- Edge base with tip 20 C-motion border. Position flowers and trim with tip 349 leaves. *Serves 12.*

TALENTED TRIO

- Heart Mini-Tier Set, p. 189
- Tips 2, 16, 31, p. 134-136
- Pink, Lemon Yellow, Royal Blue Icing Colors, p. 124
- Comical Clowns and Alphabet Cookie Cutter Sets, p.120-121
- Celebration Candles, p.144
- Cake Boards, Fanci-Foil Wrap, p.132-133
- Lollipop Sticks, p.118
- Meringue Powder, p.125
- Roll-out Cookie Dough Recipe, p.105
- Buttercream, Royal Icings, p. 93

- Tint cookie dough pink with icing color. Roll out dough, then cut clowns and desired letters. Bake and cool. Using royal icing, outline and pipe in details on clowns and letters with tip 2 strings. When dry, attach lollipop sticks to backs with icing.
- Position 1-layer smaller cakes on cake boards cut to fit and separator plates, largest tier on foil-covered cake board. Ice cakes smooth.
- Cover sides with tip 31 rows of stars (alternate colors). Overpipe pink stars with tip 16 blue stars.
- Pipe tip 16 outline candleholder rings on top tier. Assemble tiers on pillars. Push in candles and cookies. *Serves 12.*

SITTING PRETTY

- Wonder Mold Pan, p. 178
- Tips 2, 2B, 5, 13, 101s, 127, 364, p. 134-139
- Teal Blue, Black, Pink, Violet, Sky Blue, Watermelon, Icing Colors, p. 124
- '92 Pattern Book (Mermaid Pattern), p. 115
- Freckle-Face Doll Pick, p. 141
- Decorating Comb, p. 128
- Piping Gel, Meringue Powder, p. 125
- Celebration Candles, p. 144
- Buttercream, Royal Icings, p. 93

- Using royal icing, make one tip 13 drop flower with tip 2 dot center. Make approximately 10 spatula-striped shells with tip 364, 8 spiral-motion conch shells with tip 13, 5 starfish with tip 13 pull-out stars. Figure pipe 2 to 3 crabs with tips 2 and 5 (see pg. 104). Let dry.
- Generously ice cake, heavier around base where candles will go. Smooth message area, pat and swirl remaining area for a rough textured look.
- With toothpick, mark Mermaid Pattern. Figure pipe tail with tip 2B (see pg. 104).
- On doll pick, pipe tip 364 upright shells and tip 13 star top. Push into tail. Pipe tip 127 ruffle fins. Cover tail with rows of tip 101s ruffles.
- Print tip 2 message on rock. Pipe a band of tinted piping gel around base with tip 2B. Add white icing highlights with tip 2. Swirl and blend icing and piping gel with Decorating Comb.
- Attach flower to hair with a dot of icing. Position sea creatures randomly on rock and in water. Push in candles. *Serves 12.*

ALL HEART

- 9 in. Heart Pans, p. 189
- Tips 3, 16, 129, 224, 225, 352, p. 134-137
- Pink, Golden Yellow, Leaf Green Icing Colors, p. 124
- Darling Dolls Candle Set, p. 145
- Meringue Powder, p. 125
- Buttercream, Royal Icings, p. 93

- Using royal icing make 60 tip 224 and 40 each tips 129 and 225 drop flowers with tip 3 dot centers. Let dry.
- Ice 2-layer cake smooth. Edge base with tip 16 shell border. With toothpick, 1 1/2 in. up from base, mark 2 in. intervals. Connect marks with tip 16 drop strings. Add another row of tip 16 drop strings approximately 1/2 in. above, alternating connecting points.
- Write tip 3 name. Add tip 224 flowers to sides and top border. Randomly position remaining flowers on cake top. Pipe tip 352 leaves. Arrange candles. *Serves 16.*

BEARTHDAY PARTY

- Mini Bears Pan, p. 178
- Tips 1, 3, 13, 48, p.134-139
- Pink, Violet, Teal Blue Icing Colors, p. 124
- Flower Nail No. 7, p.130
- Circus Balloons (6 bunches needed), p.140
- Cake Boards, Fanci-Foil Wrap, p. 132-133
- Buttercream Icing, p. 93.
- 1½ in. diameter round sandwich cookie (for "cake"), sugar cubes and tinted sugar (for gifts), gift wrap (for hat)

- Ice sides of bears smooth. Outline details with tip 3. Pipe in eyes, noses, snouts, inside of ears, tummies and paws with tip 3 (smooth with finger dipped in cornstarch).
- Cover bears with tip 13 stars. Edge bases with tip 13 shell borders.
- For birthday bear's cake: Attach cookie to flower nail with dots of icing. Ice top smooth. Cover sides with tip 48. Pipe tip 3 dot balloons. Add tip 1 balloon strings, side garlands and printed message. Pipe tip 3 bead borders. Pipe a large mound of icing on tummy of birthday bear with tip 3. Lift "cake" onto bear with a spatula. Make cone hat out of paper and position on cake.
- For party bears: Print tip 1 names. Ice sugar cubes with thinned icing. Sprinkle with tinted sugar. Pipe tip 1 string ribbons. Position gifts and push in balloons. *Each serves 1.*

MISCHIEVOUS KITTY

- Kitty Cat Pan, p. 182
- Mini Ball Pan, p. 183
- Tips 2, 4, 8, 233, p. 134
- Pink, Violet, Teal Icing Colors, p. 124
- Buttercream Icing, p. 93

- For balls of yarn: Position mini ball cakes on cake circles cut to fit. Cover with tip 4 side-by-side strings. Overpipe strings until cake is covered completely.
- Outline kitty with tip 4 strings. Pipe in eyes, nose, tongue and inside of ears with tip 8 (smooth with finger dipped in cornstarch). Add tip 4 strings to eyes (flatten with cornstarch).
- Cover with tip 233 pull-out fur. Write tip 2 message. Position cakes together. Pipe tip 4 string strand of yarn from kitty to yarn ball. *Serves 16.*

BIRTHDAYS!

Little ladies will adore these precious delights!

7

These all-time favorites signal big adventure!

BIRTHDAYS!

8

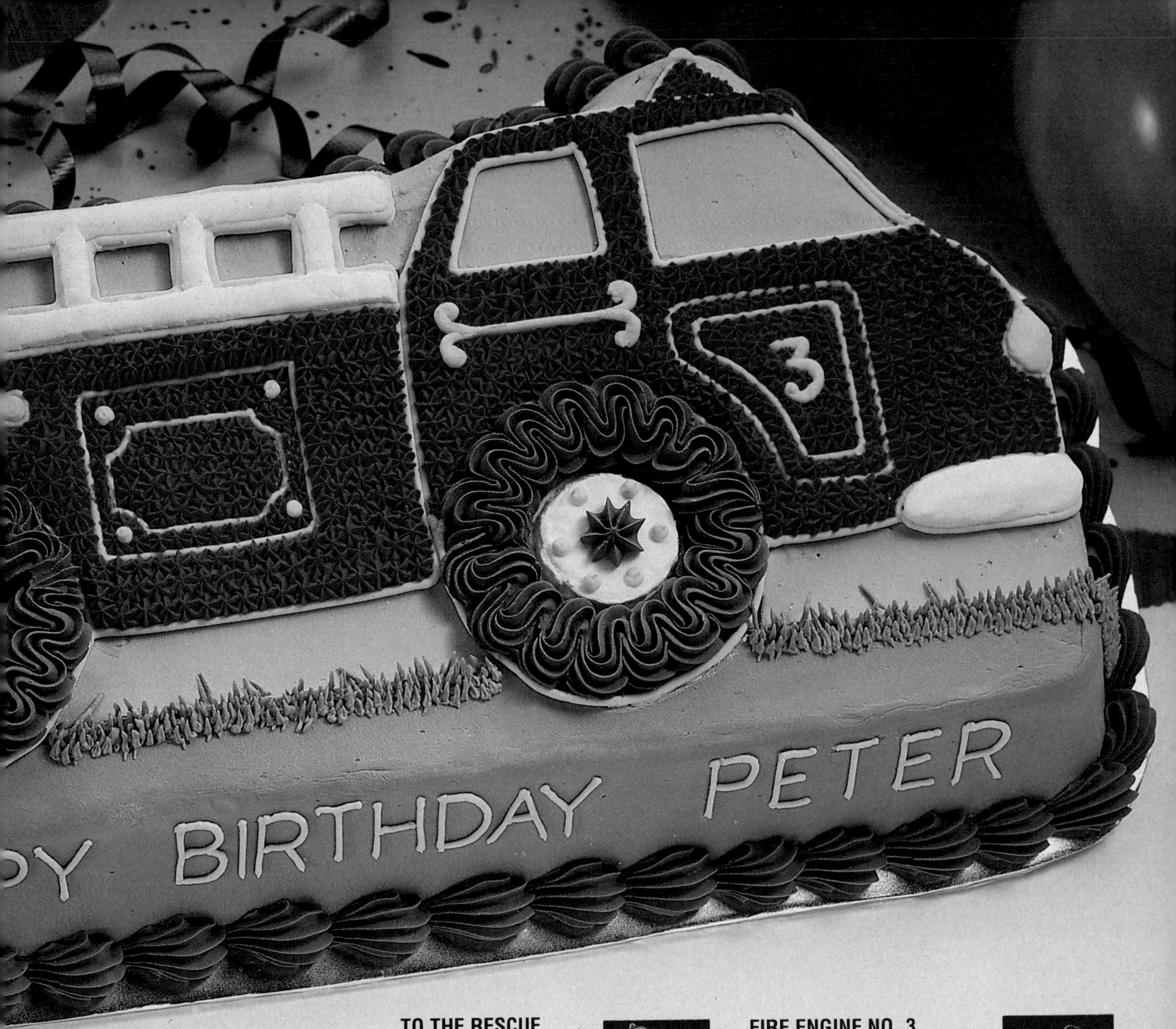

[Image: photograph of a fire engine birthday cake reading "HAPPY BIRTHDAY PETER"]

FETCHING DALMATION
- Puppy Dog Pan, p.182 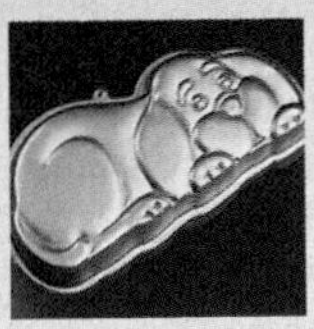
- Tips 2, 4, 7, 16, p. 134-135
- Black, Golden Yellow Icing Colors, p. 124
- '92 Pattern Book (Doggy Pattern), p. 115
- Buttercream Icing, p. 93
- Small gift package

- Ice sides and background areas on top smooth. With toothpick, mark Doggy Pattern on cake top (for easier marking, lightly ice area white).
- Outline doggie's details with tip 4 strings. Pipe in eyes, nose and mouth with tip 7 (smooth with finger dipped in cornstarch). Add tip 2 comma-motion highlights to eyes and nose.
- Cover face, ears, paws, leg, body and tail with tip 16 stars. Edge base with tip 16 star border. Position gift package. *Serves 12.*

TO THE RESCUE
- Happy Clown Pan, p.178
- Tips 3, 5, 16, 20, p. 134-135
- Wilton (No-Taste) Red, Brown, Golden Yellow, Black Icing Colors, p. 124
- '92 Pattern Book (Numbers Patterns), p. 115
- Buttercream Icing, p. 93

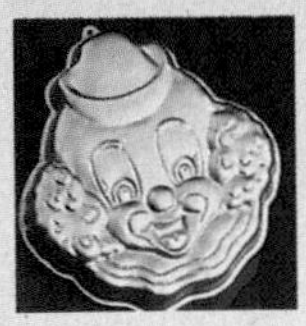

- Ice sides and background area smooth. With toothpick, mark desired Number Pattern on hat (for easier marking, lightly ice area).
- Outline hat, face and collar with tip 3 strings. Pipe in number, eyes, mouth and tongue with tip 5 (smooth with cornstarch). Add tip 3 dot highlights to eyes.
- Cover hat, face and collar with tip 16 stars. Outline eyebrows and lashes with tip 3 strings.
- Add tip 16 rosette hair. Edge base with tip 20 shell border, trimmed with tip 3 zigzags. *Serves 12.*

FIRE ENGINE NO. 3
- Little Fire Truck Pan, p.177
- Tips 3, 10, 16, 21, 233, p. 134-135
- Wilton Red, Golden Yellow, Brown, Leaf Green, Royal Blue Icing Colors, p. 124
- Message Block Letter Pattern Press Set, p.128
- Buttercream Icing, p. 93

- Ice sky areas on top and sides blue; grass area green. Outline ladder and truck with tip 3 strings. Pipe in ladder, bumpers and whitewalls with tip 10 (smooth with finger dipped in cornstarch). Pipe in headlight and hose hookups with tip 3, then outline hose cap.
- Cover body of truck with tip 16 stars. With tip 21, pipe zigzags on tires, star spokes on wheels. Trim design on side and wheels with tip 3 dots. Add tip 3 outline door handle.
- Imprint message with pattern press on side. Print tip 3 message and number. Add tip 233 pull-out blades of grass. Edge base with tip 21 shell border. *Serves 12.*

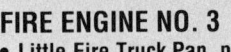

PARTY BEAR

- Huggable Bear Pan, p. 178
- Tips 3, 5, 8, 18, 21, 127, 127D, p. 134-138
- Royal Blue, Christmas Red, Brown*, Golden Yellow Icing Colors, p. 124
- Buttercream Icing, p. 93
- Party hat

*Substitute chocolate icing for brown color

- Ice sides smooth. Outline mouth and eyes with tip 5. Pipe in whites of eyes with tip 5 (flatten with finger dipped in cornstarch). Add tip 5 dots to eyes(flatten with cornstarch).
- Cover inside of ears and paws with tip 18 spirals. Cover bear with tip 18 stars. Add tip 8 ball nose (shape with cornstarch).
- Print name on hat with tip 3. Push hat onto cake. With stiffened buttercream, pipe ruffles on hat with tip 127, around neck with tip 127D. Edge ruffles with tip 5 strings. Trim with tip 3 dots.
- Add tip 18 pull-out star buttons. Edge base with tip 21 shells, trimmed with tip 5 zigzags. *Serves 12.*

JOLLY

- Happy Clown Pan, p. 178
- Tips 4, 17, 21, p. 134-135
- Christmas Red, Golden Yellow, Leaf Green, Black Icing Colors, p. 124
- Buttercream Icing, p. 93
- Decorative baking trims, candy-coated chocolates.

- Ice face smooth. Outline hat, facial features and collar with tip 4 strings.
- Pipe in mouth, tongue and nose with tip 4 (smooth with finger dripped in cornstarch).
- Cover hat and collar with tip 17 stars. Pipe tip 21 rosette hair. Sprinkle hair with baking trims. Add candy-coated chocolates to eyes. *Serves 12.*

CLOWNING AROUND

- 6 & 10 in. Round Pans, p. 171
- Tips 2, 2A, 3, 12, 13, 18, 102, p. 134-135, 138
- Leaf Green, Lemon Yellow, Royal Blue, Christmas Red Icing Colors, p. 124
- '92 Pattern Book (Tracks Pattern), p. 115
- Clown Separator Set, Circus Balloons, Derby Clowns, p. 140
- Train & Candle Set, p. 145
- Dowel Rods, p. 166
- Cake Circles, Fanci-Foil Wrap, p. 132
- Buttercream Icing, p. 93

- Prepare 2-layer cakes for pillar construction (see p. 106). With toothpick, mark Tracks Pattern on 10 in. top. Outline with tip 2 strings.
- Edge cake tops with tip 2 and 2A Bold Stripe Borders (see p. 103). Edge bases with tip 18 zigzag borders.
- Print tip 2 message. Pipe numeral with tip 12. Trim with tip 3 dots.
- Figure pipe three clowns with tip 12. Trim with tips 3 and 18. Add Derby Clown heads. See p. 104 for figure piping instructions.
- Position 6 in. on clown separator. Add train with candles on 10 in. Push in balloons. *Serves 32.*

Fun times for kids are times spent with clowns!

HAPPY BIRTHDAY MANUEL

3

BUDDING ARTIST

- Huggable Bear Pan, p.178
- Tips 1, 2A, 4, 8, 12, 233, p.134
- Lemon Yellow, Brown, Christmas Red, Royal Blue, Leaf Green Icing Colors, p.124
- '92 Pattern Book (Palette Pattern), p. 115
- Crayon Candles, p. 144
- Buttercream Icing, p.93

- Cut off one ear where beret will go. Ice inside of other ear, snout, paws and tummy smooth. Generously ice area where pallette will go to build up. With toothpick, mark Pallette Pattern. Figure pipe pallette with tip 12 (smooth with finger dipped in cornstarch). Add tip 4 paint dabs, then fluff with a spatula.

- Outline mouth with tip 4. Pipe tip 8 dot eyes, nose and tongue (smooth with cornstarch).

- Outline beret with tip 2A, then pipe in with a spiral motion (smooth with finger dipped in cornstarch). Add tip 12 pull-out "stem" on top.

  - Print tip 1 message on tummy. Cover bear with tip 233 pull-out fur. Push in candles. *Serves 12.*

BIRTHDAYS!

Light up your works of art with our crayon candles!

SCRIBBLES

- Jumbo Muffin Pan, p.174
- Tip 3, p. 134
- Jumbo Crayon Candles, p. 144
- Buttercream Icing, p.93

- Ice tops. Pipe tip 3 string designs randomly. Push in candles. *Each serves 1.*

TOT ART

- Book Pan, p.180
- Tips 5, 16, p. 134-135
- Lemon Yellow, Leaf Green, Royal Blue, Christmas Red Icing Colors, p. 124
- Decorating Comb, p. 128
- Crayon Candles, p. 144
- Buttercream Icing, p.93

- Ice cake smooth. Add ribbed effect on sides with decorating comb.

- With toothpick, mark stick figure and message. Outline hat, hair, face, mouth, arms, body and legs with tip 5 strings. Add tip 5 dot eyes, bead hands and shoes. Fill in hat with tip 5 zigzags.

- Print tip 5 message. Edge base with tip 5 bead border. Pipe tip 16 outline ring candleholders. Push in candles. *Serves 12.*

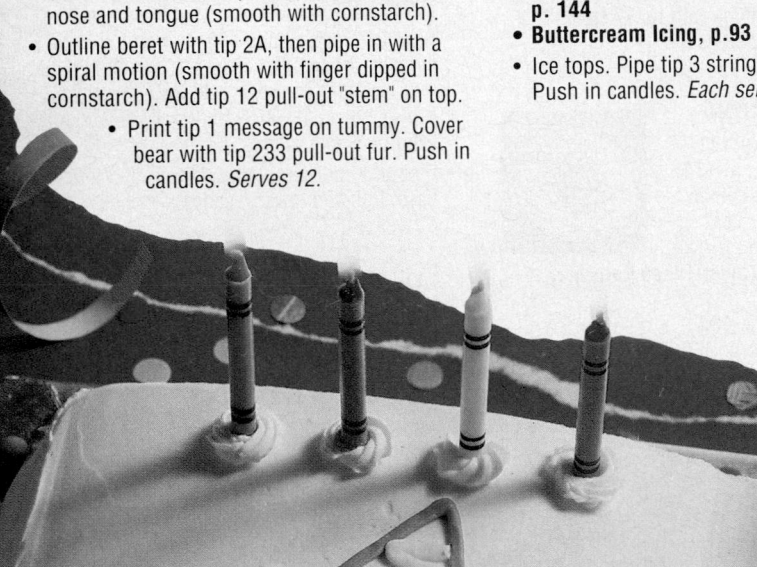

SANDCASTLES

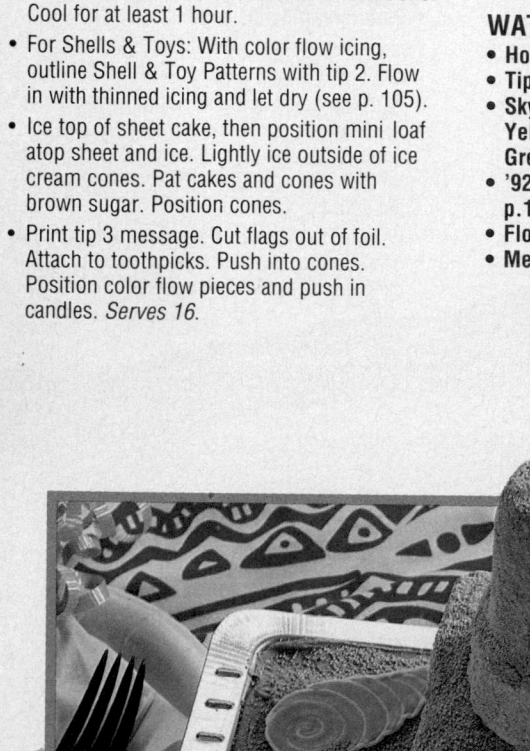

- Mini Loaf Pan, p.174
- 9 x 13" Insulated Sheet Pan, p. 173
- 8" Square Pan (optional), p. 169-173
- Tips 2, 3, p. 134
- Sky Blue, Golden Yellow, Orange Icing Colors, p. 124
- '92 Pattern Book (Shells & Toys Patterns), p.115
- Color Flow Mix, p. 125
- Fanci-Foil Wrap, p. 132
- Dowel Rods, p. 166
- Celebration Candles, p. 144
- Buttercream, Color Flow Icings, p. 93, 105
- Granulated light brown sugar, toothpicks, plain ice cream cones

- Optional: Cake batter can be baked inside ice cream cones. Fill half full of cake batter. Place upright in an 8" square pan. Bake in a 350º oven for about 20 minutes or until done. Cool for at least 1 hour.

- For Shells & Toys: With color flow icing, outline Shell & Toy Patterns with tip 2. Flow in with thinned icing and let dry (see p. 105).

- Ice top of sheet cake, then position mini loaf atop sheet and ice. Lightly ice outside of ice cream cones. Pat cakes and cones with brown sugar. Position cones.

- Print tip 3 message. Cut flags out of foil. Attach to toothpicks. Push into cones. Position color flow pieces and push in candles. *Serves 16.*

WHAT A BALL!

- Sports Ball Pan, p.183
- Tips 4, 17, p. 134-135
- Sky Blue, Golden Yellow, Orange Icing Colors, p. 124
- '92 Pattern Book (Beach Ball Patterns), p.115
- 6 or 8 in. Cake Circles, Fanci-Foil Wrap, p. 132-133
- Buttercream Icing, p. 93

- Slice curved side off one half of ball so cake sits level and secure to a foil-covered cake circle with icing. Fill and position cake halves together to form ball.

- Ice top area smooth. With toothpick, mark patterns, Top of Ball & Side Sections. (Hint: for easier marking, lightly ice sides white.)

- Outline top circle and sections with tip 4 strings. Fill in sections with tip 17 stars. Print tip 4 name. *Serves 8.*

WATER SLIDE FUN!

- Horseshoe Pans, p.182
- Tips 1, 2, 3, 7,12, p. 134
- Sky Blue, Brown, Lemon Yellow, Red-Red, Leaf Green Icing Colors, p. 124
- '92 Pattern Book (Inner Tubes Patterns), p.115
- Flower Formers, p. 130
- Meringue Powder, p. 125

- Cake Boards, Fanci-Foil Wrap, p. 132-133
- Round Cookie Cutter Set, p. 121
- Roll-Out Cookie Recipe, p. 105
- Buttercream, Royal Icings, p. 93
- Granulated brown sugar, 3" round cookies*

- For Towers: Out of cookie dough, using 3" round cutter, cut 36 cookies and bake. Cool cookies completely. *Optional timesaving idea: Buy ready-made 3" round cookies. To make handling easier, build towers on a cake circle cut to fit. Using royal icing between each, stack up cookies. Each tower is 17 cookies high. Let dry before icing. Cover towers with royal icing, pat with granulated brown sugar and let dry.

- Using royal icing, figure pipe kids with tips 1, 2, 7, and 12. See p. 104 for figure piping. Ice the inside of two larger flower formers with royal and let dry.

- Bake two horseshoes and postion together in an "s-shape." Generously ice top blue. Add a rippled effect to resemble water. Ice sides brown, then pat with granulated brown sugar. Print tip 3 message.

- Pipe bead borders—tip 7 at top, tip 12 at base. Position towers, slides and kids. *Serves 24.*

BIRTHDAYS!

Fun in the sun ideas are bound to make a big splash!

GIFTED FELINE

- Garfield® Pan, p. 184
- Tips 2, 4, 16, 17, 47, p. 134-139
- Golden Yellow, Orange, Lemon Yellow, Brown Icing Colors, p. 124
- Buttercream Icing, p. 93

- With toothpick, mark gift on cake top (for easier marking, lightly ice area). Ice area where face maker will go.

- Outline Garfield and gift with tip 4 strings. Position facemaker. Cover "stripe" markings (just on top) with tip 16 zigzags. Fill in Garfield and gift with tip 17 stars.

- Pipe tip 47 ribbed ribbon stripes and bow. Write tip 2 message. *Serves 12.*

GARFIELD CHARACTER:
©1978 United Feature Syndicate, Inc.

PRANCING ON AIR

- Precious Pony Pan, p. 179
- Tips 2, 4, 21, 224, 349, p. 134-137
- Pink, Violet, Teal Blue Icing Colors, p. 124
- Meringue Powder, p. 125
- Buttercream, Royal Icings, p. 93

- Using royal icing, make 25 tip 224 drop flowers with tip 2 dot centers. Let dry.
- Ice sides, background areas on top and inside of ear smooth. Outline pony with tip 4 strings. Pipe in tip 4 white-of-eye (smooth with finger dipped in cornstarch). Add tip 4 dot iris and pupil.
- Cover pony with tip 16 stars. Pipe in tip 4 eyelid and add dot nostril. Print tip 2 message.
- Pipe tip 21 elongated shells and reverse shells (overpipe to build dimension) on mane and tail.
- Edge base with tip 21 upright elongated zigzag border (see p.103). Position flower collar and trim with tip 349 leaves. *Serves 12.*

UPSCALED DINO

- Partysaurus Pan, p. 182
- Tips 3, 16, 21, p. 134-135
- Teal Blue, Golden Yellow, Orange Icing Colors, p. 124
- Buttercream Icing, p. 93
- Roll-up fruit snacks

- Cut scales (use pan as a guide) and message banners out of fruit snack.
- Ice sides, background areas on top smooth and eye smooth. Position scales on cake.
- Outline Partysaurus' details with tip 3 strings. Pipe tip 3 dot iris and pupil to eye (flatten with finger dipped in cornstarch). Pipe in nostril with tip 3 (flatten with cornstarch).
- Cover head, body and legs with tip 16 stars. Add tip 3 pull-out dot nails on foot.
- Write messages on banners with tip 3 and position on cake. Edge base with tip 21 star border. *Serves 12.*

HARE EXTRAORDINAIRE

- Bugs Bunny Pan, p. 184
- Tips 3, 16, 20, p. 134
- Black, Lemon Yellow, Teal Blue, Pink Icing Colors, p. 124
- Buttercream Icing, p. 93

- Ice sides and background area on cake top teal, message balloon white.
- Pipe in eyes, nose, teeth, mouth and inside of ears with tip 3 (smooth with finger dipped in cornstarch).
- Cover Bugs and tie with tip 16 stars. Add tip 16 pull-out star tuft of hair.
- Print tip 3 message. Pipe tip 3 outline eye brows and whiskers.
- Edge base with tip 20 shell border, trimmed with tip 3 zigzags. *Serves 12.*

HAPPY BIRTHDAY CHRIS!

BIRTHDAYS!

Invite a party animal to your next celebration!

FAST TRACK

- Oval Pan Set (largest size is used), p. 168
- Mini Loaf Pan, p. 174
- Race & Sport Cookie Cutter Sets, p. 120
- Tips, 1, 2, 3, 6, 7, p. 134
- Black, Orange, Christmas Red, Golden Yellow, Kelly Green Icing Colors, p. 124
- '92 Pattern Book (Oval Track Patterns), p. 115
- Decorating Comb, p. 128
- Fanci-Foil Wrap, Cake Boards, p. 132-133
- Meringue Powder, p. 125
- Lollipop Sticks, p. 118
- Snow-White Buttercream (for decorating cookies), Buttercream Icing Recipes, p. 93
- Roll-Out Cookie Dough Recipe, p. 105
- Candy-coated chocolates, candy sticks, licorice strings

- Out of cookie dough, cut 6 race cars and extras for treats. Bake and cool. Using thinned Snow-White Buttercream, outline details on cookies with tip 1. Fill in areas with tips 1, 2 and 3 (depending on size of the area). Let dry. Attach lollipop sticks to backs of cookies with icing and let dry.
- Place oval and 3 mini cakes on foil-covered boards. Ice the oval area (approximately) on oval white. Cut Oval Track Pattern out of waxed paper and center over iced area. Ice remainder of track cake top and mini cake switch boxes black. Ice sides of cakes smooth.

- Using Decorating Comb, make ridges in black icing. Outline track (1 in. from edge) and pipe wavy danger lines with tip 2 strings. Outline buttons, switch and control lever openings with tip 3. Pipe in on/off switch with tip 3 (smooth with finger dipped in cornstarch). Add tip 7 pull-out dot button (shape with cornstarch).
- Print tip 3 message, then add tip 1 string motion lines. Print component names with tip 2.
- Pipe tip 6 bead borders on tops, tip 7 at bases. Pipe tip 7 balls, then push in candy railing posts. Attach top railing to posts with dots of icing. Position mini cakes and track together. Add candies and cookies. *Serves 28.*

START YOUR ENGINE!

- Super Race Car Pan, p. 177
- Tips 3, 8, 14, 16, p. 134-135
- Black, Golden Yellow, Orange, Red-Red Icing Colors, p. 124
- Buttercream Icing, p. 93

- Ice background areas on top and sides white, road gray.
- Outline car, details, and helmet with tip 3. Pipe in windshield, hubcaps, tires, headlight and visor with tip 3 (smooth with finger dipped in cornstarch).

- Fill in body, white walls and helmet with tip 16 stars. Print tip 16 number.
- Edge road top with tip 3 bead border. Edge base with tip 8 bulb border trimmed with tips 14, then 3 zigzag borders. *Serves 12.*

EVERYTHING'S GO

- Long Loaf Pan, p. 174
- Round Cookie Cutter Set, p. 121
- Tips 2, 5, 21, p. 134-135
- Black, Christmas Red, Lemon Yellow, Leaf Green, Golden Yellow*, Orange* Icing Colors, p. 124
- Color Flow Mix, p. 125
- Gold Fanci-Foil Wrap, p. 132

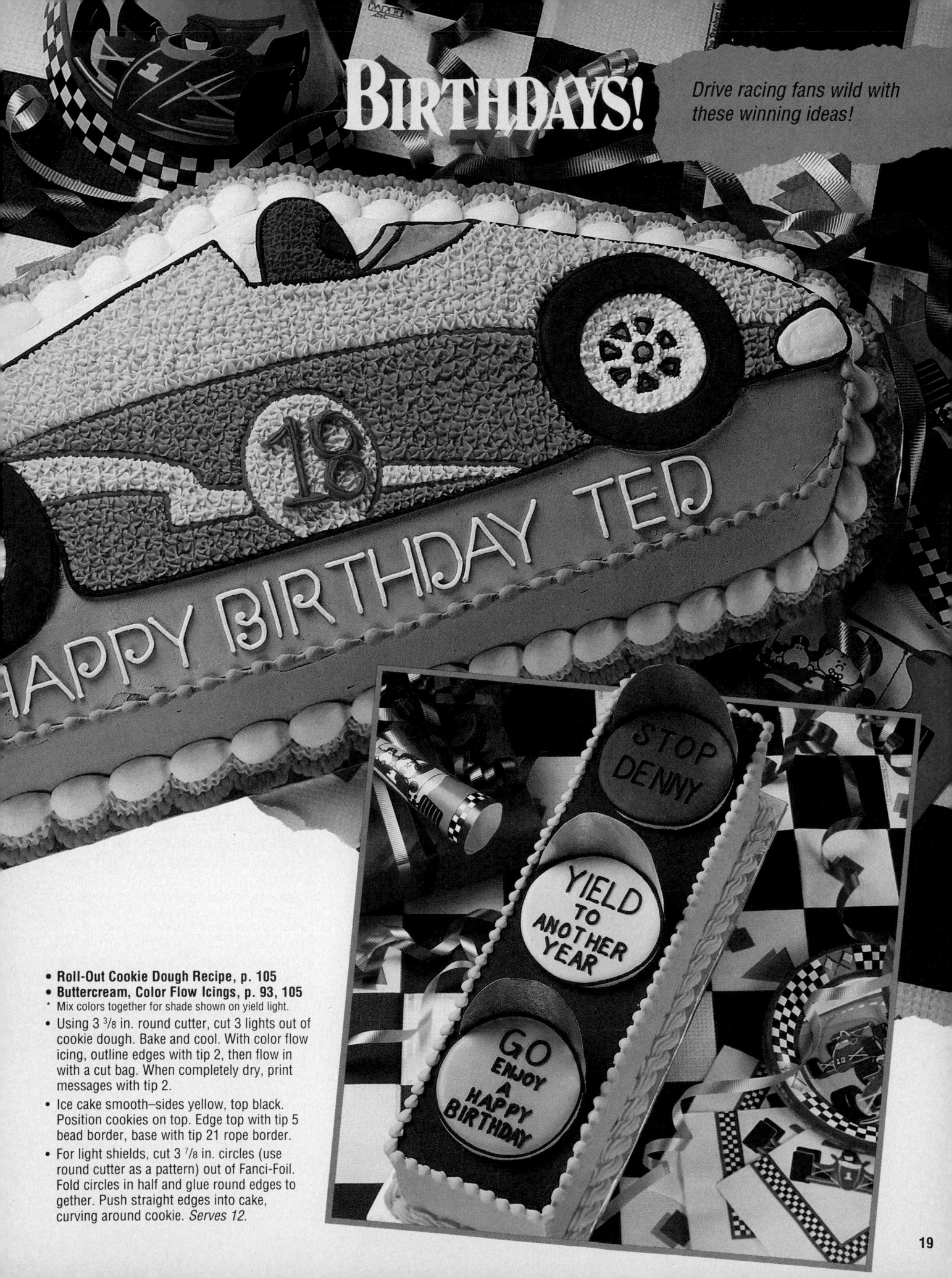

BIRTHDAYS!

Drive racing fans wild with these winning ideas!

HAPPY BIRTHDAY TED

18

STOP DENNY

YIELD TO ANOTHER YEAR

GO ENJOY A HAPPY BIRTHDAY

- **Roll-Out Cookie Dough Recipe, p. 105**
- **Buttercream, Color Flow Icings, p. 93, 105**
- * Mix colors together for shade shown on yield light.
- Using 3 ⅜ in. round cutter, cut 3 lights out of cookie dough. Bake and cool. With color flow icing, outline edges with tip 2, then flow in with a cut bag. When completely dry, print messages with tip 2.
- Ice cake smooth–sides yellow, top black. Position cookies on top. Edge top with tip 5 bead border, base with tip 21 rope border.
- For light shields, cut 3 ⅞ in. circles (use round cutter as a pattern) out of Fanci-Foil. Fold circles in half and glue round edges to gether. Push straight edges into cake, curving around cookie. *Serves 12.*

WISE GUY

- Bart Simpson Pan p. 185
- Tips 3, 5, 16, p. 134-135
- Kelly Green, Christmas Red, Golden Yellow, Black Icing Colors, p. 124
- Buttercream Icing, p.93

- Ice background area on top and sides smooth. Outline Bart and message banner with tip 3 strings. Pipe in eyes, mouth, tongue and banner with tip 5 (smooth with finger dipped in cornstarch). Add tip 3 dot eyes (flatten with cornstarch.)
- Cover Bart and shirt with tip 16 stars. Print tip 3 message. Edge background area on top with tip 16 side-by-side zigzags. Edge base with tip 16 shell border. *Serves 12.*

FAMILY SIMPSONS

- Simpson Cookie Cutters, p. 121
- Cookie Sheets, p. 173
- Tips 1, 3, 13, p. 134-135
- Golden Yellow, Black, Christmas Red, Brown, Sky Blue Icing Colors, p. 124
- Meringue Powder, p. 125
- Roll-Out Cookie Recipe, p. 105
- Snow-White Buttercream Icing, p.93

- Cut characters out of dough. Bake and cool.
- Outline details with tip 3. Pipe in eyes, teeth, beard, collar, beads, bow and pacifier with tip 3 (smooth with cornstarch).
- Cover faces, hair and outfit with tip 13 stars. Add tip 1 outline eyelashes.

WILD & CRAZY

- 10 in. Round Pans, p. 171
- Alphabet Cookie Cutter Set, p. 121
- Tips 1, 3, 14, 18, 20, p. 134-135
- Kelly Green, Royal Blue, Pink, Lemon Yellow Icing Colors, p. 124
- Simpson Family Candle Set, p. 145
- Slenders Candles, p. 144
- Buttercream Icing, p.93
- Roll-Out Cookie Recipe, p. 105

- Cut name out of cookie dough. Bake and cool.
- Ice 2-layer cake smooth. Position cookies on cake top. Outline with tip 3 and fill in with tip 14 stars. Trim with tip 3 dots. Print tip 3 message.
- Pipe shell borders—tip 18 at top, tip 20 at base. To pipe free-form string streamer, use tip 1 and each icing color. Hold bag several inches away from cake and move hand straight up and down allowing strings to fall as they may.
- Position Simpson family cookies and push in candles. *Serves 24.*

MATT GROENING

BIRTHDAYS!

Easy-to-decorate cartoon friends will make the party just right!

FEARLESS LEADER

- **Teenage Mutant Ninja Turtles®(Face) Pan, p. 185**
- **Tip 7, p. 134**
- **Kelly Green, Brown Icing Color, p. 124**
- **Candy Melts ™*—White, Red (optional), p. 118**
- **Candy Colors Kit, p. 118**
- **Buttercream Icing, p.93**

* brand confectionery coating

- Note: Bake cake first, then wash and dry pan thoroughly before molding mask.
- For Candy Mask: On the inside of pan, using a cut bag, flow in eyes with melted white Candy Melts. Allow eyes to set completely. Tint white candy with red color, or use red candy, then fill in rest of mask and tongue. Let set (see p. 108).
- Ice cake smooth. Outline mouth with tip 7, then pipe in (smooth with finger dipped in cornstarch). Edge base with tip 7 bulb border.
- Unmold candy from pan and position on cake. Pipe tip 7 dot pupils on eyes (flatten with cornstarch).

COOKIE WARRIOR

- **Teenage Mutant Ninja Turtles® Pan, p. 185**
- **Kelly Green, Brown, Red-Red, Orange Icing Colors, p. 124**
- **Decorator's Brush (optional), p. 128**
- **2 pkgs. sugar cookie dough or favorite recipe**

- Cookie dough can be tinted before baking with icing colors. Add color to dough and mix thoroughly. Or after baking and cooling cookie it can be painted. Thin icing color with a little water and paint areas with a Decorator's Brush.
- To make cookie, press dough into lightly greased pan and bake for 17 to 20 minutes or until edges begin to pull away from sides of the pan. Turn out onto a cooling rack.

VICTORY GARDEN

- 12 x 18 in. Sheet Pan, p. 170
- Tips 1, 2, 3, 10, 14, 101s, 233, 349, 352, p. 134-138
- Flower Nail No. 9, p. 130
- Black, Brown, Kelly Green, Pink, Lemon Yellow, Violet, Orange, Royal Blue, Christmas Red, Ivory Icing Colors, p. 124
- Tree Formers, p. 130
- Garden Gate, p. 161
- Dowel Rods, p. 166
- Piping Gel, Meringue Powder, p. 125
- Cake Boards, Fanci-Foil Wrap, p. 132-133
- Royal, Buttercream Icings, p. 93
- Toothpicks, paper

- The following trims are made with royal icing. Make 100 tip 14 drop flowers with tip 3 dot centers. Make 45 cabbages and 50 cauliflowers. Using flower nail for both (see rosemaking, p.100), pipe tip 3 dots then cover with tip 101s petals for cabbages; tip 349 for cauliflowers. For trees: Make several sizes on tree formers. Cover with tip 352 pull-out leaves. Allow trims to dry.
- Ice top of 1-layer sheet smooth. Using decorating comb, make garden rows. With a toothpick, mark pond and path. Pipe tip 3 dot carrots, radishes and turnips. Trim tops with tip 1 pull-out dots. Pipe tip 2 pull-out dot peppers. Add tip 2 outline vines and tip 349 leaves.
- For path: Position Garden Gate. Pipe tip 10 ball rocks (flatten with finger dipped in cornstarch). Pipe tip 3 vines on trellis, trim with tip 352 leaves. Edge pond with tip 3 ball rocks. Pipe in pond with tinted piping gel.

- Build up bushes with tip 10. Cover with tip 233 pull-out needles.
- Edge sides and trim path with tip 233 pull-out grass. Edge base with tip 10 ball rocks (shape and flatten with cornstarch). Add flowers to bushes and pond. Attach flowers to trellis with dots of icing.
- Cover dowel rod tree trunks with tip 3 side-by-side strings. Push into cake. Add tree tops.
- Cut sign out of paper. Print names and glue onto toothpick. Push into cake. *Serves 30.*

FRUIT BASKET

- 8 in. Square Pans, p. 169
- Tips 2A , 2B, 45, p. 134, 139
- Ivory Icing Color, p. 124
- '92 Pattern Book (Basket Handle Pattern), p. 115
- Meringue Powder, p. 125
- Lollipop Sticks, p. 118
- Royal, Buttercream Icings, p. 93
- Assorted fruits

- With royal icing and Handle Pattern, cover handle with tip 2A ropes. Let dry completely. Turn handle over. Attach a lollipop stick to each end, then repeat rope procedure.
- Ice 2-layer square smooth. With spatula-stripe buttercream icing, cover sides with tip 2B ribbed stripe basketweave. Pipe tip 45 smooth stripe bands around top, sides (at top) and base.
- Top with fruit. Push in handle. *Serves 16.*

POUR IT ON

- 8 in. Ring Mold Pan, p. 174
- 8 in. Round Pans, p. 173
- Tips 3, 5, 8, p. 134
- '92 Pattern Book (Sprinkling Can Pattern), p. 115
- Tree Former (1 needed), p. 130
- Buttercream Icing, p. 93
- Posterboard, iridescent gift streamers

- Fill and ice two 8 in. rounds and one ring cake together. Push tree former into side of cake and ice smooth.
- With toothpick, mark Sprinkling Can Pattern on side. Outline flowers, leaves and vines with tip 3 strings.
- Edge top and center opening with tip 5 bead border. Edge base with tip 8 bulb border.
- Trim top and spout with tip 3 outline scroll designs. For handle: Cut a 1 in. wide x 24 in. long piece of posterboard. Push into cake. For sprinkler head: Cut out a posterboard circle 2 in. diameter. Attach to spout with icing. Add gift streamers to center and spout (attach with icing). *Serves 18.*

GREEN THUMB

- Baseball Glove Pan, p. 183
- Tips 2, 3, 5, 224, 349, p. 134-137
- Brown, Pink, Leaf Green, Icing Colors, p. 124
- Cake Boards, Fanci-Foil Wrap, p. 132-133
- Buttercream Icing, p.93

- Cut trowel and handle out of cake boards. Cover trowel with Fanci-Foil and secure with tape.
- With stiffened buttercream, make 35 tip 224 drop flowers with tip 3 dot centers.
- Ice sides and background area on top brown; glove white. Note: Make thumb size smaller. Outline glove with tip 5 strings. Print tip 2 message. Randomly cover glove with tip 2 dot design flowers.
- Edge base with tip 3 pull-out string strands of grass (overpipe to add dimension). Add drop flowers and pipe tip 349 leaves. Push trowel into cake. *Serves 12.*

BIRTHDAYS!

Cake ideas for gardeners . . .
one of America's favorite hobbies!

High-energy designs for the young-at-heart!

Happy Birthday 50

ARNOLD 50

HAPPY BIRTHDAY

FIT & FAIR
- Little Mouse Pan, p. 179
- Tips 2, 4, 5, 16, 21, 103, p. 134-135, 138
- Brown, Pink, Violet, Burgundy, Royal Blue, Copper Icing Colors*, p. 124
- '92 Pattern Book (Gymnast Pattern), p. 115
- Buttercream Icing, p.93

*Mix Pink, Violet and Burgundy colors together for pink shades shown.

- Ice background areas on top and sides smooth. With toothpick, mark Gymnast Pattern (for easier marking, lightly ice area first).
- Outline details with tip 4 strings. Pipe in eyes, mouth and socks with tip 4. Pipe in earphones with tip 5. Flatten all piped in areas with finger dipped in cornstarch. Fill in bands on leotard with tip 2 strings.
- Cover skin, leotard and tights with tip 16 stars. Add tip 16 zigzags to soles of shoes. Cover hair with tip 21 side-by-side stripes. Trim with tip 103 ribbon bows.
- Add tip 5 dot cheeks and outline earphone headband. Pipe tip 2 outline lashes, musical notes and shoe laces. Edge base with tip 21 star border. *Serves 12.*

BAR BELLS
- Sports Ball Pan Set, p. 183
- Tips 2, 8, 17, p. 134-135
- Brown* Icing Color, p. 124
- Meringue Powder, p. 125
- Decorator's Brush, p. 128
- Plastic Dowel Rods, p. 166
- Celebration Candles, p. 144
- Buttercream, Royal Icings, p. 93

*If desired, substitute chocolate for Brown color.

- Paint dowel rod with royal icing. Let dry. Prepare ball cakes as per instructions included with your pan.
- Gently push dowel rod into cakes. Cover balls with tip 17 stars.
- Write and print tip 3 messages. Add tip 8 number. Push in candles. *Serves 20.*

RIGHT ON TRACK
- 6 in. Round Pans, p. 169,171
- 4-Pc. Oval Pan Set (10 3/4 x 7 7/8 in. size used), p. 168
- Tips 3, 11, 21, 363, p. 134-135
- Pink Icing Color, p. 124
- Celebration Candles, Candleholders, p. 144-145
- Cake Boards, Fanci-Foil Wrap, p. 132-133
- Buttercream Icing, p. 93

- Stack 2-layer round on 1-layer oval so that outer edges are perpendicular. Ice top and tongue areas smooth. Lightly ice remaining areas.
- With toothpick, mark tongue, sole and detail stripes. Print tip 3 message. Build up top of tongue with tip 11 (smooth and shape with finger dipped in cornstarch).
- Outline top of shoe and stripes with tip 11 strings. Cover shoe with tip 21 stars.
- Edge tongue and sole with tip 21 zigzags. Pipe tip 11 outline laces. Add tip 11 bow. Push candles into candleholders Position in cake. *Serves 20.*

EVERY SECOND COUNTS!
- Good Time Clock Pan, p. 181
- Tips 2, 4, 11, 18, 233, p. 134-135
- Brown, Copper, Kelly Green, Icing Colors, p. 124
- Buttercream Icing, p. 93

- Ice face of clock, background areas and sides smooth. Outline button, rim of clock, hands and wrist with tip 4. Trim hands with tip 4 dot. Add tip 2 outline time lines. Write and print tip 2 message.
- With tip 11, outline fingers and pipe in wrist (shape and flatten with finger dipped in cornstarch).
- Edge base with tip 18 rope border. *Serves 12.*

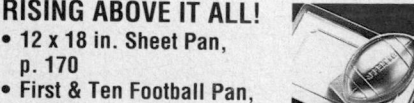

KING PIN
- **Bowling A "Strike" Pan, p. 183** 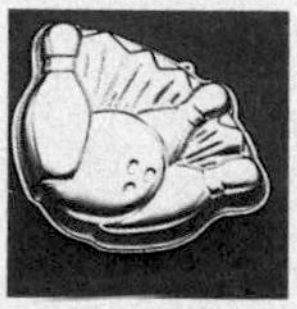
- **Tips 3, 16, 21, p. 134-135**
- **Sky Blue, Black, Christmas Red Icing Colors, p. 124**
- **Bumbling Bowler, p. 142**
- **Celebration Candles, p. 144**
- **Buttercream Icing, p. 93**
- Ice sides and small background areas on top smooth. Outline strike zone, pins and ball with tip 3. Pipe in holes with tip 3 (flatten with finger dipped in cornstarch).
- Cover pins, ball and strike zone with tip 16 stars. Print tip 3 name. Edge base with tip 21 rosette border.
- Pipe tip 16 outline candleholder rings and push in candles. Position Bumbling Bowler. *Serves 12.*

RISING ABOVE IT ALL!
- **12 x 18 in. Sheet Pan, p. 170**
- **First & Ten Football Pan, p. 183**
- **Tips 1D, 2, 3, 6, 7, p. 134,139**
- **Sky Blue, Kelly Green, Black, Golden Yellow Icing Colors, p. 124**
- **'92 Pattern Book (Blimp & Field Patterns), p. 115**

- **Super Bowl Football Set, p. 142**
- **Fanci-Foil Wrap, Cake Boards, p. 132-133**
- **Dowel Rods, p. 166**
- **Buttercream Icing, p. 93**
- **Roll-Out Cookie Recipe, p. 105**
- Using Blimp Patterns, cut cabin, wings and tail out of cookie dough. Bake and cool. Ice smooth with thinned icing. Timesaving idea: Cut pieces out of cake board. Cover with foil or icing.
- Ice blimp smooth on cake board cut to fit. With toothpick, mark Field Pattern on sheet cake. Ice sky and field areas on top and sides smooth. Cut and position dowel rods in sheet where blimp will go. Position blimp cake.
- With toothpick, mark down lines (refer to pattern). Cover marks with tip 2 strings. Push tail, cabin and wings into blimp. Pipe tip 3 outlines on nose, tail and wings. Outline windows with tip 3 and pipe in (smooth with finger dipped in cornstarch). Pipe tip ID smooth stripe message banner. Add tip 2 dot printed message. Print rest of message with tip 3.
- Pipe tip 3 (small) and tip 6 (large) zigzag puff clouds randomly on top. Edge blimp and field with tip 3 bead borders. Pipe bead borders — tip 6 around sky area, tip 7 at base.
- Push goal posts into field and position players. *Serves 42.*

VERY CATCHY
- **Double Tier Round, p. 181**
- **Tips 1, 2, 8, 18, 44, 127, p. 134-139**
- **Sky Blue, Christmas Red, Lemon Yellow, Black Icing Colors, p. 124**
- **Fanci-Foil Wrap, Cake Circles, p. 132-133**
- **Buttercream Icing, p. 93**
- Ice hat area yellow. Generously ice bottom tier blue. Swirl and pat with a spatula to resemble water.
- Build up base of hat with tip 8 band (to make brim stand away). Pipe tip 127 ruffle brim. Trim sides at top and on brim with tip 44 smooth stripes. Edge top of hat with tip 2 outline.
- Figure pipe lures using tips 1, 2 and 8 (see p. 104). Print message and add outline airholes on sides with tip 2.
- Edge base with tip 18 C-motion border. Overpipe with tip 2. *Serves 12.*

HAVE A
· GOOD YEAR'
HAPPY BIRTHDAY AL......

Happy Birthday Dad

BIRTHDAYS!

Sporty greats for your great sport!

BIRTHDAYS!

Beautiful ideas for lovely ladies!

SWEETLY SINGING

- Sports Ball Pan Set, p. 183
- 10 in. Round Pans, p. 171
- Tips 3, 5, 8, 17, 32, p. 134-135
- Pink Icing Color, p. 124
- 8 in. Round Decorator Preferred Separator Plates (2 needed), p. 167
- 7 in. Crystal-Look Pillars Set, p. 165
- Cake Circles, Fanci-Foil Wrap, p. 132-133
- Dowel Rods, p. 166
- Kissing Love Birds p. 160
- Meringue Powder, p. 124
- Buttercream, Royal Icings, p. 93
- Ribbons, silk flowers, uncooked spaghetti, craft block

- For cage bars: Coat pieces of spaghetti using royal icing and tip 8 (see p. 103). You'll need 32 bars, 7 in. long and 5 bars for door, 2 in. long. Make extras to allow for breakage. Push bars into craft block to dry.
- Ice half ball on cake circle atop separator plate. Position and ice 2-layer round on foil-covered cake circle. Dowel rod (see p. 106) and position separator plate on round.
- Cover half ball with tip 5 strings. Hint: Use center of scallop-edge on plate as a guide for vertical strings. Horizontal bar is 2 in. above base. Edge base of ball with tip 17 shell border.
- Edge top of round with tips 3 and 32 crown border (see p. 103). Pipe tip 32 reverse shells at base.

- Position Kissing Love Birds, flowers, ribbon and pillars on plate. Assemble ball dome on pillars. Attach long bars to separator plates with dots of royal icing. When dry, attach door bars.
- Outline scallop edges on plates with tip 17. Attach flower/ribbon trim to ball dome. *Serves 30.*

SWIRL WITH FLAIR

- Viennese Swirl Pan, p. 174
- Tip 17, p. 135
- Pink Icing Color, p. 124
- Crystal-Look Base*, p. 16
- 4 mm. Pearl Beading** (4 yds. needed), p. 161
- Scrolls (12 used), p. 163
- Poured Fondant, Buttercream Icings, p. 93
- Fresh flowers

* Invert and use as a vase.

- Place cake on a rack over a drip pan; cover with poured fondant icing. Let set.
- Using buttercream icing, outline swirls with tip 17. Cut 12 strands of pearls, 6 in. long. Position pearls on swirls.
- Edge base with tip 17 zigzag border. Add pearls. Position Scrolls on sides. Arrange flowers in vase (base) and position in center of cake. *Serves 12.*

**Caution: Remove pearls before cutting.

HEART'S CONTENT

- 12 in. Heart Pans, p. 189
- Tips 1, 3, 14, 17, 32, 101, 102, 104, 352, p. 134-135
- Pink, Kelly Green, Golden Yellow Icing Colors, p. 124
- Flower Nail No. 7, 1 5/8 in. Lily Nail, Pearl Stamens, p. 130
- Meringue Powder, p. 125
- Jumbo Celebration Candles, p. 144
- Cake Boards, Fanci-Foil Wrap, Tuk-N-Ruffle, p. 132-133
- Buttercream, Royal Icings, 93

- Using royal icing, make 8 petunias on lily nail (allow extras for breakage) —3 with tip 104, 5 with tip 102. Use tip 14 for centers and add stamens. Make 36 apple blossoms with tips 1 and 101.
- Ice 2-layer cake smooth. Pipe tip 3 overlapping drop strings on sides. Edge top with tip 17 shell border.
- Pipe tip 32 shell border at base. Trim with tip 14 zigzags.
- Write tip 3 message on top. Arrange flowers on top and base. Trim with tip 352 leaves. Push in candles. *Serves 32.*

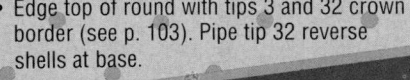

BIRTHDAYS!

Grand ways to please a special man!

TASTEFULLY TAILORED

- **10 in. Round Pans**, p. 171
- **Tips 2, 10, 12, 16, 104, 352**, p. 134-138
- **Brown, Ivory Icing Colors**, p. 124
- **Flower Nail No. 7**, p. 130
- **Cake Dividing Set**, p. 128
- **Celebration Candles**, p. 144
- **Buttercream Icing**, p. 93

- Using stiffened buttercream, make 3 two-tone roses with tips 12 and 204, 8 half roses and 10 buds with tip 104. Let set.
- Ice 2-layer cake smooth. Using Cake Dividing Set, mark sides, 2 in. above base, into 15ths. Pipe tip 10 V-scroll Bulb Border (see p. 103). Edge top with same border, alternating V-scrolls as shown.
- Edge base with tip 10 bulb border. Write tip 2 message. Overpipe capital letters with tip 2. Arrange roses on top and trim with tip 352 leaves. Pipe tip 16 rosettes, then push in candles. *Serves 24.*

30

RAILROAD WISHES

- Little Train Pan, p. 177
- Tips 2, 4, 6, 10, 11, 16, 18, p. 134-135
- Brown*, Ivory Icing Colors, p. 124
- Buttercream Icing, p. 93

* Alternate idea: substitute chocolate icing for Brown icing color.

- Ice windows, background area and sides smooth.
- Outline engine, car, windows, wheels, smoke stack, brakeshaft, headlight, cowcatcher with tip 4 strings.
- Pipe in brakeshaft and headlight with tip 10 (smooth with cornstarch).
- Cover engine and car with tip 16 stars. Cover smokestack and cowcatcher with tip 16 zigzags.
- Print tip 6 message. Add fancy line and dot details to engine and car using tip 2.
- Add e-motion smoke puff with tip 11. Pipe 3 dots on engine with tip 10, outline wheel caps with tip 2, pipe in with tip 11 (smooth with cornstarch).

GRAND "FATHER" CLOCK

- 11 X 15 in. Sheet Pans, p. 170
- Good Time Clock Pan, p. 181
- Tips 1D, 2, 4, 6, 10, 46, 79, 789, p. 134-139
- Brown, Royal Blue, Red-Red, Golden Yellow Icing Colors, p. 124
- '92 Pattern Book (Clock Background and Woodwork Lines Patterns), p. 115
- White Candy Melts™* (2 bags needed), p. 118
- 15 pc. Decorator Pattern Press Set, p. 128
- Round Cookie Cutter Set, p. 121
- Meringue Powder, p. 125
- Cake Boards, Fanci-Foil Wrap, p. 132-133
- Roll-Out Cookie Dough Recipe, p. 105
- Buttercream Icing, p. 93

- For clock face: Mold candy plaque face with melted Candy Melts™ (see p. 108). Let set. Using royal icing, outline eyes and mouth with tip 4, then pipe in (flatten with finger dipped in cornstarch). Add tip 2 dot highlights to eyes. Pipe tip 2 Roman numerals. Outline hands with tip 6. Add tip 4 dot in center of hands. Pipe tip 10 shell-motion brows and mustache. Edge base with tip 6 bead border.
- For clapper: Cut 4 in. cookie out of dough. Bake and cool. Ice smooth with thinned buttercream. Let dry. Write tip 2 message.
- For cabinet: Position sheet cakes end to end. Ice background area on top and sides white. Let icing crust for a while, then position waxed paper pattern of Clock Background on white icing. Ice rest of cake brown. To add random areas of darker brown, pipe lines with tip 4 or 6, then smooth with spatula. Draw wood grain lines randomly with a toothpick. Mark 11 x 7 in. rectangle window (for an easy way to mark, just position then remove our smaller sheet pan) and ice area dark brown.
- Mark Woodwork Lines Pattern on top of clock. Outline outer edge with tip 6, inside lines with tip 4. Overpipe tip 6 with tip 4; tip 4 with tip 2. At bottom of clock, pipe tip 789 smooth band. Add tip 1D smooth bands at top, around window and (overpipe) at bottom. Outline bands at bottom with tip 79.
- Position clock face. Using pattern press, imprint scroll designs. Cover marks with tip 4, then overpipe with tip 2. Edge all areas on top with tip 4 beads, base with tip 6.
- Position cookie clapper and pipe tip 6 bead chain. *Serves 52.*

SPRING WISHES
- 8 in. Round Pans, p. 171
- Tips 1, 3, 59⁰, 103, 124, 233, 352, p. 134-138
- Pink, Kelly Green, Creamy Peach, Violet, Lemon Yellow Icing Colors, p. 124
- Flower Nail No. 7, p. 130
- Plastic Dowel Rods, p.166
- Flower Formers, p.130
- Meringue Powder, p. 125
- 10 x 14 in. Rectangle Cake Boards, 10 in. Cake Circles, Fanci-Foil Wrap, p. 132-133
- Small Doves, p. 160
- Buttercream, Royal Icings, p. 93
- Pastel mini marshmallows

- Using royal icing, make 28 daisies using tips 3 and 103 (7 in each pastel shade). Also make 35 violets with tips 1 and 59⁰. Let dry . For roof: Cut rectangle cake board into an 8 in. square. Score in half and fold gently. Cover with tip 124 smooth stripe shingles (start at bottom and work upward). Let dry.
- Ice 2-layer cake smooth. Flatten marshmallows with a rolling pin. Place marshmallow "stones" around edge of top and on sides.
- Push dowel rod "posts" into cake. Position flowers in center of cake. Attach roof to posts with icing. Let set. Pipe tip 3 vines and tip 352 leaves on roof, posts and cake. Attach doves with dots of icing.
- Edge base with tip 233 pull-out grass. *Serves 12.*

SUMMER ROSE BASKET
- Happiness Heart Pan Set, p. 188
- Tips 3, 8, 12, 47, 104, 352, p. 134-139
- Creamy Peach, Golden Yellow, Kelly Green and Leaf Green* Icing Colors, p. 124
- Flower Nail No. 7, p.130
- Meringue Powder, p. 125
- Buttercream, Royal Icings, p. 93

*Mix greens together for shade shown.

- Using royal icing, make 18 tri-color roses with tips 12 and 104. Also with tip 104, make 15 half roses and 7 rosebuds.
- Ice 2-layer (3 in. high) cake smooth—top green, side white. Cover sides with tip 8 and tip 47 basketweave. Edge top and base with tip 8 rope borders.
- Arrange roses on top and sides. Pipe tip 3 e-motion tendrils down side. Trim roses with tip 352 leaves. *Serves 12.*

This lovely cake is also the star of our cover!

BIRTHDAYS!

Extraordinary cakes celebrate the birth date and the season!

SPRING

SUMMER

AUTUMN SPLENDOR

- Oval Pan Set (13 ¹/₂ x 9 ⁷/₈ in. size is used), p. 168
- Tips 1, 2, 5, 6, 7, 10, 69, 82, 127, p. 134-139
- Golden Yellow, Moss Green, Brown, Orange, Red-Red Icing Colors, p. 124
- Flower Nail No. 7, p. 130
- '92 Pattern Book (Leaves Patterns), p. 115
- Flower Formers, p. 130
- Meringue Powder, p. 125
- Buttercream, Royal Icings, p. 93
- Uncooked spaghetti

- Using royal icing, make 8 chrysanthemums with tip 82. Add tip 1 dot centers. With tip 69, make 3 cattail leaves, 10 green and 5 brown leaves. For mottled tone on maple leaves, combine red and orange icing, then mix slightly. Make 3 oak and 6 maple leaves—outline with tip 2 and pipe in with tip 6 Score veins with a toothpick. Let dry on flower formers. Make 3 cattails using tips 2, 6 and 10 (see p. 103). Note: To allow for breakage, be sure to make extras.

- Ice 2-layer cake smooth. Print tip 2 message on top. Pipe a band of icing with tip 5, 1-in. above base. Attach tip 127 ruffle to band. Edge top and ruffle with tip 7 bead border.

- Pipe mounds of icing for mums with tip 10. Position flowers and leaves. Push in cattails. *Serves 32.*

WINTER GALA

- Round Mini Tier Set, p. 168
- Tips 1, 3, 7, 13, 224, p. 134-137.
- Royal Blue, Violet Icing Colors, p. 124
- Flower Nail No. 7, p. 130
- Meringue Powder, p. 125
- Florist Wire, p. 130
- Cake Circles, Fanci-Foil Wrap, p. 133
- Artificial Leaves - 1 ¹/₄ in. silver, p. 159
- Pearl Beading* - 4mm. (2 yds.), 6mm. (4 yds.), p. 161
- Silver Celebration Candles, p. 144
- Buttercream, Royal Icings, p. 93

- Using royal icing, make 2 tip 13 chrysanthemums. Make 40 tip 224 drop flowers with tip 3 dot centers. Pipe approxmately 100 tip 1 dot and string snowflakes. Let dry. Attach each drop flower and snowflakes to florist wires (see p. 101).

- Prepare one-layer cakes for push-in pillar construction (see p. 106). Ice cakes smooth.

- Position rows of beads around tiers (use 6mm. at bases). Pipe tip 1 snowflakes and dots randomly on sides of cakes.

- Pipe mounds of icing in centers of cakes with tip 7 and position mums. Push in wires and arrange leaves. *Serves 12.*

*Remove pearls before cutting and serving.

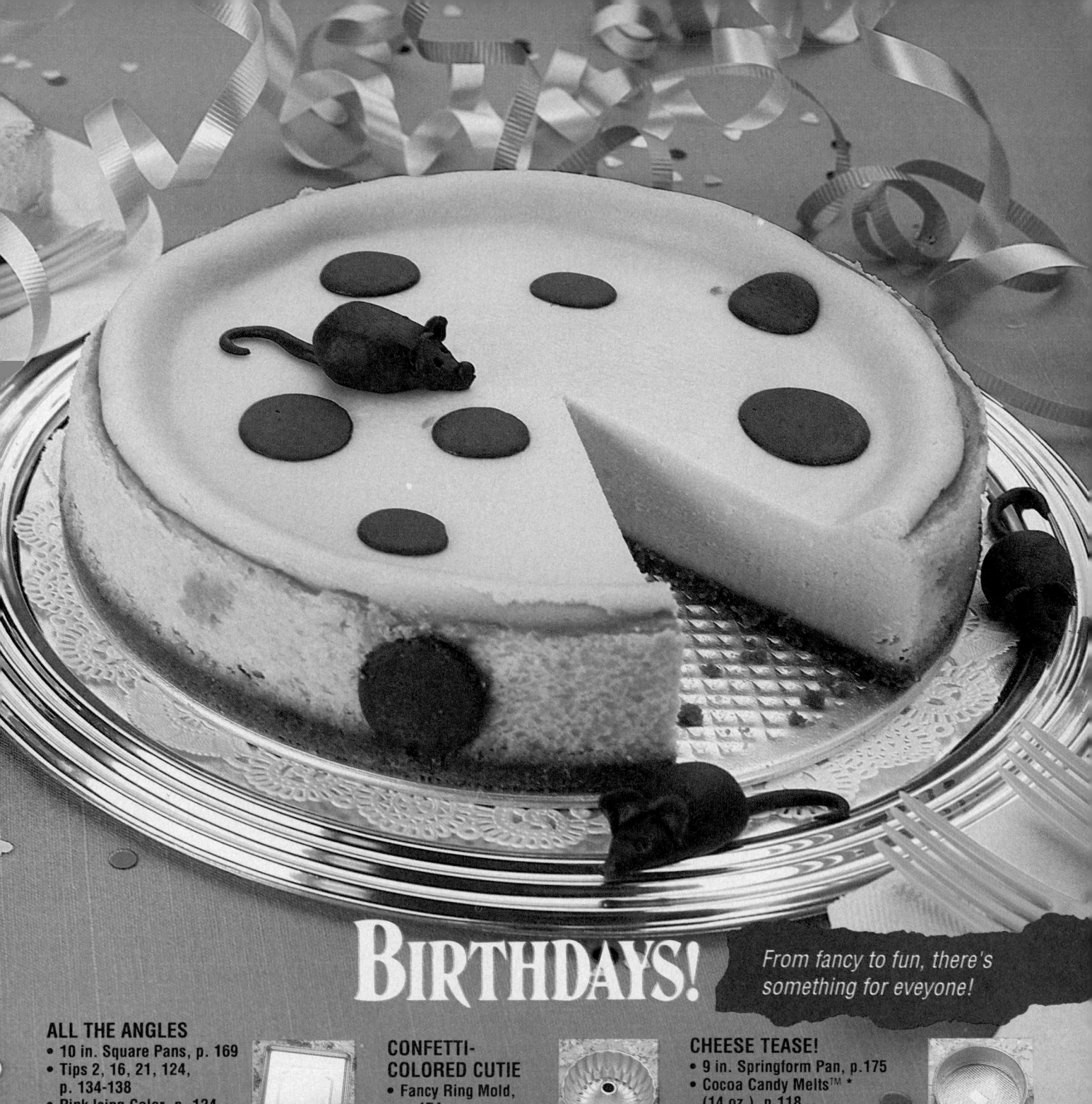

BIRTHDAYS!

From fancy to fun, there's something for eveyone!

ALL THE ANGLES
- 10 in. Square Pans, p. 169
- Tips 2, 16, 21, 124, p. 134-138
- Pink Icing Color, p. 124
- Crinkles Cookie Cutters, p. 121
- Celebration Candles, p. 144
- **Chocolate Cookie Recipe, p. 105**
- **Buttercream Icing, p. 93**

- Out of cookie dough, cut 9 cookies—1 square, 8 triangles. Cut triangles in half. Bake and cool.
- Ice 2-layer cake smooth. With toothpick, mark square area on top, 2 in. from edge. Cover square area and sides with tip 2 cornelli lace.
- Edge top with tip 124 double ruffle border. Pipe tip 16 row of shells in center of ruffles. Edge base with tip 21 rosette border.
- Position square cookie on top and triangles around sides. Print tip 2 message on square cookie. Push candles in center of tip 16 rosettes. *Serves 24.*

CONFETTI-COLORED CUTIE
- Fancy Ring Mold, p. 174
- Tips 1, 6, p. 134
- Pink, Sky Blue, Kelly Green, Lemon Yellow Icing Colors, p. 124
- Celebration Candles, p. 144
- **Confectioners Sugar Glaze Recipe, p. 93**

- Using confectioners sugar glaze made with only 2 Tbsp. milk, cover cake using tip 6 zigzag motion. Fill in any gaps immediately. Trim top with tip 1 string and dot design.
- Edge base with tip 6 scallop-motion border. Trim with tip 1 dots. Push in candles. *Serves 12.*

CHEESE TEASE!
- 9 in. Springform Pan, p.175
- Cocoa Candy Melts™ * (14 oz.), p.118
- Parchment Triangles, p.129
- **Modeling Candy Recipe, p.109**
- **Favorite (baked) cheesecake recipe**

- Before preparing modeling candy recipe, remove ½ cup Candy Melts™ from bag.
- For mice: Using modeling candy, shape cone-shaped bodies, add ball heads. Add petal-shaped ears, dot noses and string tails.
- For cheesecake: Before adding batter, place 3 or 4 Candy Melts™ around sides of pan. Melt remaining candy, then with a cut bag, pipe "holes" in various sizes on waxed paper. Let set.
- When cake is done, position piped "holes" randomly on top and sides. Cool cake per recipe directions.
- At serving time, position mice.
* brand confectionery coating

PURE ENCHANTMENT
- Gingerbread House Kit, p. 122
- Even Bake® Cookie Sheets, p.173
- Tips 1, 2, 3, 16, 349, p. 134-136
- Christmas Red, Kelly Green Icing Colors, p. 124
- Decorating Comb, p. 128
- Meringue Powder, p. 125
- Formal Railing (22 posts needed), p. 161
- Santa 'N Tree, Snowman Cake Picks, p. 143
- Appaloosa Rocking Horses, p. 140
- Cake Boards (13 x 14 in doubled), Fanci-Foil Wrap, p. 132-133
- Royal Icing, p.94
- Candy sticks, plastic wrap or acetate for windows, ribbon, electric nightlight, socket, 15 watt bulb

- Make gingerbread following recipe included with your kit. Cut pieces, using patterns for Open House Design, adding these additional pieces. For sign: Cut one triangle section using steeple pattern included with church design. Immediately after baking, make holes for ribbons. For awnings: Use scalloped eave pattern and cut one 3 scallops wide for door and two 4 scallops wide for windows. On one long wall, cut double door area using rectangular door pattern.
- Attach acetate windowpanes on the inside of the wall panels. Assemble and electrify gingerbread on foil-covered base, following instructions included with your kit.
- Ice roof, dormer, eaves and awnings, then add wavy design using decorating comb. Position dormer and edge seams with tip 3 beads.
- Use tip 3 for outlines, zigzag trims and bead borders on doorway and windows. For lights, pipe tip 2 curvy strings, then add pull-out dots.
- Cover seams of walls and roof top with tip 16 zigzags. Add candy sticks. Generously ice base. Position Formal Railings, Snowmen, Ponies, Santa 'N Tree (inside store). Pipe tip 349 leaf garlands (on chain links) and wreath. Add tip 1 dots, bows and printing.

- For sign, decorate one side with tip 1. When dry, turn over and decorate. Add ribbons and hang from candy stick.

HOLLY HORSE

- Carousel Horse Pan, p.180
- Tips 3, 7, 16, 66, p.134-136
- Kelly Green, Royal Blue, Ivory, Christmas Red Icing Colors*, p. 124
- Buttercream Icing, p.93
*Mix equal amounts of blue and green for hunter green.
- Ice background areas and sides green
- Outline horse, pole and saddle with tip 3 strings. Pipe in eye with tip 3 (smooth with finger dipped in cornstarch). Add tip 3 dots to eye and bridle.
- Cover pole, horse, bridle, collar and saddle with tip 16 stars. Use tip 16 to pipe rosettes on mane and pull-out stripes on tail.
- Edge collar and hooves with tip 16 zigzags. Trim saddle with tip 3 dots. Add tip 3 outline eyelashes. Pipe tip 66 holly leaves on mane and saddle. Trim with tip 3 dot berries.
- Pipe bead borders—tip 3 at top, tip 7 at base. *Serves 12.*

VICTORIAN VIRTUOSO
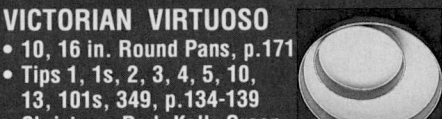
- 10, 16 in. Round Pans, p.171
- Tips 1, 1s, 2, 3, 4, 5, 10, 13, 101s, 349, p.134-139
- Christmas Red, Kelly Green, Royal Blue, Ivory, Black Icing Colors, p. 124
- '92 Pattern Book (Gazebo Pattern), p. 115
- Tree Formers, p. 130
- Meringue Powder, p. 125
- Bridesmaids (10 needed), Groomsmen (7 needed), p. 159
- Cake Circles, Fanci-Foil Wrap, p. 132-133
- Dowel Rods, p. 166
- Decorator's Brush, p. 128
- Royal, Buttercream Icings, p. 94, 93
- Paper, ribbon
- See How-To Section to make gazebo, trees and carolers. All are decorated with royal icing using tips 1, 1s, 2, 3, 4, 349.
- For tiered cake: Dowel rod and stack 2-layer 10 and 16 in. cakes (see How-To Section). With tip 1, pipe dots and snowflakes randomly on sides. Add tip 13 stars. Edge tops with tip 5 bead borders; bases with tip 10 bulb borders.
- To assemble cake, position gazebo walls. Place carolers inside, then add roof. Add remaining carolers and trees. *Serves 84.*

HOLIDAYS!

Oh, what fun it is to make an unforgettable Christmas Memory!

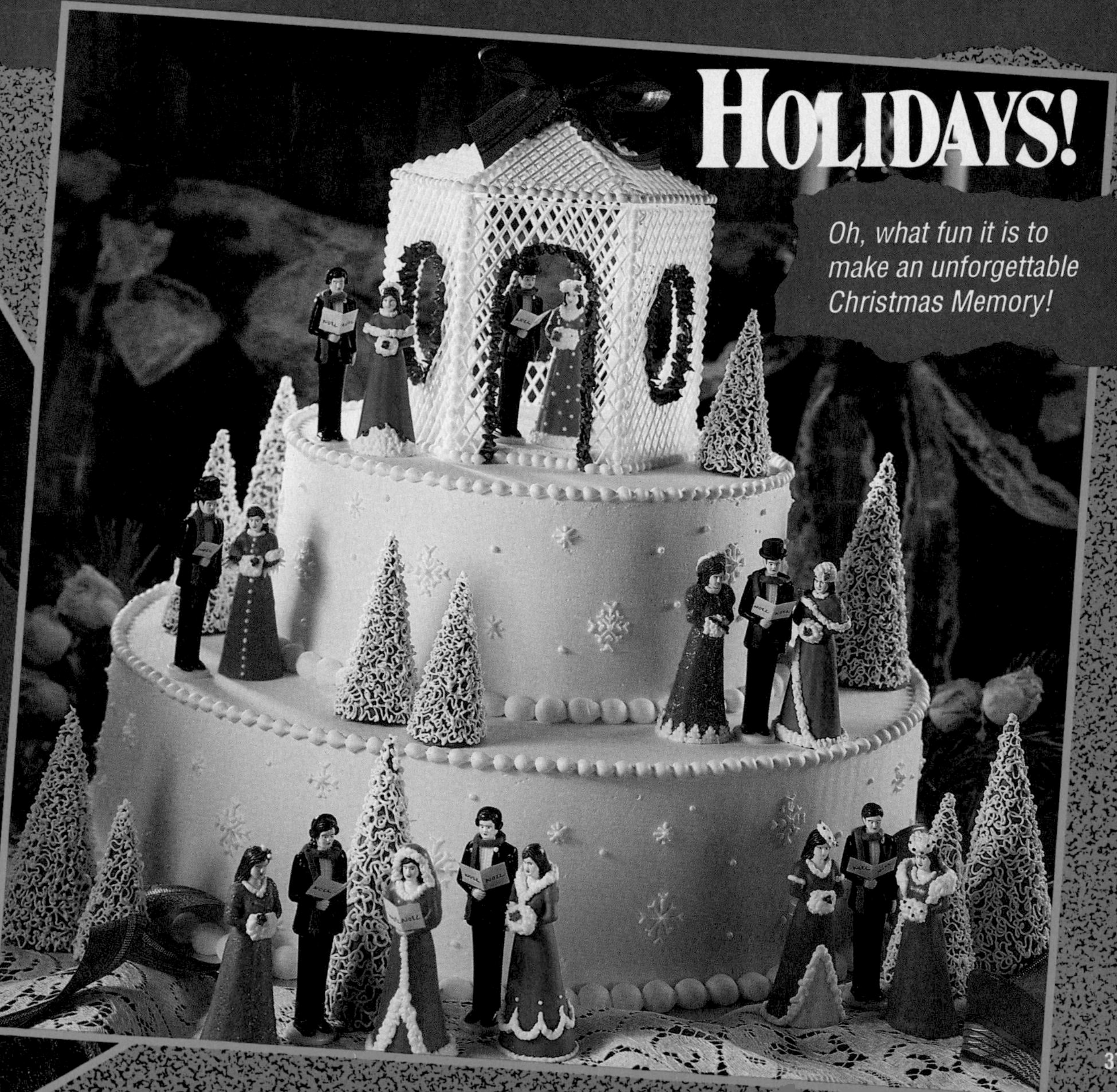

ENCHANTED FOREST

- Oval Pan Set (largest size is used), p. 168
- Tips 2, 4, 199, 301, p. 134-135
- Creamy Peach, Ivory Icing Colors, p. 124
- '92 Pattern Book (Christmas Trees and Message Banner Pattern), p. 115
- Candy Melts™*—White, p. 118
- Cake Boards, Fanci-Foil Wrap, p.132-133
- Iridescent Doves (5 needed), p.163
- Rolled Fondant Recipe (2 batches), p. 94
- Buttercream Icing, p.93
- Satin ribbon - 3 yds. of each — ⅛,½,¾ in. wide ribbons and 3 in. wide lace, pearl-head straight pins

*brand confectionery coating

- Attach lace to foil-covered cake board with dots of icing. Make 3 accents for top combining lace and ribbons.**

- Using Christmas Tree Pattern, and melted candy, make 3 trees. For each, make 1 whole and 2 half tree panels. Using flow-in candy method (see p. 109), outline trees with tip 2, then flow in. Let panels set completely. With melted candy, attach panels together then attach doves.

- Lightly ice 2-layer cake with buttercream icing, then cover with rolled fondant. With a pin, mark Message Banner Pattern on top. Outline with tip 4. Print tip 301 message. Edge base with tip 199 shell border. Position trees and attach doves with dots of icing. Anchor lacy accents to top, ribbons and bow to side with pins. *Serves 44.*

**Remove when serving

ANGEL WREATH

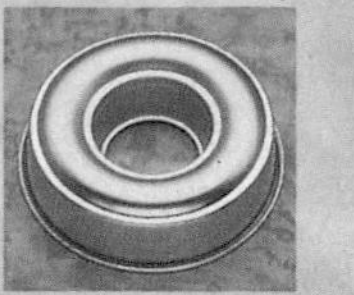

- 10 in. Ring Pan, p. 174
- Tips 3, 69, 104, p. 134-138
- Ivory, Creamy Peach Icing Colors, p. 124
- Angel Duet, p. 162
- Edible Glitter, Decorator's Brush, p. 128, 130
- Buttercream Icing, Confectioner's Sugar Glaze, p.93

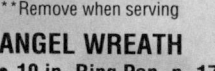

- Ice sides of ring smooth. Cover inside base and top with rows of tip 69 leaves. Edge outside base with tip 69 shell-motion border. Outline center of border with tip 3 string.

- Pipe tip 104 ribbon and bow on top. To add color to angels, make a very small amount of Confectioner's Sugar Glaze. With brush, paint wings and banners. Allow glaze to set, then place on wreath. *Serves 14.*

CHARMING CAROLERS

- Santa Bear, p. 186
- Mini Bear Pan, p. 178
- Tips 1, 2, 3, 4, 7, 16, 21, 44, 349, p. 134-136, 139
- Creamy Peach, Ivory, Willow Green Icing Colors, p. 124
- Buttercream Icing, p.93
- Candy-coated chocolates, mini chocolate chips

- On Santa Bear: With a serrated knife, trim away bow. Build up area where book and scarf will be with icing. Ice sides smooth. Mark book and scarf with toothpick.

- Outline bear, cap, scarf, book and mittens with tip 4 strings. Pipe in nose, mouth and inside of ears with tip 7 (smooth with finger dipped in cornstarch).

- Cover bear, stocking cap, scarf, book and mittens with tip 16 stars. Edge cap with tip 16 zigzags. Pipe tip 16 star in center of pompon. Fill in remaining area with tip 16 wavy stripes.

- Trim cap and scarf with tip 4 dots. Add tip 4 outline fringe to scarf. Pipe tip 1 curvy lines on book. Print tip 2 letters, overpipe letters, c and s. Pipe tip 349 leaves on book. Trim with tip 2 dot berries. Figure pipe bell with tip 4. Add tip 2 dots. Outline and pipe-in notes with tip 2.

- Edge base with tip 21 star border. *Serves 12.*

- For Mini Bears: Ice sides smooth. Outline details on bears with tip 3 strings. Pipe in nose with tip 3 (smooth with finger dipped in cornstarch).

- Cover ears, faces, paws and body with tip 16 stars. Add tip 16 zigzag caps with tip 3 dot pompons.

- Pipe tip 44 smooth ribbon scarves. Trim ends with tip 3 pull-out strings. Edge bases with tip 16 star borders. Add chocolate chip eyes. *Each serves 1.*

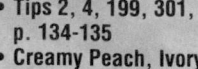
HOLIDAYS!

Coordinate your cake with your color scheme. Pastel shades for the holidays are as popular as traditional Yuletide hues.

CHRISTMAS MAIL

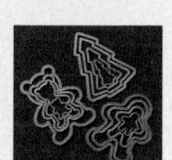

- Loaf Pan, p. 174
- Tips 2, 3, 17, 97, 113, p. 134-136, 138
- Christmas Red, Kelly Green, Black, Brown, Golden Yellow Icing Colors, p. 124
- '92 Pattern Book (Letters & Mailbox Patterns), p. 115
- Color Flow Mix, Meringue Powder, p. 125
- Tree Formers, Flower Formers, Decorator Brushes, p. 128, 130
- Cake Boards, Fanci-Foil Wrap, p. 132-133
- Lollipop Sticks, p. 118
- Love Doves, p. 160
- Buttercream, Royal, Color Flow Icings, p. 93, 105

- Using Letters and Mailbox Patterns and tip 2 for outlines, make three letters, flag, door and latch out of color flow icing (see How-To Section). Let pieces dry completely.
- The following trims are all decorated with royal icing – Letter: Add tip 2 addresses. Holly leaves (make 6): Pipe tip 113 holly leaves on waxed paper. With Decorator Brush, pull out points on edges of leaves. Let dry on concaved flower formers. Pinecones (make 3): Pipe tip 97 "petals" on tree formers (see How-To Section). Cardinal: With brush, paint Love Dove with thinned icing. Pipe comb on head with tip 2 (smooth with cornstarch). Add tip 2 outline beak and eyes.
- For mailbox: Bake 2 loaf cakes using a cake mix for each. Allow cakes to cool and firm overnight. Trim to make sides staight. Secure bottom layer to serving base with icing. Torte and stack for 4-layers or stack only for 2-layers. With buttercream, ice opening end brown, rest white. Position latch on cake top and door on board. With tip 17, edge ends with tip 17 zigzags; base with stars. Write tip 2 name on side. Secure flag by resting it on top of cake and inserting a lollipop stick into hole through cake. Cover end of stick with tip 3 dot. Arrange letters, holly, pinecones and cardinal. *Serves 24.*

PARTY SANDWICH

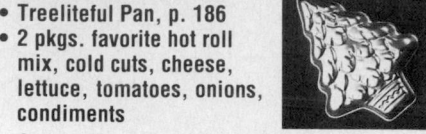

- Treeliteful Pan, p. 186
- 2 pkgs. favorite hot roll mix, cold cuts, cheese, lettuce, tomatoes, onions, condiments

- Grease Treeliteful pan with vegetable shortening. Prepare hot roll dough according to directions on package, except press into pan before second rising.
- Bake per directions. Remove from oven and allow dough to cool for 5 minutes, then unmold from pan. Cool 1 hour. Using a serrated knife, slice bread in half horizontally.
- Fill and garnish to suit your taste. Serve immediately.

FAMILY FUN!

- Cookie Cutter Sets— Christmas Bears Nesting, Christmas Trees, Gingerbread Boys, p. 122
- Tips 1, 2, 3, 13, 101, p. 134-135, 138
- Kelly Green, Christmas Red, Golden Yellow, Royal Blue, Brown, Icing Colors, p. 124
- Meringue Powder, p. 125
- Snow-White or Buttercream Icings, p. 93
- Roll-Out Cookie and Gingerbread Dough Recipes, p. 105

- For Bear and Gingerbread Boys: Cut out of gingerbread dough. Bake and cool.
- For Trees: Tint roll-out cookie dough green with icing color. Cut out trees, bake and cool.
- Decorate cookies with tips 1, 2 and 3 string and dot details. Add tip 13 stars. Pipe banners and ruffles with tip 101.

HOLIDAY LIGHTS

- Mini Christmas Tree Pan, p. 186
- Tip 46, p. 139
- Royal Blue, Christmas Red, Golden Yellow, Kelly Green, Black Icing Colors, p. 124
- Decorating Comb, p. 128
- Buttercream Icing, p. 93
- Marshmallows, shoestring licorice, candy-coated mini squares of gum, toothpicks*

- Trim away two bottom corners of each tree cake and position on foil-covered cake board (cut to fit). Ice cakes smooth (pat with finger dipped in cornstarch or allow icing to crust slightly) then place plastic wrap over icing and smooth area gently. Carefully remove wrap.
- Push a toothpick into marshmallow. Holding onto toothpick, ice sides then give a ribbed effect with decorating comb. Pipe tip 46 stripe around marshmallow "base." Push toothpick with marshmallow into cake. Ice end of marshmallow.
- For "plug," ice marshmallow, following same procedure, remove toothpick and add gum.
- Cut 6" pieces of licorice wires. Position lights and push in licorice. *Each serves 1.*

*Be sure to remove toothpicks.

HOLIDAYS!

Welcome your guests with festive party fare!

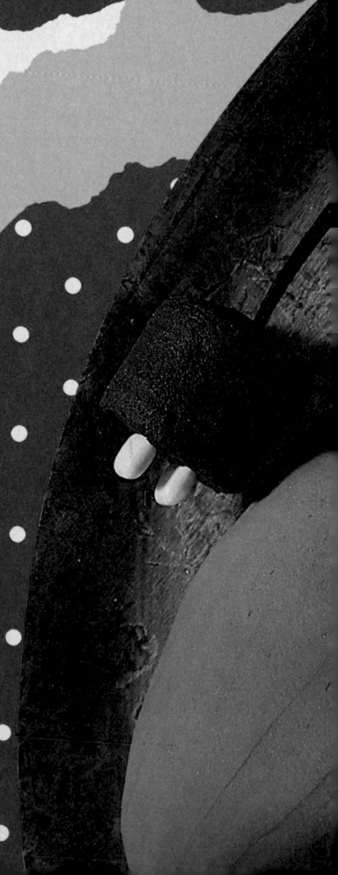

See How-To Section
to decorate Candy Melts™ !

FATHER CHRISTMAS

- Jolly Santa Pan, p. 187
- Tips 2, 2A, 4, 9, 12, 21, 112, p. 134-139
- Christmas Red*, Burgundy*, Ivory, Kelly Green Icing Colors, p. 124
- '92 Pattern Book (Father Christmas Pattern), p. 115
- Buttercream Icing, p. 93

*Combine colors for shades shown

- Ice cap and sides smooth. Ice face and mark Father Christmas Pattern with toothpick.
- Outline eyes with tip 2. Pipe tip 12 ball nose (smooth with finger dipped in cornstarch).
- For hair and beard, pipe tip 21 pull-out stripes side-by-side, then trim ends with rosettes. For mustache, pipe tip 21 curved stripes. Add tip 21 elongated shell eyebrows. Pipe in pompon with tip 2A (smooth with cornstarch).
- Edge cap with tip 112 holly leaves. Trim with tip 4 dots. Edge base with tip 9 bulb border. *Serves 12.*

HARK THE HERALD

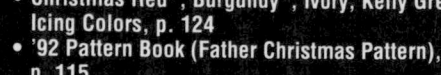

- Half Round Pan, p. 169
- Tips 2, 3, 13, 18, p. 134-135
- Ivory, Kelly Green, Violet, Pink, Burgundy, Royal Blue Icing Colors*, p. 124
- '92 Pattern Book (Angel Pattern), p. 115
- Color Flow Mix, Meringue Powder, p. 125
- Cake Boards, Fanci-Foil Wrap, p. 132-133
- Buttercream, Color Flow, Royal Icings, p. 93, 94

*For mauve shade, mix pink and burgundy together.

- Using Angel Pattern and color flow icing, outline angel with tip 3 and flow in (see Color Flow, How-To Section). Let dry.
- Ice one-layer cake smooth. Edge top with tip 18 shell border, trimmed with tip 3 dots. Outline base of cake with tip 18. Mark 2½ in. intervals on base board with dots of icing. Pipe Fan Border (see How-To Section) with tips 2, 13 and 18.
- At serving time, position angel on top. *Serves 18.*

Note: Since buttercream icing will break down color flow, either position angel on cake shortly before serving, set atop sugar cubes or place a piece of plastic wrap, cut to fit, on area first.

O LITTLE TOWN

- Gingerbread House Kit, Mini Gingerbread House Kit, p. 122
- Tips 2, 3, 4, 16, p.134-135
- Royal Blue, Kelly Green, Pink, Burgundy, Golden Yellow Icing Colors, p. 124
- '92 Pattern Book (Tree Pattern), P.115
- Meringue Powder, Piping Gel, p. 125
- Edible Glitter, p. 130
- Cake Boards, Fanci-Foil Wrap, p. 132-133
- Royal Icing (3 recipes), p. 94
- Grandma's Gingerbread Dough (2 recipes)

- Using patterns in your gingerbread house kits, cut out church and 4 mini houses. Bake, cool and dry gingerbread overnight. The following day, pour thinned royal icing over pieces. Immediately sprinkle with Edible Glitter. Let dry.

- Prepare candy windows and attach to panels (recipe and instructions included in kit booklet). Note: Foil-covered cake boards are great to use for bases. Attach walls, roof and steeple together with icing. Using tips 2 and 3 for mini houses and 4 for church, pipe in fleur-de-lis, scrolls, dots, zigzags or bead designs on seams, roofs and around windows. For drifting snow, add piping gel for shimmery look. With a spatula, generously mound icing around edge of roofs. Then pull out snowy peaks.

- For trees: Cut 5 pieces of cardboard out for each using top of steeple pattern for smaller trees, Tree Pattern for tall tree. Tape cardboard pieces together. Cover with tip 16 pull-out stars. Sprinkle with Edible Glitter. Let dry.

- Place village and trees on desired base.

HOLIDAYS!

Create jewel-bright cakes as dazzling as the season itself!

43

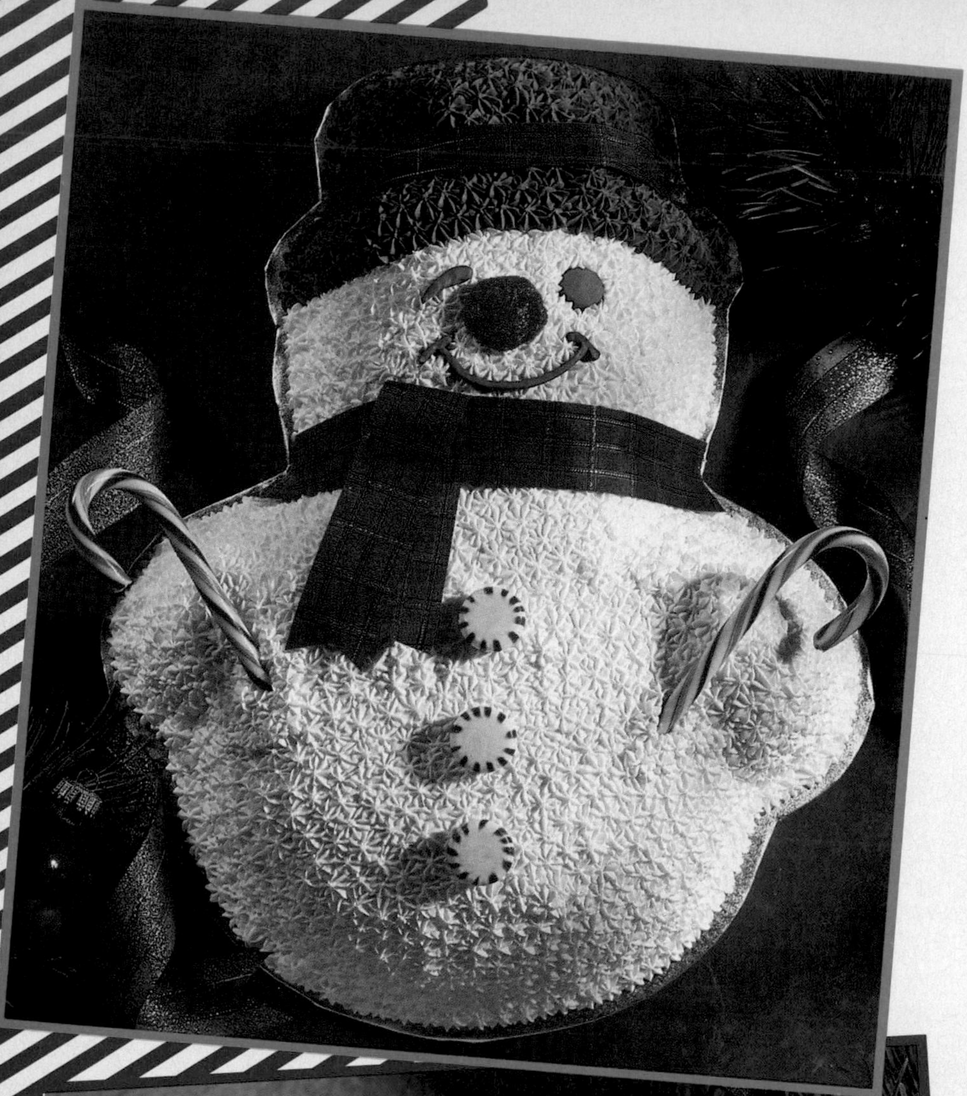

CANDY CANE MAN

- Snowman Pan, p. 186
- Tips 4, 21, p. 134-135
- Kelly Green Icing Color, p. 124
- Cake Board, Fanci-Foil Wrap, p. 132-133
- Buttercream Icing, p. 93
- Candy Canes, peppermint discs, round jelly candy, Christmas ribbon—¹⁄₂ in. wide for hat band, 1¹⁄₄ in. wide for scarf.

- Pipe a tip 4 bead and dot for eyes, outline string for mouth.
- Cover hat and snowman with tip 21 stars. Add ribbon hatband and scarf. Push in candy canes, jelly patty nose and peppermint buttons. *Serves 12.*

PEPPERMINT COTTAGE

- Holiday House Pan, p. 186
- Tips 2,45, p.134, 139
- Kelly Green Icing Color, p. 124
- Piping Gel, p. 125
- Cake Board, Fanci-Foil Wrap, p. 132-133
- Buttercream Icing, p. 93
- Candy canes (small), dragees, peppermint discs, spearmint leaves, heart candy

- Position cake on foil-covered base. Ice walls smooth. Cover eaves and windows with tip 45 smooth stripes (smooth with finger dipped in cornstarch). Outline window panes with tip 2 strings.
- Generously ice base and roof, then swirl and pat to resemble drifting snow. Add piping gel to icing, then pipe tip 2 pull-out string icicles on roof.
- Add candy trims. Break candy canes into pieces to fit. *Serves 12.*

PEPPERMINT PALS

- Gingerbread Boy, Mini Gingerbread Boy Pans, p. 187
- Tips 1, 4, 5, 8, 12, p. 134
- Christmas Red, Brown Icing Colors, p. 124
- Buttercream Icing, p. 93
- Note: Use large tips on full-size, small tips on minis.

- Ice cakes smooth. With white icing, pipe tip 8 or 4 outline mouths and dot eyes. Add small dot to eye with tip 4 or 1.
- Spatula-stripe white icing with red. Outline top with tip 12 or 5 strings. Pipe tip 12 or 4 dot buttons and base borders (flatten with finger dipped in cornstarch).
Full-size serves 12; each mini serves 1 or 2.

WIDE-EYED DELIGHT

- Rudy Reindeer Pan, p. 187
- Tip 4, p. 134
- Christmas Red, Brown Icing Colors, p. 124
- Decorator's Brush (optional), p. 128
- Buttercream Icing, p. 93
- 2 pkgs. sugar cookie dough or favorite recipe

- Cookie dough can be tinted before baking. Or after baking and cooling cookie, it can be painted. Thin icing color with a little water. Paint areas with a Decorator's Brush.

- To make cookie, press dough into lightly greased pan and bake for 17 to 20 minutes or until edges begin to pull away from sides of the pan. Turn out onto a cooling rack.

- Outline antlers, ear, eye, nose, mouth, head and bow with tip 4 strings. Print tip 4 message.

HOLIDAYS!

Long-time Christmas favorites are almost too cute to eat!

TRUE LOVE TEDDIES

- 9 x 13 in. Sheet Pans, p. 170
- I Love You Cookie Cutter Canister, p. 123
- Tips 2, 4, 13, 15, 17, 104, 349 p. 134-138.
- Pink, Red-Red, Brown Icing Colors, p. 124
- Small Icing Roses (40 needed), p. 130
- Buttercream Icing, p. 93

- Ice 1-layer cake smooth. Using bear and triple heart cookie cutters, imprint hearts, then bears (slightly overlap hearts as shown). Outline designs with tip 2. Pipe in eyes with tip 4 (smooth with finger dipped in cornstarch). Fill in hearts and bears with tip 13 stars. Add tip 4 bead heart bows and several hearts randomly on background.
- Print tip 2 message. Pipe tip 2 dot pupils on eyes, nose, pads of paws and knots of ties.
- With toothpick, mark 13 in. sides into 6ths, 9 in. sides into 4ths. Connect marks with tip 104 ruffle garlands. Trim garland points with tip 15 rosettes. Edge top with tip 17 reverse shell border.
- Add roses to top and base. Trim with tip 349 leaves. *Serves 14.*

FONDEST THOUGHTS
- Heart Ring Mold/Pan, p. 175
- Tips 2, 199, 362, p. 134-135
- Red-Red, Pink Icing Colors, p. 124
- Frolicking Cherub, p. 162
- Petite Pedestal Base, p. 160
- Quick-Pour Fondant, Buttercream Icings, p. 93
- Roses, ferns

- Lightly ice cake smooth. Cover with poured fondant icing. Let set.
- Set Petite Pedestal Base into center. With buttercream icing, pipe tip 2 double drop string garlands (2¹/₂ in. wide) on sides.
- Edge top with tip 362 shell borders. At base, pipe tip 199 shells, outlined with tip 2 strings.
- Glue stem of flower onto Frolicking Cherub. Position cherub in center of cake. Arrange flowers. *Serves 12.*

LAVISH, LUSCIOUS DESSERT CAKES
Present a thrill beyond compare!

CHERRY ANGEL FOOD HEART
- Heart Angel Food Pan, p. 175
- Boiled Icing, p. 93
- Favorite angel food recipe or mix, maraschino cherries(drained), mint leaves

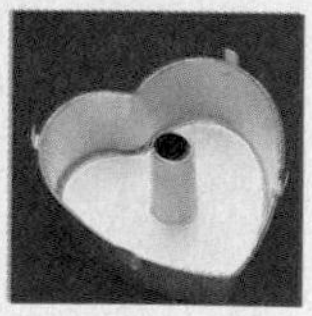

- Bake cake and unmold per baking instructions. Cool completely.
- Ice generously, then swirl with spatula (boiled icing holds patterns beautifully). Add cherries and leaves. *Serves 12.*

SWEETHEART CHEESECAKE
- Heart Dessert Pan, p. 175
- Tip 2, p.134
- Pink, Red (No-taste) Liquid Icing Colors, p. 124
- 2 pkgs. cheesecake mix or recipe for 9 in. cheesecake.

- Prepare cheesecake per recipe. Tint about ¹/₄ cup of batter red and the rest pink.
- With tip 2 (or a cut bag), pipe hearts with red batter.
- Refrigerate or bake per recipe instructions. Unmold. *Serves 12 or more.*

HOLIDAYS!

All will fall for these romantics!

WORTH A THOUSAND WORDS

- Heart Mini-Tier Pan Set, p.189
- Tips 1D, 2, 2B, 4, 5, 8, 10, 102, 129, 349, p.134-139
- Flower Nail No. 7, p.130
- Red-Red, Ivory, Brown, Pink Icing Color, p.124
- Cake Boards or Circles, Doilies, p.132-133
- Buttercream Icing, p. 93
- Photographs (cut to fit using pans as a guide to size)

- Using stiffened buttercream, make 10 roses with tips 10 (for bases) and 102. Make 12 drop flowers with tips 129 and tip 2 dot centers.
- Ice 1-layer cakes smooth. Position photos on cakes. Hint: Cover tops with waxed paper or plastic wrap, cut to fit, then attach photo to cakes with dots of icing.
- Edge tops with ribbed stripe frames—tip 1D for largest heart; tip 2B on others. For a more finished look, outline edges of frames with tip 4 (smallest heart) and tip 5.
- Pipe bead border at bases—use tip 8 on smallest, tip 10 on others. Position flowers and trim with tip 349 leaves. *All serve 12.*

SIGNS OF LOVE

- I Love You Cookie Cutter Canister, p.123
- Cookie Sheets, p.173
- Tip 2, p.134
- Red-Red Icing Color, p.124
- Buttercream Icing, p. 93
- Roll-Out Cookie Dough Recipe, p.105

- Cut cookie out of dough and bake. Cool completely. Outline with tip 2 strings.

48

PEARLY HEART
- 9 in. Heart Pan, p.189
- Tips 3, 12, 104, 127, p.134-138
- Flower Nail No. 9, p.130
- Red-Red, Pink Icing Colors, p.124
- 6 mm. Pearl Beading (5 yds.), p.161
- 1¼ in. Green Artificial Leaves, p.159
- Meringue Powder, p.125
- Cake Boards, Fanci-Foil Wrap, Doilies, p. 132-133
- Buttercream or Snow-White Buttercream, Royal Icings, p. 93
- Green florist wire, sterilized adhesive tape

- With royal or snow-white buttercream, make 7 (3 large, 4 medium size) roses with tips 12 and 104. Let set.
- With buttercream, ice 2-layer cake smooth. Edge top with tip 3 bead border. Pipe ruffles on top with tip 104, at base with tip 127. Trim edge of ruffles with tip 3 beads. Add pearls (3 rows) to top and around base. Write tip 3 message.
- To wire pearls: Cut about 15 wires into 4 to 7 in. lengths. Twist wire around string under one pearl, then loosely wrap pearls around wire. When pearls are 1 in. from end of wire, twist wire around pearl string and trim. Cover ends with tape. Push in pearls, add leaves and roses to top and base. *Serves 16.*

HOLIDAYS!

Fetching confections filled with love!

TOKEN OF AFFECTION
- 6 in. Heart Pan, p.189
- Heart Cookie Cutter Set, p.121
- Candy Melts™*—White, Red, Light Cocoa, p.118
- I Love You Lollipop Mold, p.116
- Candy Colors Kit (Red for pink and Green are used), p.118
- Doilies, p. 132
- Chocolate Cookie Recipe(yields 2 gift boxes), p.105

*brand confectionery coating

- Mold a variety of candies(see p.108). For green or pink candy, add candy colors to white melted coating.
- Prepare chocolate cookie dough(see

- For bottom: Roll dough on paper (makes filling easier) to about ½ in. thickness. Press dough into bottom and up sides. Trim excess dough from edges. Bake per recipe. Cool completely. Remove from pan.
- Using a cut bag, outline hearts on lid with melted Candy Melts. Let set. Fill with candy.

HOLIDAYS!

*Easter finery. . .
engaging to elegant!*

FLEECY & FLUFFY

- Gentle Lamb Pan,
  p. 191
- Tips 3, 6, 16, 20,
  p. 134-135
- Brown, Pink, Violet
  Icing Colors, p. 124
- Buttercream Icing, p. 93
- Shredded coconut

- Outline ears, face, bow and hooves
  with tip 3 strings. Pipe in eyes, nose,
  tongue and hooves with tip 3 (smooth
  with finger dipped in cornstarch).
- Cover ears, face and bow with tip 16
  stars. Add tip 3 outline eyelashes.
- Generously ice lamb fluffy. Hint: Pipe
  icing around outlined areas with tip 6,
  then fluff with a spatula. Pat with
  coconut. To keep coconut from getting
  onto stars or hooves, using pan as a
  guide, cut appropriate parts out of
  waxed paper and place over areas.
- Edge base with tip 20 shell border.
  Trim shells with tip 3 dots. *Serves 12.*

GLORIA

- Cross Pan,
  p. 191
- Tips 2, 6, 59⁰, 67,
  102, p. 134-138
- Flower Nail No. 7,
  p. 130
- Violet, Moss Green, Golden* and
  Lemon Yellow* Icing Colors, p. 124
- All-Occasion Pattern Press Set,
  p. 128
- 6 mm. Pearl Beading (10 yds.
  needed), p. 161
- Cake Board, Fanci-Foil Wrap,
  p. 132-133
- Meringue Powder, p. 125
- Buttercream, Royal, Rolled Fondant
  Icings, p. 93, 94

*mix equal parts together to achieve shade shown

- Using royal icing, make 70 tip 59⁰
  violets with tip 2 dot centers and 40
  tip 102 violet leaves.
- Lightly ice cake with buttercream
  icing. Cover with rolled fondant.
  Imprint message with pattern press.
- Write tip 2 message, then overpipe.
  Edge top, sides and base with tip 67
  shell-motion borders. Add pearls.
- Arrange violets and leaves on top and
  base. *Serves 12.*

ARTISTIC HARE

- Special Delivery Bunny Pan, p. 191
- Tips 2, 4, 7, 16, 18, p.134-135
- Lemon Yellow, Pink, Sky Blue, Leaf Green Icing Colors, p. 124
- Decorator's Brushes, p. 128
- Easter Favorites Cookie Cutters, p. 123
- Buttercream Icing, p. 93
- Roll-out Cookie Dough Recipe, p. 105

- Cut cookies out of dough and bake. Let cool completely. Outline with tip 2. Trim with tip 2 or 4 dots, tip 16 stars, tip 18 rosette flowers with tip 2 pull-out dot leaves. Make extras for treats and decorate with same tips as shown.

- Ice sides of cake and background area smooth. Outline bunny and basket with tip 4 strings. Pipe in ear and nose with tip 7; eyes and mouth with tip 4 (smooth with finger dipped in cornstarch). Add tip 4 dot pupils to eyes and smooth.

- Cover shirt with tip 16 stripes. Position brush in paw. Cover bunny and pants with tip 16 stars.

- Position two egg-shaped cookies in basket. Cover basket with tip 18 zigzags – add two rows of zigzags (overpiping cookies) for rim.

- Cover tail with tip 16 reverse shells. Add tip 2 string eyelashes, brows and whiskers. Pipe tip 4 dot buttons on basket handle and pants.

- Edge base with tip 7 bulb border. *Serves 12.*

JIGGLER™ TREATS

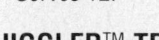

- **Easter Treats, Playful Bunnies Candy Molds, p. 117**
- **Jiggler Treats Recipe (below)**

- 2 small packages (4 serving size) JELL-O® Brand Gelatin
  1¼ cups boiling water

  Completely dissolve gelatin in boiling water. Lightly spray candy mold with vegetable oil spray. For ease in handling, place molds on cookie sheet or tray. Pour slowly gelatin into molds. Chill until firm, at least 1 hour. To unmold, lift jigglers from molds. *Fills 24-30 molds.*

Jell-O and Jigglers are trademarks of Kraft General Foods, Inc.

BUNNY TREATS

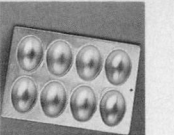

- Egg Mini-Cake Pan, p. 190
- Tips 6, 16, 233, p.134-135
- Pink, Violet, Lemon Yellow, Orange, Leaf Green Icing Colors, p. 124
- Cake Boards, Fanci-Foil Wrap, p. 132-133
- Meringue Powder, p. 125
- Buttercream, Royal Icings, p. 93
- **Shredded tinted coconut, striped gum, cinnamon candies, jelly beans.**

- Ice cakes smooth on foil-covered cake boards (cut to fit). Pat with tinted coconut.
- Cut ears out of gum and push into cake. Add candy eyes and noses.
- Pipe tip 16 star puff tails.
- With royal icing, figure pipe carrots with tip 6 (see p. 104). Trim with tip 233 pull-out string tops. *Each serves 1.*

COTTONTAIL EXPRESS

- Little Lamb Pan, p.190
- Egg Pan Set, p.190
- Easter Cookie Cutter Canister, Crinkle Cookie Cutter Set, p.123
- Tips 3, 4, 17, 21, 233, p.134-135

HOLIDAYS!

Hippity, hoppity. . .Easter is on its way!

- Lemon Yellow, Pink, Violet, Leaf Green Icing Colors, p.124
- '92 Pattern Book (Ears Pattern), p.115
- Cake Boards, Fanci-Foil Wrap, p.132-133
- Meringue Powder, p.125
- Royal, Buttercream Icings, p. 93
- Roll-Out Cookie Dough Recipe, p.105
- **Uncooked spaghetti, craft sticks, ribbon**

- For cookie cart: Make 1 recipe of cookie dough. Roll out 3rd of dough on waxed paper. Cover the outside of half egg pan with foil. Firmly press rolled out dough onto pan and trim away excess. Bake inverted, 10 minutes at 325⁰, then increase temperature to 350⁰. Continue baking for 10 minutes or until edges are lightly brown. Remove from oven and immediately trim top edge with a knife. When completely cooled, remove pan, pull out foil and set in baking ring.
- For wheels and treats: Tint remaining dough yellow, violet, green and pink. Cut 2 wheels and assorted shapes with cookie cutters. Bake and cool.
- Decorating note: Use royal icing on cart, buttercream or royal on cookies. Cover sides of cart with tip 21 rows of stars. Pipe tip 21

zigzags around top and on baking ring base. Push on wheels. Outline with tip 3 strings and add dot spokes. Trim treats with tip 3 dot, string and zigzag designs.

- For bunny cake: Outline eyes, nose, mouth, legs and paws with tip 4 strings. Pipe in eyes and nose with tip 4 (smooth with finger dipped in cornstarch).
- Using Ears Pattern, cut ears out of cake board, attach a craft stick to bottom edge with dots of icing, then cover with pink foil. Push into cake. Cover outside of ears and bunny with tip 233 pull-out fur. Add tip 17 pull-out star tail.
- For whiskers: Use tip 4 to cover spaghetti with icing (see pg. 103) and push into cake. Position cake with cart. Add ribbons and bow. *Bunny serves 12.*

RAINBOW RABBIT

- Cottontail Bunny Pan, p.190
- Tips 4, 16, 363, p.134-135
- Sky Blue, Lemon Yellow, Pink, Violet, Leaf Green Icing Colors, p.124
- Cake Boards, Fanci-Foil Wrap, p.132-133
- Buttercream Icing, p. 93

- Ice sides and background area on top smooth. Outline bunny and bow with tip 4 strings. Pipe in eye and nose with tip 4 (smooth with finger dipped in cornstarch). Add tip 4 dot to eye (flatten with cornstarch).
- Cover inside of ears and bow with tip 363 stars. Fill in bunny with tip 16 pull-out stars. Add tip 363 pull-out star tail.
- Edge base with tip 363 elongated shell border. *Serves 12.*

PUMPKIN MAN

- **Scarecrow Pan, p. 192**
- **Tips 2, 4, 7, 16, 18, 67, 114, 199, p. 134-136**
- **Orange, Brown, Lemon Yellow, Moss Green Icing Colors, p. 124**
- **Cake Boards, Fanci-Foil Wrap, p. 132-133**
- **Buttercream Icing, p.93**
- Ice sides smooth. Outline facial features, pumpkin sections and gown with tip 4 strings.
- Pipe in eyes, nose and mouth with tip 7 (smooth with finger dipped in cornstarch). Cover pumpkin face with tip 16 stars, gown with tip 18 stars. Write tip 2 message.
- Cover top of "stem" with tip 199 side-by-side stripes and spiral. Add tip 114 leaves around stem.
- Make cornstalks with tip 4 strings (overpipe to build dimension). Trim with tip 2 string bows. Pipe tip 199 star pumpkins at base. Add tip 2 dot stems. Trim base with tip 67 leaves. *Serves 12.*

I WANT MY MUMMY!

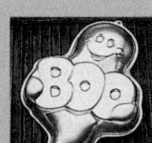

- **Boo Ghost Pan, p. 192**
- **Tips 2, 2B, 3, 16, p. 134-135,139**
- **Black, Golden Yellow, Orange Icing Colors, p. 124**
- **Buttercream Icing, p.93**
- Outline eyes, mouth and letters with tip 3 black strings. Outline letter again with orange.
- Pipe in eyes, mouth, centers of letters and build up nose with tip 3 (smooth with finger dipped in cornstarch).
- Add tip 3 dot pupils to eyes (flatten with finger dipped in cornstarch).
- Cover letters with tip 16 stars. Pipe tip 2B smooth stripe "wrappings."
- Trim letters with tip 2 string webs and dot spiders. *Serves 12.*

THAT'S THE SPIRIT!

- **Mini Ghost Pan, p. 192**
- **Tip 2, p. 134**
- **Black Icing Color, p. 124**
- **Candy Melts™*--Light Cocoa or Dark Cocoa, Green, Yellow, Orange, p. 118**
- **Halloween Variety Candy Mold Set, p. 117**
- **Buttercream Icing, p.93**
- **Shredded coconut**

*brand confectionery coating

- For Ghosts: Ice smooth. Pat with coconut. Pipe tip 2 dot eyes and outline mouths. *Each serves 1.*
- For treats: Mold a variety of delightful Halloween candies (see p. 108).

HOLIDAYS!

Brew up lots of excitement with these super thrillers!

HOLIDAYS!

Spooky treats designed for thrills!

GLOWING FACES

- 14 in. Round Pans, p. 171
- Tips 1, 2, 3, 7, 10, 81, 103, 131, 352, p. 134-137
- Flower Nail No. 7, p. 130
- Orange, Brown, Golden Yellow, Willow Green Icing Colors, p. 124
- Candy Melts™*—Orange, Dark Cocoa, Green, p. 118
- Jack-O-Lantern Candy Mold, p. 117
- Tapers or Slenders Candles, p. 144-145
- Meringue Powder, p. 125
- Buttercream, Royal Icings, p. 93
- Yellow tinted sugar

- Mold (see p. 108) 6 jack-o-lanterns out of melted Candy Melts. Unmold when set. Pipe in facial features using cut-bag candy flow-in method.
- Using royal icing, make 13 chrysanthemums with tips 1, 7, 81; 8 daisies with tips 3 and 103; 18 drop flowers with tips 3 and 131.
- Ice 2-layer cake smooth. Figure pipe ghosts on top and sides with tip 10. Add tip 1 dot eyes and outline mouths. Write tip 2 message.
- Pipe ball borders—tip 7 at top, tip 10 at base. Position candy jack-o-lanterns, push in candles and arrange flowers on top and side. Trim flowers with tip 352 leaves. *Serves 46.*

WHICH IS WITCH?

- Mini Pumpkin Pan, p. 192
- Tips 3, 16, 47, 104, 233, p. 134-139
- Black, Violet, Orange, Lemon Yellow Icing Colors, p.124
- Buttercream Icing, p. 93
- Posterboard

- Outline facial features with tip 3, then pipe in with tip 3 (flatten with finger dipped in cornstarch).
- Cover faces with tip 16 stars. Add tip 104 ruffle collars. Trim with tip 3 dots.
- Pipe tip 233 pull-out string hair. Make cone hats out of posterboard. Push into cake. Edge hats with tip 104 ruffles, tip 47 smooth stripe hatbands and tip 3 outline buckles.
- Trim eyes with tip 3 dot pupils and lashes. *Each serves 1.*

BATTY BEAUTY

- Wicked Witch Pan, p. 192
- Tips 4, 8, 11, 16, 18, p. 134-135
- Black, Orange, Golden Yellow, Violet Icing Colors, p. 124
- Cake Boards, Fanci-Foil Wrap, p. 132-133
- Buttercream Icing, p. 93

- Ice sides and background area on top smooth. With toothpick, mark bats in the sky. Outline wings and pipe dot bodies with tip 4. Smooth with finger dipped in cornstarch.
- Outline details on hat, face and outfit with tip 4 strings. Pipe in eyeballs, mouth and tongue with tip 4, buckle on hat with tip 8 and hatband with tip 11 (flatten with cornstarch).
- Cover hat, whites of eyes, face and outfit with tip 16 stars. Pipe side-by-side strings with tip 11 for hair (overpipe to build dimension). Overpipe rim of hat with tip 11 strings. Add tip 8 string bow.
- Edge base with tip 18 star border. *Serves 12.*

DARK SHADOWS

- Haunted House Kit, p. 123
- Tips 1, 3, 5, 233, 349, p. 134-136
- Black, Orange, Violet, Golden Yellow
  Icing Colors, p. 124
- '92 Pattern Book (Haunted House
  Patterns), p. 115
- 16 in. Cake Circles, Fanci-Foil Wrap, p. 132-133
- Meringue Powder, p. 125
- Royal Icing Recipe, p. 93
- Electric nightlight socket, 15 watt bulb, extension cord.

- Follow gingerbread recipe, cutting, constructing and electrifying
  instructions included with your kit. We also added hard candy
  windows and door. Note the following variations...
- Divide gingerbread dough in half. Knead orange icing color into
  one half; black into the other.
- Cut out 3 additional tombstones for steps and 4 extra door
  canopy tops (P-pattern). Cut tops vertically into 3rds for
  shutters.
- Bake, then assemble house pieces on foil-covered base
  attaching candy "glass" windows and door as you construct.
  Stack up tombstone steps. Add hanging shutters.
- Using Fence Pattern, with tip 5, pipe 16 sections, 3" long; 2
  sections, 5" long. With tip 3 and patterns, make roof points
  (43 needed) and bats (3 or 4). Let dry.
- Attach roof points with dots of icing. Outline windows,
  shutter slats and doorway of house, with tip 3 strings.
  With tip 3, edge roofs with beads, walls and tombstones
  with zigzags. Print tip 1 messages on tombstones.
- Outline tree bark with tip 3; add tip 349 leaves.
- Edge ghosts with tip 3 strings, then flow in
  with thinned icing. Add tip 1 facial features.
- Ice base and generously cover with spatula-striped
  pull-out grass. Position trees, ghosts, tombstones
  and fence sections. Attach bats.

57

EVENTS!

*Pearl accents combined
with jewel tone colors
. . .spectacular!*

LOVE VOWS

- 6 in. Square Pan, p. 170
- 14 in. Round Pans, p. 171
- Tips 3, 17, 20, 21, p. 134-135
- Cathedral Cake Kit, p. 164
- 7 in. Square Separator plates (2 needed), p. 166
- 6 mm. Pearl Beading* (16 yds. needed), p. 161
- Meringue Powder, p. 125
- Cake Circles, Fanci-Foil Wrap, p. 132-133
- Cake Dividing Set, p. 128
- Dowel Rods, p. 166
- Lasting Love Couple, p. 159
- Buttercream, Royal Icings, p. 93

- Electric nightlight socket, 15 watt bulb, extension cord, 12-13 in. diameter base for cake, flowers, ribbon, florist wire
- Cut circle out of Fanci-Foil to add color to chapel window. Wire flowers and ribbons together for chapel bouquet. Assemble chapel with window, archway and steeple. Outline seams, window, doorways and reverse C-scrolls (on steeple) with tip 3 royal icing strings. Cover strings with pearl beading. Let dry. If desired, electrify chapel per kit instructions.
- Dowel rod 14 in. 2-layer round where 7 in. plate will rest. Ice smooth and position 7 in. plate on top. Using Cake Dividing Set,

dot mark sides into 12ths. Connect marks with tip 17 e-motion garlands. Add pearls.
- Place 6 in. 2-layer square (3 in. high) on cake board cut to fit. Position on separator plate. Edge tops of tiers with tip 21 crown borders. Trim shells with tip 3 dots. Pipe tip 20 zigzag puff borders at bases. Trim 6 in. base with pearls.
- At shower, position 14 in. tier atop fabric-covered base. Position plastic supports (included in kit) on separator plate, add couple and archway. Tape chapel bouquet to bottom of 6 in. plate. Place 6 in. cake, steeple and chapel. Arrange flowers. *Serves 77.*

TIERS OF JOY

- 7, 10, 14 in. Round Pans, p. 171
- Tips 16, 32, p. 135
- Pink Icing Color, p. 124
- 8 in. Decorator Preferred Round Separator Plates, p. 167
- 5 in. Grecian Pillars, p. 165
- Dowel Rods, p. 166
- Cake Circles, Tuk-N-Ruffle, Fanci-Foil Wrap, or Ruffle Board™, p. 132-133
- Cake Dividing Set, p. 128
- Heart & Round Cookie Cutter Sets, p. 121
- 15-pc. Decorator Pattern Sets, p. 128
- 4 mm. Pearl Beading*(6 yds.), p. 161
- Mini Bouquet, p. 159
- Masterpiece, p. 149
- Buttercream Icing, p. 93
- Prepare 2-layer rounds for pillar and stacked construction (see p. 106). Using Cake Dividing Set, dot mark sides on 7 in. and 10 in. tiers into 8ths, 14 in. cake into 16ths. Use half of 2½ in. round cutter on 7 in.; 2½ in. heart cookie cutter on 10 in.; C-scroll pattern press on 14 in. to imprint guidelines at marks.
- Cover half round marks on 7 in. with tip 16 zigzags. Position pearls. Pipe tip 16 scroll hearts on 10 in. Add tip 16 swirled shells. Position pearls. Cover C-Scrolls with tip 16. Pipe tip 16 outlines.
- Edge separator plate on 10 in. with tip 16 scallops. Pipe-in shell borders – use tip 16 on tops; tip 32 at bases. Edge shells at base of 14 in. with tip 16 zigzags. Add pearls.
- Pipe tip 16 fleur-de-lis. Trim 7 in. sides with tip 16 rows of stars.
- To serve, position top tier on pillar. Position mini bouquet. *Serves 116.*

*remove pearl beading before cutting.

BRIDE'S BOUQUET

- Dessert Shell Pan, p. 174
- Tips 1, 2, 5, 10, 15, 25, 101, 102, 104, 129, 349, 352, p. 134-138
- Flower Nail No. 7, p. 130
- Pink, Golden Yellow, Burgundy, Royal Blue, Willow Green Icing Colors, p. 124
- '92 Pattern Book (Banner Pattern), p. 115
- 4 mm. Pearl Beading* (approx. 5 yds.), p. 161
- Meringue Powder, Color Flow Mix, p. 125
- Florist Wire, p. 130
- Color Flow, Royal, Buttercream, Quick-Pour Fondant Icings, p. 93
- Lace ribbon
- Use Banner Pattern and color flow icing, outline banner with tip 2, then flow-in (see p. 105). Let dry. Trace words onto banner with a pin. Outline with tip 1 and flow in. Let dry.
- Use royal icing for the following flowers: 5 roses with tips 10 and 102, 10 drop flowers with tips 2 and 129, 10 apple blossoms with tips 1 and 101, 5 bachelor buttons with tips 1, 5, 15.
- Lightly ice cake with buttercream icing. Cover with poured fondant.
- With buttercream icing, pipe tip 104 ruffle border. Edge ruffle with tip 15 zigzags. Add pearl beading.
- Arrange flowers on cake top. Pipe tip 349 thin leaves and ferns. Add tip 2 outline stems, dotted with tip 25 star flowers with tip 1 dot centers. Add tip 352 leaves.
- Secure ribbon and pearls together in the center with florist wire. Push wire into cake. Position banner. *Serves 12.*

*Remove pearls before cutting.

FAMILY GLEE

- 9 x 13 in. Sheet Pan/Cover, p. 173
- Tips 1, 2, 2B, 18, 47, 224, 233, p. 134-139
- Sky Blue, Red-Red, Golden Yellow, Black, Orange, Brown, Leaf Green Icing colors, p. 124
- Buttercream Icing, p. 93
- Candy discs

- Make 13 drop flowers with tip 224. Add tip 3 dot centers.
- Ice cake (in pan) smooth. With toothpick, mark tree trunk. Cover with tip 18 side-by-side stripes.
- Generously ice tree top. Position candy discs. On candy, pipe facial features and hair with tip 2. Pipe tip 2B smooth stripe message banners. Print tip 2 names.
- Edge top with tip 18 reverse shell borders. Pipe tip 233 pull-out grass. Add flowers. *Serves 14.*

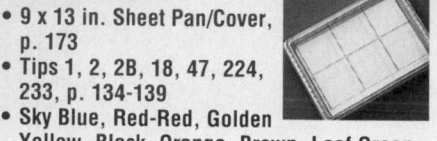

TIME TO CELEBRATE!

- Happy Time Clock Pan, p. 181
- Tips 1, 3, 16, 20, p. 134-135
- Brown, Leaf Green, Royal Blue, Lemon Yellow, Christmas Red Icing, p. 124
- Buttercream Icing, p. 93
- Party horn

- Ice face of clock, background area and sides smooth.
- Outline bells, hands, eyes, mouth, tongue and feet with tip 3.
- Cover bells and feet with tip 16 stars. Pipe in circles in eyes, hands, mouth and tongue with tip 3 (smooth with finger dipped in cornstarch).
- Print tip 3 message and numbers.
- Edge base with tip 20 shell border. To add free-form string streamers, use tip 1 and each icing color. Hold bag several inches away from cake and move hand straight up and down allowing strings to fall freely. Position party horn. *Serves 12.*

RED CARPET TREATMENT

- 18-Wheeler Truck Pan, p. 177
- Tips 3, 5, 10, 12, 16, 20, 44, 45, 47, p. 134-139
- Lemon Yellow, Brown, Red-Red Icing Colors, p. 124
- Buttercream Icing, p. 93

- Ice sides, window and background areas on top smooth.
- Outline van with tip 3 strings. Pipe in hubcaps with tip 10, tires with tip 12, bumper with tip 5 (flatten all with finger dipped in cornstarch)
- Pipe smooth stripes on door and trailer — use tip 44 for narrow, tip 47 for medium and tip 45 for wide.
- Cover van with tip 16 stars. Print name and write message with tip 3. Edge base with tip 20 shell border. *Serves 12.*

EVENTS!

Welcoming ways to make everyone feel at home!

HAPPY NEW YEAR

MOVING VAN

Welcome Neighbors

HIT THE ROAD!

- **Super Race Car Pan,** p.177
- **Tips 2, 2B, 3, 10, 16, 20,** p. 134-139
- **Sky Blue, Royal Blue, Christmas Red, Copper, Black Icing Colors,** p. 124
- **Buttercream Icing,** p. 93
- Ice sky areas on top and sides and hubcaps blue, message area white. With toothpick, mark couple and roof cover. Outline car with tip 3 strings.

- For suitcases, pipe row upon row of tip 10 horizontal stripes (working from bottom up). Outline handles and bands with tip 2 strings.
- Cover car with tip 16 stars. Pipe tip 3 beads and dots on wheels. Edge tires with tip 16 zigzags.
- Figure pipe faces with tip 10 (flatten with finger dipped in cornstarch). Add tip 2 facial features, hair and sunglasses. Pipe tip 2B smooth stripe banner. Outline with tip 2 and print messages. Pipe bodies and arms. Add tip 2 dot hands.
- Pipe shell borders–tip 16 on top, tip 21 at base. *Serves 12.*

4TH OF JULY SPARKLER

- **Shining Star Pan,** p. 180
- **Tips 3, 13, 21, 134-135**
- **Christmas Red, Royal Blue Icing Colors,** p. 124
- **Florist Wire,** p. 130
- **Flower Spikes,** p. 160
- **Meringue Powder,** p. 125
- **Cake Boards, Fanci-Foil Wrap,** p. 132-133
- **Buttercream, Royal Icings** p. 93
- Ice top of one-layer cake smooth. Cover sides with three rows of tip 21 stars.
- Using royal icing, make fireworks display. Place a flower spike inside another spike. Ice spike and let dry. Trim spike with tip 3 outline and tip 13 star design. When dry, push into cake. Cut approximately 50 pieces of florist wire, 7 1/2 in. long. Push into flower spike. On waxed paper, pipe 175 each, red and blue, tip 13 stars. When dry, attach to wires with tip 3 dots of icing. *Serves 12.*

*So many wonderful
reasons to celebrate!*

**FOR THE GOOD
EARTH'S SAKE!**
- **Sports Ball Pan**, p. 183
- **12 in. Round Pans**, p. 169
- **Tips** 1, 2, 3, 4, 14, 101, 233, 224, p. 134-138
- **Pink, Orange, Golden Yellow, Royal Blue, Black, Brown, Leaf Green, Red-Red Icing Colors**, p. 124
- **'92 Pattern Book (Globe Pattern)**, p. 115
- **Holiday Shapes Cookie Cutter Set**, p. 122
- **Lollipop Sticks**, p. 118
- **Meringue Powder**, p. 125
- **Dowel Rods**, p. 166
- **6 & 14 in. Cake Circles, Fanci-Foil Wrap**, p. 132-133
- **Roll-Out Cookie Dough Recipe**, p. 105
- **Buttercream, Royal (optional) Icings**, p. 93

- Cut 8 cookies (4 each, boys & girls) out of cookie dough. For brown cookies, add chocolate per recipe or blend brown icing color into dough. Bake and cool. Using stiffened buttercream or royal icing, outline smiles and outfits with tip 1. Pipe in outfits with tip 3 or 4 (smooth with finger dipped in cornstarch) or fill in with tip 14 stars. Add hair, cap or turban with tips 1 or 3. Outline shoes with tip 3 strings. Baseball cap brim is tip 101 ribbon stripe. Also use tip 101 for ruffles. For Hawaiian lei, pipe tip 13 star flowers with tip 1 dot centers. Make dot eyes, buttons, tiny flower print, bows with streamers and all other small details with tip 1. Attach lollipop sticks to backs of cookies with icing.

- Make 20 drop flowers with tip 224 drop flowers with tip 3 dot centers.
- For globe: Prepare ball cake per instructions included with your pan. Ice cake blue. With toothpick, mark Globe Pattern. Outline continents with tip 3. Cover with tip 14 stars.
- Ice 2-layer round smooth—top yellow, sides green. Cut and position 3 dowel rods where ball cake will go. Position globe cake atop round. Push a sharpened dowel rod down through both cakes. Pipe "snow" on top of ball with tip 4, then swirl with a spatula.
- With toothpick, mark top 2 inches from edge. Cover area with tip 233 pull-out grass. Write tip 3 message on side. Edge base with tip 233 pull-out grass border. Add flowers and push cookies into cake top. *Serves 44.*

BOUNCING BABY BEAR

- Santa Bear Pan, p. 186
- Tips 3, 16, 124, p. 134-138
- Sky Blue, Pink, Lemon Yellow Icing Colors, p. 124
- Buttercream Icing, p. 93
- Candy pacifier

EVENTS!

Beautiful celebrations await your bundle of joy!

- Ice snout and gift smooth. Outline mouth, eyes and gift with tip 3 strings.
- Cover bear and bow with tip 16 stars. Pipe tip 3 dot eyes and nose (flatten with finger dipped in cornstarch). Add tip 3 dot highlights to eyes. Outline brows and lashes with tip 3 strings. Trim bow with tip 3 dots. Write tip 3 message, then overpipe in pink.
- Pipe tip 124 ruffles around face. Edge ruffle with tip 16 shells. Add tip 3 bonnet strings and dots. Position pacifier. *Serves 12.*

BEAUTIFUL BABY BIB

- Dessert Shell Pan, p. 174
- Tips 2, 5, 16, 21, 104, 127, 224, 349, p. 134-138
- Sky Blue, Lemon Yellow Icing Colors, p. 124
- '92 Pattern Book (Bib Pattern), p. 115
- Buttercream Icing, p. 93

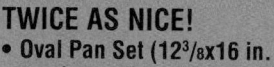

- Make 15 tip 224 drop flowers with tip 2 dot centers.
- Ice cake top and sides smooth.
- With toothpick, mark open area for Bib Pattern on cake top. Cover bib area with tip 16 white stars.
- Edge bib with tip 127 ruffles. Trim ruffle with tip 16 shell border. Add tip 104 smooth stripe neck edge and bow. Trim with tip 2 dots.
- Add tip 2 outline vines. Position drop flowers on bib area. Add tip 349 leaves.
- Pipe message with tip 5; overpipe with tip 2 dots. Edge base with tip 21 shell border. *Serves 12.*

TWICE AS NICE!

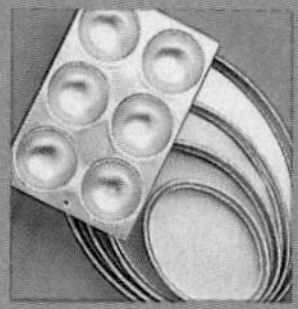

- Oval Pan Set (12³/₈x16 in. pan is used), p. 168
- Mini Ball Pan, p. 183
- Tips 2, 2A, 3, 4, 12, 47, 104, 127, p. 134-139
- Pink*, Lemon Yellow*, Sky Blue Icing Colors, p. 124
- Cake Boards, Fanci-Foil Wrap, 132-133
- Buttercream Icing, p. 93

* For flesh, mix a small amount of yellow with pink icing.

- Ice top of 2-layer oval smooth. Ice two ball cakes smooth on cake boards cut to fit. Position atop oval.
- With toothpick, mark facial features and handles. Outline eyes and mouths with tip 3. Pipe in eyes with tip 3, add dot nose and cheeks (flatten with finger dipped in cornstarch). Add tip 2 dots and lashes on eyes. Figure pipe handles with tip 2A. Pipe tip 104 ruffle bonnets and ribbon bows. Trim ruffles with tip 3 beads. Add tip 3 bonnet strings and outline curls. Write tip 3 message.
- Cover sides with four rows of tip 127 ruffles (work from base upward). Edge top ruffle with tip 47 smooth stripe. Pipe tip 12 ball border around top. Trim border, alternating tip 3 string/dot designs and tip 104 ribbon bows. *Serves 44.*

EVENTS!

*Adorable creations
welcome the new arrival!*

See p. 116 for
New Baby Arrival
Candy Molds.

BABY CAKES

- Jumbo Muffin Pan, p.174
- Tips 3, 14, p. 134-135
- Sky Blue, Pink, Lemon Yellow Icing Colors, p.124
- Alphabet and Baby Things! Cookie Cutters, p. 120, 121
- Jumbo Muffin Cups, p. 126
- Roll-Out Cookie Recipe, p. 105
- Buttercream Icing, p. 93
- Cut out Baby Things and Alphabet Letters from cookie dough. Bake and cool. Outline cookies with tip 3 strings. Fill in areas with tip 14 stars, or pipe in with tip 3, (smooth with finger dipped in cornstarch). Add tip 3 details.
- Ice cupcakes smooth. Position cookies on cupcakes. *Each serves 1.*

CHOO CHOO COOS

- Little Train Pan, p. 177
- Tips 1, 2, 4, 7, 8, 11, 16, 18, 44, p. 134-138
- Lemon Yellow, Sky Blue, Pink Icing Colors, p. 124
- Buttercream Icing, p. 93
- Ice background, sides, windows, and message area of cake smooth.
- Use tip 4 to outline areas around windows, train engine and car, wheels, brake shaft. Use tip 4 to cover car canopy with side-by-side stripes. Write tip 2 message.
- Pipe in wheel rims and hubs, brake shaft, top of smokestack, roof of cab, cowcatcher and front of engine with tip 7 (smooth with finger dipped in cornstarch).
- Trim smokestack and engine with bands of tip 44 smooth stripes (alternate colors). Add tip 2 dot rivets. Cover train and wheels with tip 16 stars.
- Add tip 44 stripes on train engine and smokestack. Trim with tip 2 rivets.
- Figure pipe stork with tips 2, 4, and 7 (see p. 104). Pipe tip 8 ball baby heads (flatten with finger dipped in cornstarch). Add tip 2 facial features and tip 1 dot fingers.
- Edge base with tip 18 rosette border. Trim centers with tip 2 dots. *Serves 12.*

EVENTS!

Mark these milestones in marvelous ways!

SAFELY IN HIS CARE
- **Two-Mix Book Pan, p. 180**
- **Tips 1, 2, 5, 8, 349, p. 134-136**
- **Pink, Leaf Green Icing Colors, p. 124**
- **'92 Pattern Book (Prayer Book Patterns), p. 115**
- **Decorating Triangle, p. 128**
- **Cake Boards, Fanci-Foil Wrap, 132-133**
- **Buttercream Icing, p. 93**

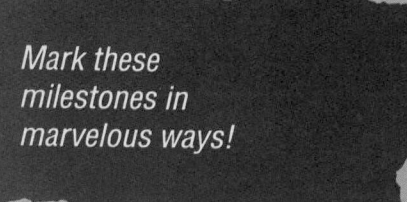

- Ice cake smooth. Comb sides with Decorating Comb to resemble pages.
- With toothpick, mark Pray Book Patterns on cake top. Outline bookmark with tip 2. Pipe in with tip 4 (smooth with finger dipped in cornstarch).
- Cover letters on left page with tip 2. On right page, use tip 1 for printing and overpiping letters.
- Pipe string border designs and bead/dot flower with tip 2. Add tip 349 leaves.
- Edge top of book with tip 5 bead border. Pipe tip 8 bulb border at base. *Serves 24.*

REJOICE IN THE SPIRIT!
- **18 in. Half Round Pan, p. 169**
- **Tips 1, 2, 5, 13, 32, 70, p. 134-**
- **Royal Blue, Golden Yellow, Violet, Leaf Green Icing Colors, p. 124**
- **'92 Pattern Book (Chalice Pattern), p. 115**
- **Buttercream Icing, p. 93**

- Ice top white, adding small amounts of blue icing for marble effect, and sides all white. With toothpick, mark Chalice Pattern. Outline chalice with tip 2 strings. Pipe in host and inside of chalice with tip 2 (smooth with finger dipped in cornstarch).
- Cover chalice with tip 13 stars. Overpipe outline on chalice and add dot "stones" with tip 5. Outline wheat with tip 2 strings. Pipe tip 5 dot grapes, then overpipe to add dimension. Add tip 70 grape leaves and tip 1 outline tendrils.
- Write tip 2 message and letters on host. Trim letters with tip 1 decorative build-up.
- Edge top with tip 32 crown border. Trim with tip 13 rosettes. Edge base with tip 32 shell border. *Serves 18.*

STAINED GLASS GLORY

- 11 x 15 in. Sheet Pan, p. 170
- Tips 1, 3, 10, 13, 18, 21, 59, 102, 349, p. 134-138
- Flower Nail No. 7, Flower Formers, p. 130
- Lemon Yellow, Violet, Kelly Green, Pink, Sky Blue, Wilton Red Icing Colors, p. 124
- '92 Pattern Book, (Stained Glass Window Pattern), p. 115
- Meringue Powder, Piping Gel, p. 125
- Cake Boards, Fanci-Foil Wrap, p. 132-133
- Buttercream, Royal Icings, p. 93

- With royal icing, make 12 tip 59 violets with tip 1 centers. Let dry on flower formers. Make 6 roses with tips 10 and 102.

- Ice top and sides of cake smooth. With toothpick, mark Stained Glass Window Pattern. Cover marks with tip 3 strings. To fill-in stained glass, fill a parchment bag with tinted piping gel. Cut end of bag just enough to allow gel to flow out.

- Edge cake top with tip 18 reverse shell border. Trim with tip 3 dots. Pipe tip 21 shell border at base. Edge shells with tip 13 zigzags.

- Pipe tip 3 outline vines under window. Write tip 3 message. Position flowers and trim with tip 349 leaves. *Serves 22.*

EVENTS!

Extraordinary events deserve spectacular celebrations!

HEAVENLY PRAISES

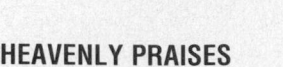

- Cross Pan, p. 191
- Tips 1, 2, 3, 17, 18, 66, 101, 102, p. 134-138
- Golden Yellow, Kelly Green Icing Colors, p. 124
- Flower Nail No. 7, Flower Formers, p. 130
- '92 Pattern Book (Dove Pattern), p. 115
- Meringue Powder, Color Flow Mix, p. 125
- Cake Boards, Fanci-Foil Wrap, p. 132-133
- Buttercream, Royal, Color Flow Icings, p. 93, 105
- Tinted sugar

- Using Dove Pattern and color flow icing, outline dove with tip 2, then flow-in (see Color Flow, p. 105).

- With royal icing (allowing extras for breakage), make about 20 tip 101 apple blossoms with tip 1 dot centers. Make 10 tip 102 daisies with tip 3 dot centers. Pat centers with tinted sugar. Let dry on flower formers.

- Ice top and sides of cake smooth. Cover bevel area with tip 17 stars. Edge base with tip 18 star puff border. Write tip 2 message.

- Position flowers and trim with tip 66 leaves. Position color flow*. *Serves 12.*

*Note: Since buttercream icing will break down color flow, position on a piece of plastic wrap cut to fit, sugar cubes or mini marshmallows.

EVERLASTING JOY

- 10, 14 in. Round Pans, p. 169
- Tips 2, 8, 11, 20, 102, 103, 104, 349, 352, p. 134-139
- Flower Nail No. 7, p. 130
- Christmas Red, Kelly Green Icing Colors, p. 124
- Shining Cross, p. 141
- Dowel Rods, p. 166
- Cake Circles, Tuk-N-Ruffle, Fanci-Foil Wrap, or try Ruffle Boards™, p. 132-133
- Buttercream Icing, p. 93

- Use stiffened buttercream or royal icing, make 3 dozen roses, 1 dozen with each of the following tips—102, 103 and 104. Use tip 8 for bases of smaller roses, tip 11 for large. Make 2 dozen sweet peas with tips 103 and 104. Use tip 103 and 104 to make 2 dozen half-roses. Make 2 dozen rosebuds with tip 102. Let set.

- Prepare 2-layer rounds for stacked construction (see p. 106). With toothpick, mark 5 in. long, 2 in. wide "white carpet" on 10 in. cake top. Outline area with tip 2. Cover with tip 2 cornelli lace.

- Write tip 2 message on sides. Overpipe with tip 2 to build up letters.

- Edge tops and bases with tip 20 reverse shell border. Push cross into top tier. Arrange flowers on tops and sides. Trim with tip 349 small and tip 352 large leaves. *Serves 70.*

BLESSINGS

- 12 in. Hexagon Pans, p. 168
- Tips 1D, 2, 3, 5, 47, 349, p. 134-139
- Royal Blue, Leaf Green, Golden Yellow, Violet Icing Colors, p. 124
- '92 Pattern Book (Star, Lettering and Menorah Patterns), p. 115
- Color Flow Mix, p. 125
- Buttercream Icing, p. 93

- Using Star Pattern and Color Flow icing, outline star with tip 3. When dry, flow in design with thinned icing (see Color Flow, p. 105). Let dry. Overpipe center lines of star and print tip 3 message using Lettering Pattern as a guide.

- Ice 2 layer cakes smooth. With toothpick, mark Menorah Pattern in center of sides. Outline menorah with tip 3 strings; candles and flames with tip 2. Pipe tip 3 dot grapes. Add tip 2 e-motion tendrils and tip 349 leaves.

- Edge cake top and base with tip 1D smooth (blue) stripes. Overpipe with tip 47 smooth stripe band. Edge cake top with tip 5 bead border. Position color flow*. *Serves 28.*

*Note: Since buttercream icing will break down color flow, position on a piece of plastic wrap cut to fit, sugar cubes or mini marshmallows.

RISING STAR

- 14 in. Square Pans, p. 170
- Wonder Mold Pan, p. 178
- Tips 8, 17, 20, 21, 104, p. 134-138
- Burgundy, Red-Red Icing Colors, p. 124
- 9 in. Decorator Preferred Separator Plates (2 needed), p. 167
- 5 in. Grecian Pillar Set, p. 165
- Teen Doll Pick, p. 141
- 4 mm. Pearl Beading (10 yds. needed), p. 161
- Lollipop Sticks, p. 118
- Parchment Triangles, p. 129
- Dowel Rods, p. 166
- Cake Circles, Boards, Tuk-N-Ruffle, Fanci-Foil Wrap, p. 132-133
- Crystal-Look Base*, p. 160
- Buttercream Icing, p. 93
- Silk or fresh flowers, open-center candies, glue

*Invert and use as a vase.

- Place wonder mold cake on cake circle atop separator plate. Push doll pick into cake. Ice bodice of doll, building up icing at waist for a smooth look (shape with finger dipped in corn starch). Ice skirt smooth with a downward motion to create pleated effect. With toothpick, mark V-inset on skirt. Pipe in marked area with tip 104 (smooth with cornstarch). Edge neck and inset with tip 104 ribbon drape. Trim bodice and base of skirt with pearls.

- Ice 2-layer cake smooth. Dowel rod and position separator plate (see p. 106). Dot mark sides into 4ths. Edge base with tip 21 shell border. Pipe tip 17 zigzag garlands. Trim points of garlands with tip 17 fleur-de-lis. Add pearls.

- Position pillars. Edge separator plate with tip 17 scallops. For pearl sprays: Cut 5 strands of pearls for each corner in the following lengths: Two 7 in. (outer), two 7½ in. (inner) and one 8 in. (center). Glue ends to each pillar. Push other ends into icing on edge of cake. Cut four strands of pearls, 4 in. long. Tie each into bows and glue to pillars.

- Edge cake top with tip 20 reverse shell border. For Torah: Cut a 2 in. x 8 in. rectangle out of parchment triangle. Cut 2 lollipop sticks 3½ in. long. Glue sticks to ends of parchment and roll up. Write message on scroll. Place open-center candies on ends of sticks. Push end of sticks into open end of tip 8 to cover handles of Torah. Let icing set. Glue Torah onto doll.

- Position floral arrangement on separator plate. Place doll cake on pillars. *Serves 66.*

CAUTION: Remove pearls before cutting cake.

IT SPELLS SUCCESS

- **12 x 18 in. Sheet Pan,** p. 170
- **Tips 1, 3, 13, 16, 18, 21,** p. 134-135
- **Golden Yellow, Black, Wilton Red, Moss Green Icing Colors,** p. 124
- **Alphabet Cookie Cutters, School Days Cookie Cutters,** p. 120, 121
- **Roll-out Cookie Dough Recipe,** p. 105
- **Buttercream Icing,** p. 93

- With cookie cutters cut "TGIG" and School Days shapes from cookie dough. Bake and cool. With stiffened buttercream or royal icing, ice blackboard and computer screen. Outline details with tip 3. Pipe in bus windows, lights and tires with tip 3; pipe in apple's eyes, stem and mouth with tip 1 (smooth with finger dipped in cornstarch). Fill in remaining areas with tip 13 stars. Print tip 1 messages on cookies.

- Ice sheet cake smooth. Write tip 3 message. Edge top with triple shell border, using tip 18 for side shells, tip 16 in center. Edge base with tip 21 rosettes. Trim rosettes with tip 16 stars. Place cookies on cake. *Serves 28.*

LOTS OF LUCK!

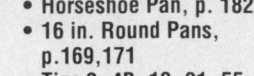

- **Horseshoe Pan,** p. 182
- **16 in. Round Pans,** p.169,171
- **Tips 3, 4B, 12, 21, 55, 104, 352,** p. 134-137
- **Wilton Red, Golden Yellow, Moss Green Icing Colors,** p. 124
- **Flower Nail No. 7,** p. 130
- **Candy Melts™*** (28 oz. yellow), p. 118
- **7 in. Spiked Pillars** (2 are used), p. 165
- **Glad Grad,** p. 142
- **13 x 19 in. Cake Boards, 18 in. Cake Circles, Fanci-Foil Wrap and Tuk-N-Ruffle or use New! Ruffle Boards™,** p. 132-133
- **Buttercream Icing,** p. 93

*brand confectionery coating

- Mold horseshoe plaque out of melted Candy Melts™ (see p. 108), refrigerate until completely set, then unmold. For support, attach back to a cake board (cut to fit) with dots of icing. With icing write tip 55 message.

- Using stiffened buttercream (or royal), make 40 roses (20 in each color) with tips 12 and 104.

- Ice 2-layer cake smooth. Pipe shell borders—tip 21 at top, tip 4B at base. Between top shells, add tip 104 flutes. Edge shells at base with tip 104 ruffles.

- Push spiked pillars into cake to support each side of horseshoe plaque. Build up icing where roses will go with tip 12. Arrange roses and trim with tip 352 leaves. Pipe tip 104 half roses and buds. Position plaque and Glad Grad. *Serves 60.*

CLASSY CLASS

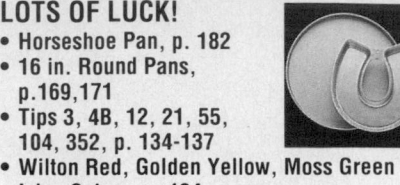

- **8 in. Round Pans,** p.169
- **12, 16 in. Square Pans,** p. 170
- **Tips 2, 6, 19, 21,** p. 134-135
- **Christmas Red Icing Color,** p. 124
- **9 in. Crystal-Look Separator Plates** (2 needed), **7 in. Crystal-Look Pillars** (1 set), p. 165
- **4 mm. Black Pearl Beading*** (14 yds.), p. 161
- **Successful Grad, Glowing Grad** (4 of each), p.142
- **Birthday Number Set** (2 needed), p.141
- **Cake Dividing Set,** p.128
- **Cake Boards, Fanci-Foil Wrap, Tuk-N-Ruffle,** p. 132-133
- **Buttercream Icing,** p. 93
- **Silk or fresh flowers**

- Ice 2-layer cakes smooth. Prepare cakes for pillars and stacked construction (see p. 106). Using Cake Dividing Set, dot mark sides of round into 8ths. Spacing on 12 in. square is 4 1/2 in., 3 in. (in center) and 4 1/2 in.; on 16 in. divide sides into 3rds. Connect marks (except on 12 in. where stairway will go) with double drop strings of pearls.

- Print name on side of round with tip 2, then overpipe. Pipe shell borders—tip 19 at tops, tip 21 at bases. Add pearls to bases.

- To serve: Position top tier on pillars. Add stairway and place graduates on stairs. Push in numbers and position flowers. *Serves 116.*

*Remove pearls before cutting.

1992

KIMBERLY

HONORS MOTHER

- 4-pc. Oval Pan Set, p. 168 (10 ³/₄ x 7 ⁷/₈ pan used)
- Tips 2, 3, 7, 47, p. 134-138
- Brown, Ivory Icing Colors, p. 124
- '92 Pattern Book (Mother Pattern), p. 115
- Color Flow Mix, p. 125
- Buttercream, Color Flow Icings, p. 93
- Sugar cubes, flowers
- Using color flow icing, outline Mother Pattern with tip 3. Flow in design with thinned icing (see Color Flow, p. 105). Let dry.
- Ice 2-layer cake smooth—top white, sides brown. With toothpick, mark 2 in. intervals on sides. Cover marks with tip 47 smooth stripes. Edge top with tip 47 smooth scallops. Outline outer edge of scallops with tip 3. Overpipe scallops with tip 3 strings.
- Write tip 2 message and add dots to cake top.
- Edge base with tip 7 bead border. Position color flow silhouette atop sugar cubes. *Serves 14.*

MAMA BEAR

- Teddy Bear Stand-Up Pan, p. 179
- Tips 2, 3, 13, 16, 103, 125, p. 134-138
- Golden Yellow, Brown, Orange, Black, Ivory, Red-Red Icing Colors, p. 124
- 4-pc. Teddy Bears Cookie Cutters, p. 120
- Roll-Out Cookie Recipe, p. 105
- Buttercream Icing, p. 93
- Ribbon
- For cubs: Out of cookie dough, cut a boy and a girl bear (make more for snacking). Bake and cool. Using stiffened buttercream, outline inside of ears and outfits with tip 2 strings. Pipe in tip 2 ears and bib front (smooth with finger dipped in cornstarch). With tip 13, cover bears with stars, skirt with zigzags, outline belt and bow with tip 13. Pipe tip 2 dot eyes, noses and mouths.
- For mama: Outline facial features with tip 3 strings. Pipe in tip 3 eyes, nose, inside of ears and tongue (flatten with finger dipped in cornstarch) with tip 3. Add tip 3 dot pupils (flatten with cornstarch).
- Cover mama with tip 16 stars. Edge dress with ruffles—tip 103 at neck, tip 125 at hem. Edge ruffles with tip 3 bead borders. Add tip 16 C-motion curl. Add ribbon bow. Position cub cookies. *Serves 12.*

EVENTS!

Honor Mom and Dad on their days with a spectacular cake!

MODEL DAD

- 10 in. Square Pans, p. 170
- Tips 1D, 2, 3, 47, p. 134-136
- Brown, Ivory Icing Colors, p. 124
- '92 Pattern Book (Car Pattern), p. 115
- Color Flow Mix, p. 125
- Buttercream, Color Flow Icings, p. 93, 105
- Sugar cubes, flowers
- Using color flow icing, outline Car Pattern with tip 3. Flow in design with thinned icing (see Color flow, p. 105). Let dry.
- Ice 2-layer cake smooth. Dot mark sides into 4ths. Connect dots with tip 3 drop strings (1½ in. deep). Pipe 1 in. deep tip 3 drop strings between strings.
- Pipe ribbed stripe borders—tip 47 on top, tip 1D at base. Edge top with tip 3 bead border. Print tip 2 message and add dots to cake top. Position color flow car atop sugar cubes. *Serves 28*

DAD'S COOKOUT

- 10 in. Round Pans, p. 169
- Tips 3, 6, 8, 16, 70, 233, p. 134-136
- Black, Leaf Green, Red-Red, Golden Yellow, Orange Icing Colors, p. 124
- Candy Melts *—1 bag each White and Chocolate, Red Candy Color, p. 118
- Decorator's Brushes, p. 128
- Ol' Smoky, p. 142
- Modeling Candy Recipe, p. 109
- Buttercream, Royal Icings, p. 93
- Uncooked spaghetti, large marshmallows, confectioners sugar, craft block
- For grates: With thinned royal icing, "paint" 9 pieces of spaghetti grey. Push into a craft block to dry. Carefully break spaghetti into graduated lengths to fit top of "grill." For coals: Flatten marshmallows, paint deep grey. When dry, pat with confectioners sugar.
- Make hamburgers and hot dogs out of modeling candy (see p.109). Indent and paint grate marks on hot dogs. Use a cut bag to flow thinned royal icing cheese over hamburgers. With leftover modeling candy, make a 1 in. wide rim piece, the circumference of top.
- Ice 2-layer cake smooth; top black, sides white. Position candy rim on edge of top. With toothpick, mark grill sides, 3 in. from top. Outline bottom of grill with tip 8. Cover grill rim and sides with tip 16 stars. Print tip 3 message, then overpipe.
- Place marshmallow "coals" and spaghetti "grates" on top. Edge top with tip 6 outline.
- Pipe tip 8 outline legs and ball feet. Add tip 233 grass at cake base.
- Position hamburgers and hot dogs. Pipe tip 70 spatula-striped leaf motion "flames" between grates. *Serves 24.*

*brand confectionery coating

EVENTS!

Mark these milestones in marvelous ways!

SILVER SENTIMENTS
- 18 in. Half Round Pans (2), p. 169
- 9, 12 in. Heart Pans, p.189
- Tips 327, 363, p. 135, 139
- Silver-tone beading*— 5 yds. each 4 mm. and 6 mm., p. 161
- 11 in. Heart Separator Plates (2 needed), p. 166
- 5 in. Grecian Pillars (3 pillars are used), p. 165
- Cake Dividing Set, p. 128
- Cake Circles, p. 132-133
- Magical (Silver), p. 149
- Buttercream Icing, p. 93
- Silk or Fresh Flowers

- Prepare two-layer cakes for stacked and pillar construction (see p. 106). Using Cake Dividing Set, mark 18 in. sides into 16ths. Mark 3 in. wide garlands on sides of hearts. Connect marks with tip 327 garland ruffles. Add silver beads.

- Edge tops of hearts with tip 327 ruffle borders. Pipe double row of scallops on separator plate with tip 327. Add beads to borders.
- Pipe tip 327 double ruffle border at base of 12 in. heart and top of 18 in. round. Add beads. Edge base of 9 in. heart and round with tip 363 shell border.
- To serve: Position flowers on 12 in. tier and at base. Add 9 in. heart atop pillars. Place Magical on top. *Serves 148, without top tier. (Party cake size servings.)*

*Remove before cutting.

BELLS ARE STILL RINGING
- 11 x 15 in. Sheet Pans, p. 170
- Tips 2, 11, 19, 102, 103, 104, 129, 352, p. 134-138
- Flower Nail No. 7, p. 130
- Teal, Creamy Peach Icing Colors, p. 124
- Filigree Bells—1 7/8 in. (6 needed), 2 5/8 in. (2 needed), p. 160
- 13 x 19 in. Cake Boards, Fanci-Foil Wrap, p. 132-133
- Petite Anniversary Years, p. 158
- Buttercream Icing, p. 93

- Using stiffened buttercream or royal icing, make 3 dozen two-toned roses—1 dozen each with tips 102, 103, and 104. Use tip 11 for bases. Make 52 sweet peas—26 each with tips 103 and 104. Make 75 tip 129 drop flowers with tip 2 dot centers.
- Ice 2-layer cakes smooth. Pipe tip 127 rows of ruffles on sides (pipe bottom row first, 1 1/2 in. down from top).
- Edge top and base with tip 19 rosette border. Print tip 2 message on top.
- Position Petite Anniversary Years and 2 large bells on top; pairs of small bells at base. Attach flowers to ornament, cake and cake board with dots of icing. Trim with tip 352 leaves. *Serves 44.*

EVENTS!

The years have flown, but not the memories!

FAIR & SQUARE
- 12 in. Square Pans, p. 169
- Tips 3, 70, 137, 224, 349, 506, 508 (included in Stellar Star Set), p. 134-137
- Golden Yellow, Violet, Moss Green Icing Colors, p. 124
- Cake Boards, Fanci-Foil Wrap, Tuk-N-Ruffle, 132-133
- Kissing Lovebirds, p. 161
- Buttercream Icing, p. 93

- Using stiffened buttercream (or royal) icing, make 230 drop flowers–80 with tip 137, 150 with tip 224. Add tip 3 dot centers.
- Ice 2-layer cakes smooth. Dot mark cake sides into 4ths. At marks, pipe upright columns-tip 508 on corners, tip 506 on sides. Connect columns with tip 3 double drop strings.
- Edge top with tip 70 shell motion ruffle border. Write tip 3 message. Position Kissing Lovebirds. Arrange flowers on top, sides, and at base. Trim with tip 349 leaves. *Serves 40.*

GOLDEN MEMORIES
- 4-Pc. Oval Pan Set, (16 x 12³/₈ and 10³/₄ x 7⁷/₈ pan are used), p. 168
- Tips 1, 3, 12, 16, 19, 102, 103, 352, p. 134-137
- Flower Nail No. 7, p. 130
- 6 ½ in. Arched Pillars (4 needed), p. 165
- 11 ½ in. Oval Separator Plates (2 needed), p. 166
- 4 mm. Gold-Tone Beading (9 yds. needed), p. 161

- Cake Boards, Tuk-N-Ruffle, Fanci-Foil Wrap, p. 132
- Cake Dividing Set, p. 128
- Dowel Rods, p. 166
- Golden Jubilee, p. 158
- Anniversary Champagne Glasses Set, p. 153
- Buttercream Icing, p. 93

- Using stiffened buttercream (or royal) icing, make 12 tip 12 and 103 roses. Let set.
- To prepare 2-layer ovals for pillar and stacked construction, see p. 106.
- Using Garland Marker (included with Cake Dividing Set), mark garlands on sides of large oval—4 in. wide, 1¹/₂ in. deep for cornelli area and 2¹/₂ in. deep for gold bead garlands. Add tip 1 cornelli lace. Position gold bead garlands. Pipe tip 102 ruffle garlands, edged with tip 3 drop strings.
- Write tip 3 message on side of top oval. Trim edge of separator plate with tip 16 shell border. Edge top of tiers with tip 102 ruffles and tip 16 shells. Add gold beads.
- Edge base of top tier with tip 19 upright shells, edged with tip 19 shells. Pipe Over-lapping Shell Border (see p. 103) at base of bottom tier. Outline base shells with tip 3. Add gold beads to borders. Position roses on large tier and trim with tip 352 leaves.
- To serve: Position top tier on pillars. Add Golden Jubilee and Anniversary Champagne Glasses. *Serves 66.*

78

TAILORED TREASURE

- 4 pc. Hexagon Pan Set (9, 12, 15 in. pans are used), p. 168
- Tips 3, 5, p. 134
- '92 Pattern Book (Candy Panel Patterns), p. 115
- White Candy Melts™ (12 bags needed), p. 118
- Rounds, Wedding, Hearts II Candy Molds, p. 116, 117
- Floating Tier Cake Stand, p. 164
- Meringue Powder, p. 125
- 1 7/8 in. White Artificial Leaves, p. 159
- Cake Boards, Fanci-Foil Wrap, p. 132-133
- Masterpiece, p. 149
- Modeling Candy Recipe, p. 109
- Buttercream, Royal Icings, p. 93, 94
- Using modeling candy, make 13 candy roses (see p. 110).
- Using Candy Panel Patterns and melted Candy Melts™, outline and flow in panels with tip 3 (see p. 108). Patterns specify number of panels needed, but be sure to make extra in case of breakage. Also mold candy shown using molds listed. Rose candies on top tier are made by filling in only the rose on round mold. Refrigerate candy until completely set.
- When candy is completely set, attach molded candy to panels with royal icing. Add rows of triple bead and garlands with tip 3 on top and bottom panels. Pipe rows of tip 3 beads on center panels. Let icing dry.
- Cut cake boards 3 in. larger than cakes and cover with Fanci-Foil Wrap. Ice 2-layer cakes smooth. Build up icing at bases with tip 5 to support beveled panels. Position candy panels on sides, add bottom bevel pieces; attach side pieces with royal icing. Edge with tip 5 royal icing beads.
- Position candy roses on 12 and 15 in. tops. Add artificial leaves.
- At reception, position cakes on Floating Tier Stand. Add Masterpiece. *Serves 122.*

Note: This cake must be stored in a very cool (65°-70°) place or refrigerated.

*Serving size is 1 in. wide x 2 in. deep x 4 in. high. By tradition, the top tier is saved for the couple's first wedding anniversary. We do not figure it in with the number of servings.

HEART STRINGS

- 8, 12, 14 in. Round Pans, p. 169
- Tips 2, 3, 199, p. 134-135
- Ivory, Creamy Peach Icing Color, p. 124
- 10 and 16 in. Decorator Preferred Separator Plates (1 each), p. 167
- 7 and 9 in. Grecian Spiked Pillars (1 set each), p. 165
- Cake Dividing Set, Decorator Brushes, p. 128
- 10, 14 (4 needed), 16 in. Ruffle Boards™, p. 132
- Meringue Powder, p. 125
- Crystal-Look Bowls (2 needed), p.163
- Happiest Day Couples (4 needed), p. 150
- Allure, p. 148
- Buttercream, Royal Icings, p. 93
- Flowers
- Have florist arrange flowers in Crystal-Look Bowls. Remove veils from Happiest Day brides. Using thinned royal icing, "paint" gowns and headpieces to coordinate with bride's choice of color.
- To prepare 2-layer cakes (8 and 14 in. center and four 12 in. side cakes) for push-in pillar construction, see p. 106.
- Using Cake Dividing Set, mark 12 in. cakes into 16ths, 14 in. into 12ths, 1¼ in. from top edges. Using side divisions as a guide, mark scallops, 1¼ in. from edge, on 12 and 14 in. tops.
- Pipe double drop string scallops and heart bows on 12 and 14 in. tops with tip 3. Trim with tip 3 dots. Edge 7 in. pillars in 14 in. cake with tip 3 beads.
- Pipe tip 199 crown border at tops of 8 and 12 in. tiers. Add tip 2 triple drop strings. Trim shells and strings with tip 2 dots.
- Pipe tip 2 triple drop string garlands and heart bows on side of 14 in. tier. Edge 14 in. top and all bases with tip 199 shell borders. Align pillars in each 12 in. round to match up with 16 in. plate.
- At reception: Position floral arrangements, tiers on pillars, couples and Allure.
  Serves 301.

EVENTS!

Celebrate a joyous marriage with a beautiful cake!

FANTASY

- 8, 12, 16 in. Round Pans, p. 171
- Tips 2, 3, 5, 7, 12, 16, 102, 103, 104, 349, 352, p. 134-139
- Leaf Green, Pink Icing Colors, p. 124
- Flower Nail No. 7, p. 130
- '92 Pattern Book (Fan and Arched Fan Spaces), p. 115
- 10 in., 14 in. Crystal-Clear Plates, 7 ¹⁄₂ in. (1 set) and 9 in. (1 set), Twist Legs p. 164
- 10 in., 14 in., 18 in. Ruffle Boards™, Cake Boards, Fanci-Foil Wrap, p. 132
- 4 mm., 6 mm. * White Pearl Beading (5 yds. of each), p. 161
- Love's Fanfare, p. 154
- Buttercream, Royal Icings, p. 93

- Using royal icing, make 60 roses—20 each with tip 102, 103, 104. Use tip 12 for bases. Make 30 sweet peas and 40 rosebuds with tip 104.
- For fans (make 9): Trace Fan Pattern onto cake board and cut out. Cover with Fanci-Foil Wrap. Outline line details on fans with tip 3. Trim with 4 mm. pearls. Edge tops of fans with tip 3 zigzags. Pipe tip 16 rosette roses and tip 349 leaves.
- To prepare 2-layer cakes for push-in pillar construction, see p. 106. Centering 8 and 12 in. pans on tops as a guide, mark circular areas on top of 12 and 16 in. tiers. Mark Wedding Arches Patterns on sides of each tier. Fill in areas shown with tip 2 cornelli lace.
- Edge arches with tip 16 scallops. Edge circular areas on 12 and 16 in. tiers with tip 3 beads. Pipe tip 5 bead border at top of 8 in. Edge bases with bulb borders—tip 7 on 8 and 12 in., tip 12 on 16 in.
- Pipe tip 5 strings around bases of pillars and position 6 mm. pearls. Mound icing on 12 and 16 in. tops with tip 12. Position fans and flowers on tops and sides. Trim with tip 352 leaves.
- At reception: Position tiers on pillars. Add Love's Fanfare. *Serves 156.*

*Remove pearls before serving.

TRULY IN LOVE

- 6, 9, 12 in. Heart Pans, 12, 16 in. Round Pans, p. 169, 171, 175
- Tips 4, 13, 16, 19, 32, 102, 104, 352, p. 134-136, 138
- Leaf Green, Pink Icing Colors, p. 124
- Pearl White Stamens (2 pkgs. needed), p. 130
- 1 5/8 in. Lily Nail, p. 130.
- 5 in. Grecian Pillars (6 needed), Arched Tier Set, p. 165
- 8 & 11 in. Heart Separator Plates (2 of each size needed), p. 166
- Filigree Stairway, Kolor-Flo Fountain, Flower Holder Ring, p. 163
- Dowel Rods, p. 166
- Cake Boards, Tuk-N-Ruffle, Fanci-Foil Wrap, p. 132-133
- 4 in. Filigree Hearts (4 pkgs. needed), p. 163
- Cake Dividing Set, 15-pc. Decorator Pattern Press Set, p. 128
- Blossom Tier Top, Mini Bouquet, p.152
- Crowning Glory, p. 148
- Buttercream, Royal Icings, p. 93
- Ivy vines, baby's breath

- Using royal icing, make approximately 35 tip 104 and 40 tip 102 spatula-striped petunias with tip 13 centers on lily nail (allow extras for breakage). Add 3 stamens to each. Let dry.
- Using royal icing, pipe tip 4 e-motion strings on filigree hearts, on 9 and 11 in. heart separator base plates, and on inside heart of Crowning Glory. Let dry.
- To prepare 2-layer cakes for pillar and stacked construction, see p. 106. Using Cake Dividing Set, dot mark 16 in. tier into 6ths, 12 in. round into 12ths. From the point of the heart, dot mark 3 in. spacing for garlands on 9 in. and 12 in. heart tiers, 2 1/2 in. on 6 in. heart tier. Imprint small scroll design from Pattern Press Set symmetrically at base point of 9 and 6 in. hearts.
- Position filigree hearts centered at dot marks on 16 in. round tier. Position 5 hearts evenly around 12 in. heart tier as shown. Pipe tip 16 e-motion garlands on tier sides, pipe e-motion border on heart separator plates. Pipe tip 32 base and tip 16 top shell borders on all tiers. Add tip 4 drop strings on 12 in. round tier. Pipe tip 32 long double shells on base tiers, tip 19 elongated upright shells on others. Pipe in scroll design with tip 16 on 6 and 9 in. heart tiers.
- Position petunias as shown with dots of icing. Add tip 352 leaves.
- At reception: Place Flower Holder Ring and Kolor-Flo Fountain on base plate. Arrange ivy and baby's breath in ring. Position side cake, assemble tiers on pillars. Add filigree stairway, Blossom Tier Top, Mini Bouquet and Crowning Glory.
  Serves 215.

EVENTS!

Treat your guests to an elaborate celebration of love!

ROYAL WEDDING

- 7, 8, 10, 12, 16 x 2 in. Round Pans, p. 169
- Tips 7, 68, 103, 124, 125, 199, 363, 364, p. 134-139
- Flower Nail No. 7, p. 130
- Royal Blue, Kelly Green Icing Colors, p. 124
- '92 Pattern Book (Drape Patterns), p. 115
- 4 Bridesmaids, Blue; 4 Groomsmen, p. 150
- Pearl Beading*—4 mm. (3 pkgs. needed), p. 161
- Pearl White Stamens (3 pkgs. needed), p. 130
- Flower Formers, p. 130
- Crystal Stairways (4 needed), p. 163
- 7 in. Crystal-Look Pillars (2 sets needed) p. 165
- 9 in. (2 needed), and 13 in. (4 needed), Crystal-Look Plates, p. 165
- Crystal-Look Tier Set, 165
- Fountain Cascade Set, Flower Holder Ring p. 163
- Cake Dividing Set, p. 128
- Dowel Rods, p. 166
- Cake Circles, p.133
- Florist Wire (1 pkg. needed), p. 130
- Garden Delight, p. 148
- Buttercream, Royal Icings, p. 93
- White florist tape, ribbon, tulle trim

- With royal icing, make 80 wild roses with tip 103. Push in stamens and dry on flower formers. Pipe 80 calyxes on wires (see p. 101) with tip 7. When dry, attach together with icing. Make 70 leaves on wires with tip 68. Let dry. Assemble bouquets as shown, using flowers, ribbon, pearls, tulle trim and white florist tape.

- To prepare 2-layer rounds (7, 10, 16 in. for center, 8 and 10 in. for side tiers, 8 in. for front cakes) for stacked and pillar construction, see p. 106. Using Cake Dividing Set, with toothpick, dot mark 16 in. cake into 16ths, 7 in. into 6ths and the two 8 in. front cakes into 8ths. Mark Drape Patterns on sides of 10 in. center tier, 8 and 12 in. side cakes (place on opposite sides of 8 and 10 in. stacked cakes).

- Pipe shell borders: tip 199 top and base on 16 in. tier, tip 199 base and tip 364 top on 10 in. tier, tip 364 base and tip 363 top on 7 in. tier, tip 364 base and tip 363 top on 8 in. front and side tiers. Pipe tip 125 ruffle and swag on 16, 12, 10, and 8 in. tiers; tip 124 ruffle and swag on 7 in. Position pearl beading (see p. 103)

- At reception: Position tiers on pillars. Add floral bouquets, Garden Delight, fountain and flower ring, stairways, and bridesmaids and groomsmen. *Serves 317.*

*Remove pearls before serving.

A lasting keepsake to recall fond nuptial memories for years to come. Contemporary bridesmaid in bold jewel tones. See p. 150.

EVENTS!

A vision of elegance perfect for large weddings.

SIMPLY MAGNIFICENT

- 7 in. Round, 12 in. Hexagon, 16 in. Square Pans, p. 168-171
- Tip 1s, 2, 5, 7, 101, 127, 349, p. 134, 136, 138
- 15-pc. Decorator Pattern Press, p. 128
- 9 in. Crystal-look Plate (1 needed), p. 165
- 9 in. Crystal-look Spike Pillars (4 needed), p. 165
- Dowel Rods, p. 166
- Pearl Tier Top, p. 152
- Reflections, White, p. 155
- Buttercream, Royal, Rolled Fondant Icings*, p. 93, 94
- Silver Dragees

- Using royal icing, make 70 tip 101 apple blossoms, add silver dragees centers. Let dry.
- To prepare 2-layer cakes for stacked and pillar construction, see p. 106. *You will need 4 recipes of rolled fondant icing for this cake, using 2 for 16 in. square tier.
- Using scroll piece from pattern press set, imprint scrolls at varying angles on 16 in. square and 7 in. round tiers; imprint scrolls centered symmetrically on 9 in. hexagon tier sides as shown. Cover scroll marks with tip 2 strings, add apple blossoms, trim with tip 349 leaves.
- Edge base of 16 in. and 7 in. tiers with tip 127 ruffle border. Pipe tip 1s sotas lacework on ruffle. Trim with tip 5 bead border. Measure 1/2 in. from each corner angle on hexagon tier. Fill in with tip 1s sotas lacework. Outline filled-in area, and base of pillars with tip 5 beads. Edge tier base with tip 7 beads.
- At reception: Position tier on pillars. Add Reflections and Pearl Tier Top. *Serves 178.*

ROMANCE IN BLOOM

- 8, 12, 16 in. Round Pans, p. 169, 171
- Tip 10, p. 134
- Violet, Pink, Lemon Yellow, Peach, Leaf Green Icing Colors, p. 124
- 6 mm. Pearl Beading*— (1 pkg. needed), p. 161
- Dowel Rods, p. 166
- Sweethearts, p. 146
- Cake Boards, Tuk-N-Ruffle, Fanci-Foil Wrap, p. 132-133
- Rolled Fondant (4 recipes needed), Buttercream Icing, p. 93, 94

- Cover 2-layer cakes with fondant icing following recipe instructions. Using excess fondant and icing colors, make approximately 18 roses, 15 rosebuds and 60 leaves in colors shown following the modeling candy clay method for making flowers on p. 109.
- To prepare 2-layer cakes for stacked construction, see p. 106.
- Edge base of each tier with tip 10 double bead border. Position pearl beading. Attach roses, rosebuds and leaves to cake with dots of icing in positions shown.
- At reception: Position Sweethearts. *Serves 156.*

*Remove pearls before cutting and serving.

EVENTS!

Beautiful wedding memories from this day forward!

SOPHISTICATED BLISS

- 6, 10, 14 in. Round Pans, p. 171
- 18 in. Half Round Pans, p. 169
- Tips 1, 1s, 1D, 2B, 3, 4B, 13, 16, 18, 21, p. 134-139
- Black Icing Color, p. 124
- '92 Pattern Book (Cornelli Drape Patterns A & B), p. 115
- 8 & 12 in. Decorator Preferred Round Separator Plates (2 of each size needed), p. 167
- 3 & 5 in. Grecian Pillars (1 set each) p. 165
- Dowel Rods, p. 166
- Scrolls (16 needed), p. 163
- Pearl Beading*—6 mm. White, 4 mm. Black (6 yds. of each), p. 161
- Cake Dividing Set, p. 128
- Loves Delight, p. 148
- Mini Bouquets (6 needed), p. 159
- Meringue Powder, p. 125
- Decorator Brushes, p. 128
- Cake Circles, Tuk-N-Ruffle, Fanci-Foil Wrap, p. 132-133
- Buttercream, Royal Icings, p. 93

- Using thinned royal icing, paint pillars grey, let dry; with tip 1s and thinned black royal icing, pipe marbelized "veins;" before icing dries, dab through "veins" with a dry decorator brush. Repeat procedure using thinned white icing. Let dry.

- Prepare 2-layer cakes for pillar and stacked construction. Note: 18 in. base tier is made with four half rounds.

- Using Cake Dividing Set, with toothpick, mark 6 in. tier into 6ths, 14 in. into 12ths, 10 and 18 in. tiers into 4ths.

- Edge separator plates with tip 16 scallops. Twist black and white pearls together. Position around bases.

- On sides at top of 6 & 12 in., pipe tip 1D ribbed stripe bands. From bottom of bands, mark 1½ in. deep garlands. Fill in garlands with tip 1 cornelli lace. Connect garlands with tip 16 triple drop strings (work from bottom, up). Add crown borders using tip 4B at points of garlands, tip 21 in between. Trim with tip 3 dots.

- On 10 & 18 in., edge tops of cakes with tip 18 shell borders. Mark Cornelli Drape Pattern A on 10 in. sides, B on 18 in. Cover center areas with tip 1 cornelli lace. Center pairs of Scrolls at top of areas and outline with tip 13. At sides, pipe tip 4B upright shells. Connect shells and scrolls with tip 16 double drop strings on 10 in. and quadruple drop strings on 18 in. Overpipe bottom string. Trim tops of shells with tip 16 rosettes. Add tip 3 dots in center of cornelli areas.

- Between drape areas on 10 in., pipe tip 16 triple drop strings trimmed with tip 16 upright shells. On 18 in., cover 2 in. wide areas between drapes with tip 1 cornelli lace. Edge areas with tip 2B ribbed stripe bands. Add tip 16 triple drop string garlands, upright shells and rosettes at top of each area.

- At reception: Position tiers on pillars. Add Mini Bouquets and Loves Delight. *Serves 243.*

*Remove pearls before cutting and serving.

HEIGHT OF DRAMA
- 7, 10, 12 in. Round Pans, p. 171
- 16 in. Square Pan, p. 170
- Tips 2, 3, 16, 20, 129, 131, 190, 224, 225, 349, p. 134-139
- Willow Green, Golden Yellow Icing Colors, p. 124
- '92 Pattern Book, (Latticework Garland Pattern), p. 115
- 6* & 12 in. Round Separator Plates, p. 167
- 7 in. Grecian Pillars, p. 165
- Dowel Rods, p. 166
- Cake Circles, Tuk-N-Ruffle, Fanci-Foil Wrap, p. 132-133
- Meringue Powder, p. 125
- Cake Dividing Set, p.128
- Sweet Symphony Musical Ornament, p.150
- Buttercream, Royal Icings, p. 93

- Using royal icing, make 200 drop flowers, 60 of each using tips 190, 129, 131, 224, 225. Add tip 2 dot centers.
- To prepare 2-layer cakes for stacked and push-in pillar construction, see p. 106. Also dowel rod 7 in. cake to support 6 in. separator plate and ornament. Using Cake Dividing Set, dot mark 7 in. round sides into 6ths, 10 in. round sides into 8ths, 12 in. round sides into 10ths. Using garland marker, mark garlands in center of each sectional division beginning 2 inches from each cake top. Mark Latticework Garland Pattern on sides of square.
- Cover areas on sides of 10 in. and square with tip 2 latticework (strings are an 1/8 in. apart).
- Connect garland marks on 7 in. with Dropped Lattice Garlands using tips 3 and 16 (see p. 97).
- On 10 in. and square, pipe tip 16 zigzag garlands. Add tip 3 double drop strings.
- Edge pillars with tip 16 shells. Pipe tip 20 shell borders on tops and bases.
- On 12 in., pipe tips 3 and 16 Dropped Lattice Garlands. Add tip 3 double drop strings. Trim garlands on 12 in. and square with tip 16 rosettes.
- Add drop flower clusters to all sides and trim with tip 349 leaves.
- At reception: Position tiers on pillars. Add Sweet Symphony and flowers. *Serves 223.*

*Note: We suggest using dowel rods and place 6 in. separator plate on 7 in. tier to support this ornament.

EVENTS!

Begin married life in the grandest of style!

Everyone Can Enjoy Cake Decorating!

Beginners and hobbyists alike will find cake decorating fun, easy and very rewarding. A personally decorated special occasion cake will delight the recipient and prove rewarding for the decorator. The following guide will provide you with the basics of cake decorating as well as more advanced techniques. With just a little practice, you can make specific decorations described in this section that will enable you to create cakes in the "idea" section of this Yearbook. And, if you've already gained some experience with cake decorating, the pages ahead are great for review and new inspirations.

Cake Decorating Equipment

You will need basic cake decorating tools and some of your own kitchen tools and supplies. Here are some basic Wilton tools you will want to make your decorating more fun and rewarding.

Cake Stands, Separator Plates & Cake Circles & Boards	Wilton Cake Stands hold your cake and allow you to rotate the cake while you decorate. Separator plates and cake boards help support your tiered cakes (when you become more advanced!) with the use of pretty pillars. Use dowel rods for tiered cake support.
Cake Tops & Trims	Wilton cake tops are made of fine plastic and molded to fun character, animal and decorative shapes for quick and easy cake decorating. They dress up a cake so special and personalize it for most any celebration. And they become treasured keepsakes after the party.
Coupler	Grooved insert and retainer ring designed to allow tip changes on Wilton Featherweight or disposable decorating bags. This two-piece time-saver eliminates the need for a clean decorating bag every time you wish to use a different tip.
Decorating Bag	A plastic polyester-coated fabric cone, clear plastic cone or parchment paper bag that holds your decorator icing and special tip.
Decorating Tips	Cone-shaped, open-ended metal tips that drop into the decorating bag or attach to a coupler. When icing is squeezed through the tip, the size and shape of the opening determines the types of decorating produced.
Flower Nail	A round, flat metal nailhead used as a turntable for making icing roses and other special flowers.
Icing Colors & Flavors	Wilton Paste Icing Colors are concentrated in a creamy, rich base which will not change your icing consistency. Wilton Liquid Icing Colors are also concentrated and color icing in soft, pastel hues. Wilton Flavors are delicious to add to icing or batter for taste appeal.

Cake Decorating Terms to Know

These words are frequently used in cake decorating. Use this as a reference when decorating your cakes.

Attach	To secure royal, buttercream icing flowers or plastic decorations, pipe dots or icing to "attach" the decoration to an iced cake. Royal icing dries hard and is more permanent than buttercream. Use your icing to attach as you would use "glue."
Border	A continuous decoration used around the top, side or base of a cake.
Elongated	When we use the term elongated shells, leaves, etc. it means to taper an icing decoration by relaxing bag pressure and moving before stopping the technique.
Figure Piping	Decorating technique used to form figures out of icing.
Filling	Frosting, preserves or pudding that's spread between cake layers and holds them together.
Leveling	Removing the "crown" of a cake to provide a flat surface for frosting or decorating.
Outline or Strings	When the outlining method is used, the icing that flows out of the tip to follow contours of a shaped cake or to cover pattern design marks are called "strings" or outlines.
Piping	Squeezing icing out of a bag to form decoration. Also see figure piping.
Score	Using your spatula edge to make a mark in icing or marzipan by gently pressing it against the surface.

Decorating Guide

Baking Your Cake

The First Step to Success!
For a beautiful cake, follow these easy instructions. A properly baked cake is the best foundation for your icing and your decorations. NOTE: If you're using one of the Wilton shaped pans, follow the specific instructions included with the pan. For 3-dimensional stand-up cakes, use batters that bake a firm-textured cake such as a pound cake.

GREASE

FLOUR
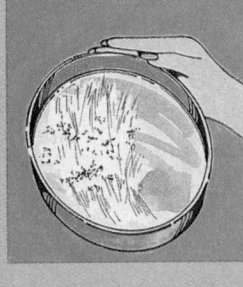

SHAKE
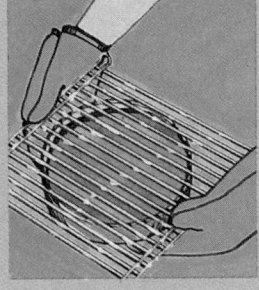

PLACE RACK

REMOVE

•Preheat oven to temperature specified in recipe or on packaged mix.
•Thoroughly grease the inside of each pan with solid vegetable shortening or use a vegetable cooking spray. Use a pastry brush to spread the shortening evenly. Be sure sides, corners and all indentations are completely covered.
•Sprinkle flour inside of pan and shake back and forth so the flour covers all the greased surfaces. Tap out excess flour and if any shiny spots remain, touch up with more shortening and flour. This tip is essential in preventing your cake from sticking. If you prefer, the bottom of a simple geometric shaped pan (round, square, hexagon, etc.) may be lined with waxed paper after greasing. This eliminates flouring pan. Your cake will unmold easily but with more crumbs on side.
•Bake the cake according to temperature and time specifications in recipe or on package instructions. Remove cake from oven and let cool 10 minutes in pan on a cake rack. Larger cakes over 12-in. diameter may need to cool 15 minutes.
•So cake sits level and to prevent cracking, while in pan, cut away the raised center portion with serrated knife. To unmold cake, place cake rack against cake and turn both rack and pan over. Remove pan carefully. If pan will not release, return it to a warm oven (250°) for a few minutes, then repeat procedure. Cool cake completely, at least 1 hour. Brush off loose crumbs and frost.

Baking Hints

•If you like to plan ahead, do so. Your baked cake will stay up to three months wrapped in heavy-duty foil in the freezer. Always thaw cake completely before icing. Your cake will still be fresh and easy to ice because it will be firm.
•Wilton Bake-Even Cake Strips will help prevent crowns from forming on basic shaped cakes as they bake.
•Packaged, two-layer cake mixes usually yield 4 to 6 cups of batter, but formulas change, so always measure. Here's a handy guide: one 2-layer cake mix will make any of the following: two 8-in. round layers, or one 10-in. round layer, or one 9x13x2-in. sheet, or one character cake, or one Wonder Mold cake, or one mini-tier cake.
•If you're in doubt as to how many cups of batter you need to fill a pan, measure the cups of water it will hold first and use this number as a guide. Then, if you want a cake with high sides, fill the pan ²/₃ full of batter. For slightly thinner cake layers, fill ¹/₂ full. Never fill cake pans more than ²/₃ full. Even if the batter doesn't overflow, the cake will have a heavy texture.
•For 3-in. deep or 3-D pans, we recommend pound or pudding-added cake batters. Fill pan half full only.
•For 3-D cakes: When using the baking core, it's essential to be exact about baking time, as it's very difficult to test 3-D cakes for doneness. Be sure to preheat the oven. If your 3-D cake is to be given away or sold, after baking you can remove the baking core and insert crumpled aluminum foil into the opening for support.
Hints for cakes-to-go! Use our Cake Pan Cover to protect sheet cakes in our 9x13-in. pan (p.170). The Cake Saver is a great way to take cakes places (p. 170).

Ruffle Boards™

Create a new, professional presentation for decorated cakes— in an instant! Our ready-to-use Ruffle Boards™ are bleached white cake boards with solid white ruffling already attached. It's a neat look with no brown cardboard peek-thru that's convenient, saves time, and gives the decorator truly beautiful results. Ruffle Boards™ are available in a range of round sizes from 8 in. to 18 in., to accomodate cakes from 6 to 16 in. See page 132 for complete ordering information.

All About Icing

Proper consistency is the key to making decorating icing that will shape the petals of a flower, show the details of a border or cover the surface of a cake. It's important that you use the recommended icing and consistency for any technique. As a general rule, flowers require a stiff icing consistency, borders a medium-stiff consistency and writing or leaves a slightly thinned consistency. Icing that can peak to an inch or more is stiff, less than that is medium consistency. Icing that flows easily from a tip without running is a thin consistency. Every Wilton icing recipe is tested for taste and other important qualities. This chart will tell you each recipe's qualities, so you can determine which is the right one for your cake.

Icing	Recommended Uses	Tinting	Flavor & Consistency	Storing Icing	Special Information
Buttercream (Wilton Mix or Homemade)	• Borders, writing • Roses, drop flowers & sweet peas • Figure piping • Icing cakes smooth	• Deep colors • Most colors deepen upon setting	• Sweet, buttery flavor • Thin-to-stiff consistency	• Refrigerate icing in an airtight container for 2 weeks	• Iced cake can be stored at room temperature for 2-3 days • Flowers remain soft enough to be cut with a knife
Snow-White Buttercream	• Borders, writing • Roses, drop flowers & sweet peas • Figure piping • Icing cakes smooth	• Deep colors • Most colors deepen upon setting • Gives true colors	• Sweet, almond flavor • Thin-to-stiff consistency	• Refrigerate icing in an airtight container for 2 weeks	• Iced cake may be stored for 2-3 days • Air-dried flowers have translucent look • Flowers remain soft to be cut with a knife • Good for wedding cakes • Tints true colors due to pure white color
Deluxe Buttercream (Use Wilton Icing Mix or Ready-To-Use Decorator Icing)	• Borders, writing • Drop flowers & sweet peas • Figure piping • Icing cakes smooth	• Deep colors	• Rich, creamy flavor • Medium-to-stiff consistency	• Refrigerate icing in an airtight container for 2 weeks	• Texture remains soft on decorated cake • Iced cake may be stored at room temperature one day • All-purpose
Cream Cheese	• Basic borders, writing, stars, shells, drop flowers • Icing cake smooth	• Pastels	• Cream cheese • Thin-to-medium consistency	• Refrigerate icing in an airtight container for 2 week	• Iced cake must be refrigerated • Cream cheese flavor is especially good with spice cakes, carrot cakes, etc. • All-purpose
Stabilized Whipped Cream	• Borders, writing • Icing cake smooth	• Pastels only • Paste colors are best to use	• Creamy, delicate sweetness • Light, thin-to-medium consistency	• Use immediately	• Iced cake must be refrigerated • Texture remains soft on decorated cake • Especially good on cakes decorated with fruits
French Buttercream	• Basic borders • Writing • Icing cake smooth	• Pastels only	• Tastes similar to vanilla icc cream • Consistency similar to whipped cream	• Use immediately	• Store iced cake in refrigerator • Texture remains soft on decorated cake • Cooked icing gives a special flavor, similar to vanilla ice cream
Quick-Pour Fondant Icing	• For icing	• Pastels	• Very sweet flavor • Pourable consistency	• Use immediately, excess fondant drippings can be reheated & poured again	• Dries to a shiny, smooth surface to coat cakes, petit fours and cookies • Seals in freshness
Rolled Fondant Icing	• For covering heavy pound or fruit cake • Cutting small decorations and ruffles	• Pastels	• Rich, sweet flavor • Dough-like consistency	• Excess can be refrigerated 3 weeks • Bring to room temperature before kneading	• Gives a perfectly smooth, velvety surface • Seals in freshness and moisture • Always decorate with royal icing • Cake can be stored at room temp. 3-4 days
Royal	• Flower-making, figure piping, making flowers on wires • Decorating cookies & gingerbread houses	• Deep colors • Some colors may fade upon sitting in bright light	• Very sweet and hard • Thin-to-stiff consistency	• Store in airtight grease-free container at room temperature for 2 weeks	• Dries candy-hard for lasting decorations • Flowers and other decorations will last for months. Air dry. • Bowl & utensils must be grease free • Cover icing with damp cloth to prevent crusting
Boiled Icing 100% Fat-free!	• Borders • Figure piping • Writing stringwork • Icing cakes smooth and fluffy.	• Pastel & deep shades	• Marshmallow-like flavor • Very fluffy consistency	• Use immediately	• Serve within 24 hours • Sets quickly! Ice smooth or fluffy, immediately • Ideal for figure piping

Icing Recipes

Buttercream Icing

¹/₂ cup solid vegetable shortening
¹/₂ cup butter or margarine*
1 tsp. Clear Vanilla Extract (p. 125)
4 cups sifted confectioners sugar
  (approx. 1 lb.)
2 Tbsps. milk**
Cream butter and shortening with electric mixer. Add vanilla. Gradually add sugar, one cup at a time, beating well on medium speed. Scrape sides and bottom of bowl often. When all sugar has been mixed in, icing will appear dry. Add milk and beat at medium speed until light and fluffy. Keep icing covered with a damp cloth until ready to use. For best results, keep icing bowl in refrigerator when not in use. Refrigerated in an airtight container, this icing can be stored 2 weeks. Rewhip before using.
YIELD: 3 cups
*Substitute all-vegetable shortening and ¹/₂ teaspoon Wilton Butter Extract for pure white icing and stiffer consistency.
**Add 3-4 Tbsps. light corn syrup per recipe to thin for icing cake.

Chocolate Buttercream

Add ³/₄ cup cocoa or three 1 oz. unsweetened chocolate squares, melted, and an additional 1 to 2 Tbsps. milk to recipe. Mix until well blended.
For a unique change of pace, add Wilton Candy Flavors (p.118), in place of vanilla extract.

Snow-White Buttercream

²/₃ cup water
4 Tbsps. Meringue Powder Mix (p. 125)
12 cups sifted confectioners sugar
  (approximately 3 lbs.)
1 ¹/₄ cups solid shortening
³/₄ tsp. salt
¹/₂ tsp. Almond Extract (p. 125)
¹/₂ tsp. Clear Vanilla Extract (p. 125)
¹/₄ tsp. Butter Flavor (p. 125)
Combine water and meringue powder; whip at high speed until peaks form. Add 4 cups sugar, one cup at a time, beating after each addition at low speed. Alternately add shortening and remainder of sugar. Add salt and flavorings; beat at low speed until smooth.
YIELD: 7 cups
Note: Recipe may be doubled or cut in half. If cut in half, yield is 2 ²/₃ cups.

Wilton Creamy White Icing Mix

You'll love its creamy taste, luscious texture and convenience. Ideal for icing smooth and decorating (p.125). Just add butter and milk, the shortening's already in the mix. For chocolate icing: Mix icing according to package directions. Stir in 2-oz. melted, unsweetened baking chocolate. If too stiff, add a few drops of milk. For Deluxe Buttercream: Use 6 Tbsps. butter and ¹/₄ cup whipping cream.

Ready-To-Serve Decorator White Icing

The ease is a breeze. Just stir and use. (p. 125)

French Buttercream

²/₃ cup sugar
¹/₄ cup flour
¹/₄ tsp. salt
³/₄ cup milk
1 cup cold butter; cut in several pieces
1 tsp. Clear Vanilla Extract (p. 125)
Place sugar, flour and salt in sauce pan and mix thoroughly; stir in milk. Cook over medium heat and stir constantly until very thick. Remove from heat and pour into a medium mixing bowl. Cool at room temperature. Add ¹/₂ cup butter at a time (cut into several pieces) and beat at medium-high speed until smooth. Add vanilla and beat well. Chill icing for a few minutes before decorating. Iced cake must be refrigerated until serving time.
YIELD: 2 cups

Stabilized Whipped Cream Icing

1 tsp. unflavored gelatin
4 tsps. cold water
1 cup heavy whipping cream
¹/₄ cup confectioners sugar
¹/₂ tsp. Clear Vanilla Extract (p.125)
Combine gelatin and cold water in small saucepan. Let stand until thick. Place over low heat, stirring constantly, just until gelatin dissolves. Remove from heat and cool, do not let set. Whip cream, sugar, and vanilla until slightly thickened. While beating slowly, gradually add gelatin to whipped cream mixture. Whip at high speed until stiff.
YIELD: 2 cups.
Cakes iced with whipped cream must be stored in the refrigerator.

Cream Cheese Icing

3-8 oz. packages slightly softened cream cheese
3 cups sifted confectioners sugar
Beat cream cheese until smooth. Add confectioners sugar and mix thoroughly. Beat at high speed until smooth. YIELD: 3 ¹/₂ cups

Packaged Topping Mix

Whipped topping mix can be used for decorating similar to stabilized whipped cream. However, use immediately after preparing. Do not allow to stay at room temperature, as topping becomes too soft for well-defined decorations.

Frozen Non-Dairy Whipped Topping

Non-dairy whipped topping must be thawed in the refrigerator before coloring or using for decorating. Can be used for decorating techniques similar to stabilized whipped cream. Do not allow to stay at room temperature, as it becomes too soft for decorating. After decorating, store cake in refrigerator.

Specialty Icing Recipes

Royal Icing

3 level Tbsps. Meringue Powder (p. 125)
4 cups sifted confectioners sugar
(approx. 1 lb.)
6 Tbsps. water*
Beat all ingredients at low speed for 7 to 10 minutes (10 to 12 minutes at high speed for portable mixer) until icing forms peaks.
YIELD: 3 cups
*When using large counter top mixer or for stiffer icing, use 1 Tbsp. less water.

Boiled Icing Recipe

Meringue:
3 Tbsps. Meringue Powder (p. 125)
¹/₂ cup cold water
Syrup:
2 cups granulated sugar
¹/₄ cup corn syrup
¹/₂ cup water
Beat meringue powder and cold water until stiff, about 4 minutes. In large microwave-safe measuring cup stir sugar, corn syrup and water. In microwave oven, bring syrup mixture to a boil (approximately 5 minutes). Remove when boiling stops. Slowly add syrup to meringue mixture while beating on low. Beat on HIGH for 4 minutes until stiff and glossy.
YIELD: 8 cups
For top of range: Mix sugar, corn syrup and water in 2 quart saucepan. Bring to a boil; cool slightly and follow directions above.

Confectioners Sugar Glaze

Great to drizzle on dessert cakes, muffins and cookies.
1 ¹/₄ cups confectioner sugar
3 Tbsps milk
Stir milk into sugar.
  YIELD: ¹/₂ cup

Quick-Pour Fondant Icing

6 cups confectioners sugar
¹/₂ cup water
2 Tbsps. light corn syrup
1 tsp. Almond Extract (p. 125)
Wilton Icing Colors (p. 125)
Place sugar in a saucepan. Combine water and corn syrup. Add to sugar and stir until well mixed. Place over low heat. Don't allow temperature of fondant to exceed 100⁰. Remove from heat, stir in flavor and icing color. Optional: Cakes may be covered with a thin coating of buttercream icing or apricot glaze. Allow to set before covering with fondant. To cover, place cake or cookies on wire rack over a drip pan. Pour fondant into center and work towards edges. Touch up bare spots with a spatula. Let set. Excess fondant can be reheated. Even easier...use Wilton Candy Wafer/Fondant Center Mix. Fondant Icing Recipe on label. (p. 118)
YIELD: 2 ¹/₂ cups

Specialty Icing Recipes

Rolled Fondant

This icing is rolled out and used as a covering for a pound or fruit cake, which is traditionally first covered with a layer of marzipan to seal in flavor and moistness of the cake. It's characteristic of the Australian method of decorating. Traditionally, cakes covered with rolled fondant are decorated with royal icing.

Rolled Fondant Recipe
1 Tbsp. unflavored gelatin
1/4 cup cold water
1/2 cup Glucose (p. 130)
1 Tbsp. Glycerin (P. 125)
2 Tbsps. solid vegetable shortening
2 lbs. confectioners sugar
2-3 drops liquid food color and flavoring, as desired.

Combined gelatin and cold water; let stand until thick. Place gelatin mixture in top of double boiler and heat until dissolved. Add glucose and glycerin, mix well. Stir in shortening and just before completely melted, remove from heat. Mixture should cool until lukewarm. Next, place 1 lb. confectioners sugar in a bowl and make a well. Pour the lukewarm gelatin mixture into the well and stir with a wooden spoon mixing in sugar and adding more, a little at a time, until stickiness disappears. Knead in remaining sugar, icing color and flavoring. Knead until the fondant is smooth, pliable and does not stick to your hands. If fondant is too soft, add more sugar; if too stiff, add water (a drop at a time).

Use fondant immediately or store in airtight container in refrigerator. When ready to use, bring to room temperature and knead again until soft. This recipe yields enough to cover a 10 x 3-in. high cake.

To Roll Fondant

Spray work surface and rolling pin with vegetable oil pan spray and dust with a mixture of confectioners sugar and cornstarch. Here are two ways to prepare cake for fondant. Coat with piping gel or apricot glaze, then cover with rolled marzipan. Coat again with piping gel or glaze. Add fondant. Or ice cake with butter-cream icing, let dry, then cover with rolled fondant.

Roll out fondant into a circle twice the diameter of the cake you are covering. As you roll, lift and move the fondant to prevent it from sticking to the surface. Gently lift fondant over rolling pin and place over cake.

Smooth and shape fondant on cake, using palm of hand. If large air bubbles are trapped under fondant, prick with a pin and continue to smooth. Trim excess from base. A fondant-covered cake may be kept up to 2 months, when tightly wrapped and frozen.

Coloring Your Icing

Color brings cake decorations to life; therefore it's essential that you learn how to tint icings to achieve different decorating effects. Wilton Icing Color is concentrated color in a creamy, rich base. It gives icing vivid or deep, rich color without changing icing consistency. See page 124 for a complete selection of quality Wilton Icing Colors. Icing Color Kits are also available.

Tinting

•Start with white icing and add the color a little at a time until you achieve the shade you desire. Use a toothpick to add icing color; (use more depending on amount of icing). Hint: Tint a small amount of icing first, then mix in with remainder of white icing. Colors intensify or darken in buttercream icings 1 to 2 hours after mixing, so keep this in mind when you're tinting icing. You can always add extra color to deepen the icing color, but it's difficult to lighten the color once it's tinted. Use White-White Icing Color to make your buttercream icing the purest snow-white!

•To mix deep or dark color icing (such as red for roses), you may need a larger amount of Wilton Icing color. The color should still be added gradually, but use a clean small spatula each time to add the color. Red No-Taste color has no after-taste! It's ideal for decorating large areas. Red-Red or Christmas Red Color is still better to use in royal icing and for accent color, as each offers more color intensity. If you plan to use flavorings, make icing stiff consistency, then use enough flavoring to improve taste.

•Always mix enough of any one color icing. If you're going to decorate a cake with pink flowers and borders, color enough icing for both. It's difficult to duplicate an exact shade of any color. As you gain decorating experience, you will learn just how much of any one color icing you will need.

Important Hints For Coloring

•Royal icing requires more base color than buttercream to achieve the same intensity.

•Use milk , not water, in buttercream icing recipe when using Violet Icing Color, otherwise the icing may turn blue.

•Substitute chocolate icing for dark brown colors. Use 6 Tablespoons unsweetened cocoa powder, or 2 one-ounce squares, of melted unsweetened baking chocolate, 1 Tablespoon milk, and add to 1 1/2 cups white icing.

•Add color to piping gel, color flow, gum paste, cookie dough, marzipan, cream cheese, sugar molds and even cake batter for striking decorating effects!

•To restore the consistency of Wilton Icing Colors that have dried out, add a few drops of Wilton Glycerin. Mix until proper consistency is reached.

•Use a clean toothpick or spatula to add Wilton Icing Colors each time, until you reach desired shade.

Coloring for Special Effects

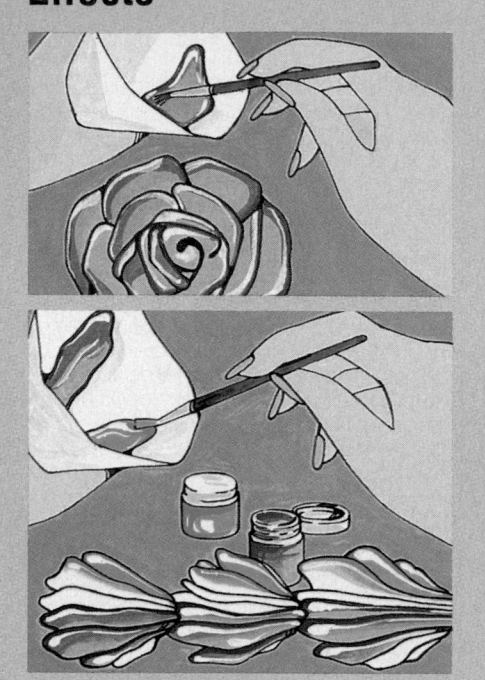

BRUSH STRIPING

Striping is a method used to give multiple or deep color effects to icing. To do this, one or more colors are applied to the inside of the parchment paper bag with a brush. Then the bag is filled with white or pastel-colored icing and, as the icing is squeezed past the color, out come the striped decorations!

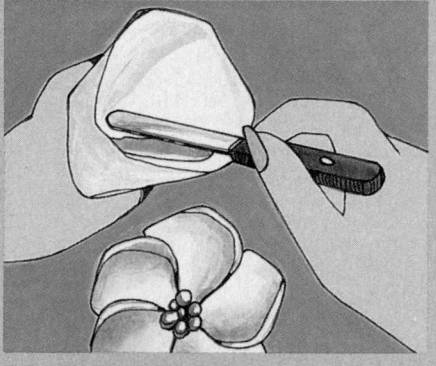

SPATULA STRIPING

Use a spatula to stripe the inside of a decorating bag with pastel-colored icing. Then fill the bag with white icing, or another shade of the same color as the striping, and squeeze out decorations with pastel contrasts. Use the above color techniques when figure piping for exciting results. It's fun to experiment with color! Try to achieve natural-looking flower colors by using the spatula striping method. (Roses look especially beautiful with this effect.)

Icing the Cake

Think of your cake as the canvas that your beautiful icing decorations will be presented upon. So it's essential that it be smooth and free of crumbs. By following our 5-easy-steps icing method, we feel you'll get the results you want.

1. Leveling
There are two ways to remove the slight crown your baked cake will have. Cool cake for 10 minutes in the pan. Carefully slice off the raised center with a serrated knife. Or after cake is cooled completely as per directions on p. 90, invert so that its brown top crust is uppermost and trim away the crust for a flat surface (see pic. 1). Our Bake-Even Strips will help prevent crowns from forming on basic shaped cakes (see p. 171 for details).

2. Filling Layers
Place one cake layer on a cake board or circle atop a cake stand or plate, top side up. Hint: To prevent cake from shifting, place a few strikes of icing on base surface before positioning cake. Fit bag with coupler and fill with icing. Make a dam by squeezing out a band of icing about 3/4-in. high around the edge. With your spatula, spread icing, jam, pudding or other filling in center. Position top layer with bottom side up.

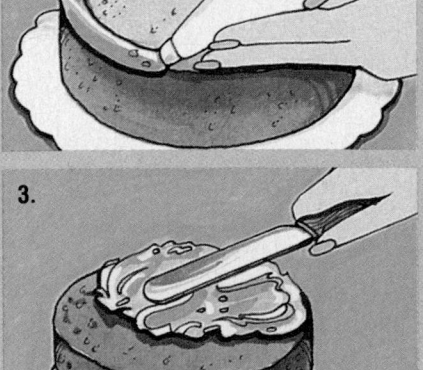

3. Icing The Top
Thin your buttercream icing with light corn syrup (approximately 2 teaspoons for each cup). The consistency is correct when your spatula glides over the icing. With large spatula, place mound of icing in center of top and spread across cake pushing excess down onto sides. Always keep spatula on the iced surface. Pulling toward the cake surface will mix in crumbs. Hint: To keep your serving base free of icing, place 3-in. wide strips of waxed paper under each side of cake.

4. Icing The Sides
Cover the sides with excess icing from the top, adding more icing if necessary. Work from top down, forcing any loose crumbs to the cake base. Again, be sure spatula touches only icing. You'll find that an angled spatula is ideal for icing sides. When you're icing a curved side, hold the spatula upright against the side of the cake and, pressing lightly, turn cake stand slowly around with your free hand without lifting the spatula from the side surface. Return excess icing to bowl and repeat procedure until sides are smooth. For angled sides such as on a cross cake, do each straight side individually; hold spatula firmly to smooth.

5. Smooth Top
Place spatula flat on one edge of cake top and sweep it across to center of cake. Lift off, remove excess icing and repeat, starting from a new point on edge of cake top. Repeat procedure until entire top surface is smooth. To smooth center, apply an even pressure to spatula as you turn cake stand around in a full circle. Lift off spatula and any excess icing.

Sheet & Other Flat Surfaced Cakes
Use the same icing procedure as shown here for sheet cakes, heart, oval, square and other shaped cakes with flat surfaces.

Torting

By simply cutting a cake into layers, you can enhance its taste and create impact! Classic and novelty shapes are easy to torte especially with our Cake Leveler! It cuts perfectly-even layers on cakes up to 10 in. in diameter and adjusts to desired height. Slice the cake horizontally into two or four layers. Make layers the same thickness. Follow directions for using our Cake Leveler on the package or use a serrated knife. Hold knife level at desired height and with a gentle sawing motion, rotate the cake against blade of knife.
• For easy handling, slide the sliced layer onto a cake board (for each layer follow this procedure).
• Fill bottom layer as shown in number 2 at left. Slide next layer off board onto filled layer.

To Ice Areas on Shaped Cakes
The sides of shaped cakes are usually the only areas iced smooth. Just place icing on side with your spatula and spread. After sides are covered, run spatula lightly over icing in the same direction.
Somtimes small background areas or facial features on top are iced smooth. Use a small spatula or decorating tip (3 or 4) and squeeze icing onto area, then smooth with finger dipped in cornstarch.

The Cake Icer Tip (No.789) Will Save You Time
If you haven't discovered this versatile tip (No. 789) you should! You'll love how quickly and easily you can cover flat-surfaced cakes with wide bands of icing. Just hold tip flat against cake surface, serrated side up, and squeeze out a ribbed band. Holding the smooth side up gives you a smooth band. To cover side, turn cake stand clockwise as you squeeze out a band of icing, wrapping it around the cake. When your cake is completely iced, use a fork to blend ribbed seams; a spatula to join smooth bands together.

Hints To Make Icing Your Cake Easier
• Thinning buttercream icing with light corn syrup makes consistency best for easy spreading.
• When icing small areas or sides of a shaped cake, be sure to ice a little past the area or edge or top to create a neat surface that can be outlined or covered with stars.
• To smooth the icing surface on 3-dimensional cakes such as the ball, egg, bear, lamb or bunny cakes, let buttercream icing crust slightly. Then place plastic wrap over the icing and smooth over the surface gently with your hands. Carefully remove wrap. For a textured surface, follow the same procedure using a cloth or paper towel.
• To make clean-up easier and quicker when decorating with buttercream icing, use a degreaser liquid soap to dissolve icing from tools. It is especially important to have grease-free utensils when using royal or color flow icings.

Decorating Guidelines

These easy-to-follow guidelines outline the basic steps in decorating. Our steps are very general because each cake you decorate has special needs. We hope these guidelines will inspire you to design original cakes on your own.

• We suggest that flowers, candy, cookies or any special accent be made ahead of time, perhaps while your cake cools. To allow for breakage, make extras of any fragile addition. Heavy trims that protrude out of cake should be attached to a craft stick or coffee stirrer with royal icing. When using cookie trims, easel backs can be cut out of dough and attached with royal icing.

• Before icing or decorating, place each cake to be decorated on a cake circle or board cut to fit. If a small cake is to be set atop a larger cake, we usually recommend that you decorate both cakes first, then put them together. To transfer, let icing set (a slight crust will form and be more workable), then slip a wide spatula under cake and lift. Position cake and slowly pull spatula out (to prevent sticking, lightly dust spatula with cornstarch). If cake is large, support with free hand and redecorate areas that may get damaged.

• Marking design: Use a toothpick, pattern press or cookie cutter. Patterns for more intricate designs are included in the '92 Pattern Book (contains easy pattern transfer instructions). Often geometric shaped cakes are divided into 6ths, 8ths, 12ths, etc. You'll find dividing a round cake is quick 'n easy when you use our Cake Dividing Set (instructions included).

Decorating Hints

• Tips from the same basic group that are close in size may be substituted for one another. The effect will be a slightly smaller or larger decoration.

• Use tip 20, 21 or the super fast Triple-Star Tip, when you're covering a large area with stars. You can also use zigzags or side-by-side stripes to fill in large areas.

• When using parchment bags, you can place a tip with a smaller opening over the tip you're using and tape it in place. This saves time changing bags and tips when you're using the same color icing.

• Stock up on the bags and tips in the sizes you use the most. Your decorating will go faster if several are filled and ready to use. Close tips securely with convenient Tip Covers.

• Overpiping: Outlining a piped decoration with the same technique will add dimension and make it stand out. Overpiping with a different technique in a contrasting color creates an eye-catching effect.

Decorating Step-by-Step

Basic Shapes
• Outline design.
• Pipe in small areas. Fill in areas with stars, zigzags, etc.
• Add top and bottom borders.
• Add message.
• Ruffles and "overpiped" decorations.
• Attach trims such as flowers, cookies, color flow and candy.
Note: If a decoration doesn't seem secure enough, just add a few dots of icing.
• Pipe leaves on flowers.
• Position Wilton cake tops or wedding ornaments.

Novelty Shapes

When decorating a cake that's basically covered with stars, here are the easy steps involved.

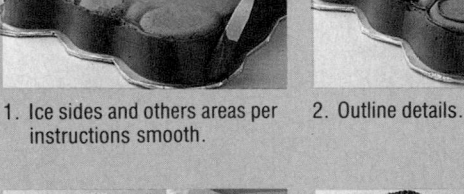

1. Ice sides and others areas per instructions smooth.

2. Outline details.

3. Pipe in facial features, small details, windows, doors, etc.

4. Cover areas with stars, stripes, zigzags or hair.

5. Add message.

6. Edge top and base with borders. Attach flowers or trims.

3 Essentials of Bag and Tip Decorating

1. Icing Consistency
Remember, if the consistency of your decorating icing isn't exactly right, your decorations won't be either. Follow the general guidelines on p. 92.

2. Bag Position
To hold the decorating bag correctly, grip the bag near the top with the twisted or folded end locked between your thumb and fingers. Guide the bag with your free hand.

Generally, there are two basic positions for the decorating bag—the 90° angle with the bag straight up, perpendicular to the surface. And the 45° angle with the bag half-way between vertical and horizontal.

Pointing the back end of your decorating bag in the right direction is also important. Sometimes instructions will tell you to hold the back end of bag pointing to the right or towards you.

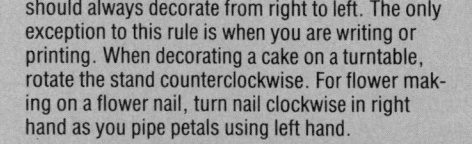

45° Angle

90° Angle

Left-handed decorators do things differently. Hold the decorating bag in your left hand and guide the decorating tip with the fingers of your right hand. If the instructions say to hold the decorating bag over to the right, you should hold your decorating bag over to the left. A right-handed person will always decorate from left to right. A left-handed person

should always decorate from right to left. The only exception to this rule is when you are writing or printing. When decorating a cake on a turntable, rotate the stand counterclockwise. For flower making on a flower nail, turn nail clockwise in right hand as you pipe petals using left hand.

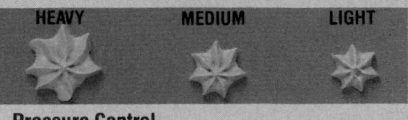

HEAVY	MEDIUM	LIGHT

3. Pressure Control
The size and uniformity of your icing design are directly affected by the amount of pressure you apply to the decorating bag and the steadiness of the pressure— how you squeeze and relax your grip on the decorating bag. Strive to apply pressure so consistently that you can move the bag in a free and easy glide while just the right amount of icing flows from the tip. Practice to achieve this control.

The Techniques

PLAIN OR ROUND TIPS

Use to outline details, filling and piping in areas, printing and writing messages, figure piping, stringwork, beads, dots, balls, stems, vines, flower centers, lattice, cornelli lace. These tips are smooth and round—small plain tips include numbers 1,2,3,4; medium, 5,6,7,8,9,10,11,12; large, 1A, 2A. For fine stringwork, use 1S, 1L, 2L, 0L, 00L,000. For Philippine method flower making, oval tips 55 and 57. Writing tip 301 pipes fine, flat lines.

Printing & Writing

Use a small round tip and thin icing consistency.
Hint: With a toothpick or Message Pattern Presses draw guidelines to follow. With practice, you'll achieve control and soon be piping out messages free-handed.

To Print: Hold bag at 45° angle with tip resting lightly on surface with back of to the right for horizontal lines, toward you for vertical. With a steady, even pressure, squeeze out a straight line, lifting tip off surface to let icing string drop. Be sure to stop squeezing before you lift the tip to end the line so a tail doesn't form.

To Write: You must move your whole arm to write effectively with icing. Hold bag at a 45° angle with back of bag to the right. The tip should lightly touch the cake as you write.

To Outline:

Use thin icing consistency and bag at a 45° angle and touch tip (usually 3 or 4) to surface. Now raise the tip slightly and continue to squeeze. The icing will flow out of the tip while you direct it along the surface. To end an outline, stop squeezing, touch tip to surface and pull away.

To Pipe In: After area is outlined, squeeze out tip 3 or 4 zigzag motion strings to fill area. Immediately smooth over strings with finger tip or spatula dipped in cornstarch.

To Fill In: Follow same procedure as Pipe In, but thin icing before piping.

Dots

Use medium icing consistency. Hold bag at a 90° angle with tip slightly above surface. Squeeze and keep point of the tip in icing until dot is the size you want. Stop pressure, pull away; use tip to clean point away or smooth with finger dipped in cornstarch. To make large dots or balls, lift tip as you squeeze to allow greater icing build-up.

Beads

Use medium icing consistency. Hold bag at 45° angle with tip slightly above surface and end of bag pointing to the right. Squeeze and lift tip slightly so icing fans out into base. Relax pressure as you draw tip down and bring bead to point. Ideal for borders or piped in side-by-side rows to cover large areas.

For Hearts: Pipe two beads side by side and smooth together with finger dipped in cornstarch.

For Shamrocks: Pipe 3 bead hearts so points meet. Add tip 3 outline stem.

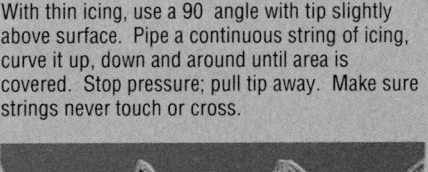

Cornelli Lace

With thin icing, use a 90 angle with tip slightly above surface. Pipe a continuous string of icing, curve it up, down and around until area is covered. Stop pressure; pull tip away. Make sure strings never touch or cross.

Drop Strings

Use stiff consistency icing that has been thinned with corn syrup. Icing is the right consistency if you can drop a loop of icing from your finger. With toothpick, mark horizontal intervals in desired widths. Hold bag at 45° angle to surface so that end of bag points slightly to the right. Touch tip to first marks and squeeze, holding bag in place momentarily so that icing sticks to surface.

Then pull tip straight out away from surface, allowing icing to drop into an arc. Stop pressure as you touch tip to second mark to end string.

Repeat procedure, attaching string to third mark and so on, forming row of drop strings. It's very important to let the string, not your hand, drop to form an arc. Try to keep your drop strings uniform in length and width.

For Double Drop Strings: Start at first mark again, squeeze bag. Let icing drop into a slightly shorter arc than arc in first row. Join end of string to end of corresponding string in first row and repeat procedure.

Always pipe longest drop strings first and add shorter ones. This technique is ideal for cake sides. Practice is important in making drop strings uniform.

Dropped Lattice Garlands: With stiff royal icing, connect garland marks with drop string guidelines. Cover strings with three rows of tip 16 zigzags (overpipe rows). Ease pressure at ends so icing doesn't build up too high. Drop a string guideline directly on top of zigzags. From cake to edge of zigzags, pipe tip 3 diagonal lines across area. From the opposite side, work strings in the other direction. Cover edges of lattice with tip 3 strings.

STAR TIPS

The star-shaped openings create the most popular decorations… stars, zigzags, shells, rosettes and more. The most often used star tips are numbers 13 through 22. Star tips range in size from small to extra large. For deep ribbed decorations, try tips 23-31, 132, 133 and 195. Large star tips include numbers 32, 96, 4B, 6B and 8B. Fine cut star tips are numbers 362, 363, 364, 172 and 199. For these techniques use medium icing consistency.

Stars

Hold bag at 90° angle with tip slightly above surface. Squeeze bag to form a star, then stop pressure and pull tip away. Increase or decrease pressure to change star size. An entire cake or just one area can be covered with stars made very close together so that no cake shows between stars. Use the triple-star or use large star tips to save time.

For Pull-Out Stars: Hold bag at 45° angle to surface. As you squeeze out icing, pull tip up and away from cake. When strand is long enough, stop pressure and pull tip away. Work from bottom to top of area to be covered with pull-out stars.

For Star Puffs: Use a large tip and hold tip in place to allow icing to build up.

For Star Flowers: Squeeze and keep tip in icing until star petals are formed. Stop pressure and pull tip away. Add tip 2 or 3 dot centers.

Ropes

Hold bag at 45° angle to surface with end of bag pointing over right shoulder. Touch tip to surface and squeezing bag, move tip down, up and around to the right forming a slight "s" curve. Stop pressure, pull tip away. Tuck tip under bottom arch of first "s" and repeat procedure. Continue joining "s" curves to form rope.

The Techniques

The size and shape of the opening on a decorative tip identifies the basic group to which the tip belongs and determines the type of decorations the tip will produce.

Zigzags

Hold bag at 45° angle to surface, so that end of bag points out to the right and fingers on the bag are facing you. Allow the tip to touch the surface lightly. Steadily squeeze and move hand in a tight side-to-side motion. To end, stop pressure and pull tip away. **Elongated Zigzags:** Follow procedure but keep an even pressure as you move hand in the desired length. Very large areas can be covered in this manner. **Relaxed Zigzags:** Simply relax pressure as you move bag along.

Zigzag Garlands

Hold bag as for basic zigzag procedure. Allow tip to touch the surface lightly and use light-to-heavy-to-light pressure to form curves of garland. To end, stop pressure, pull tip away. Practice for rhythmic pressure control so garlands are uniform.

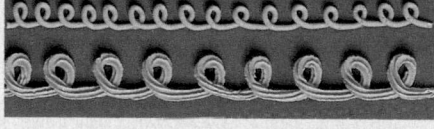

Puffs

Hold bag at 45° angle to surface, finger tips on bag facing you. Touch tip to surface and use a light-to-heavy-to-light pressure and zigzag motion to form puff. Repeat procedure again and again as you move tip in a straight line to form row of puffs. To end row, stop pressure, pull tip away.

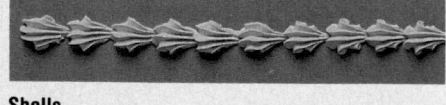

C, E & S-Motion (only "E" motion shown)

Hold bag at 45° angle to surface, finger tips on bag facing you. As you squeeze out icing, move tip down, up to the right and around as if writing the letter "c, e or s." Use a steady, even pressure as you repeat procedure. To end, stop pressure, pull tip away.

Shells

Hold bag at 45° angle with tip slightly above surface and end of bag pointing to the right. Squeeze with heavy pressure and slightly lift tip as icing builds and fans out into a full base. Relax pressure as you pull bag down to the right as you make the tail. Stop pressure completely, pull tip away. When you make the shells, always work to the right; starting each new shell slightly behind tail of previous shell. **For Elongated Shells:** Extend tail while relaxing pressure, until desired length is achieved. **For Upright Shells:** Hold bag at 90° angle to cake sides. Follow same procedure as elongated shells.

Note: Once you've mastered the motion of shell making, you can create unique borders with other tip groups such as leaf and ruffle.

Reverse Shells

Hold bag at 45° angle with tip slightly above surface. Squeeze to let icing fan out as if you were making a typical shell, then swing tip around to the left in a semi-circular motion as you relax pressure to form tail of a shell. Stop pressure, pull tip away. Repeat procedure, only this time, swing tip around to the right as you form tail of shell. Continue procedure alternating directions for a series of reverse shells.

Fleur-De-Lis

Make a shell. Keep bag at 45° angle and starting at the left of this shell, squeeze bag to fan icing into shell base. Then as you relax pressure to form tail, move tip up slightly around to the right, relaxing pressure, forming tail similar to reverse shells. Join to tail of the first shell. Repeat procedure to right side of first shell.

Scrolls

Hold bag at 45° angle to surface so that end of bag points to the right. Use tip 3 to draw an inverted "C" center and use circular motion to cover inverted "C." You may overpipe (go over lines) with tip 13 or any small star tip. Use a heavy pressure to feather the scroll, relaxing pressure as you taper end. Add side petals like reverse shells.

Reverse Scrolls

With tip 3 squeeze out an inverted "C" scroll. Then, starting at the top of this "C," squeeze and move tip down, up and around for a backward "C." Cover outlines with tip 13. Add reverse shell side petals.

Hint: Use our Scroll Pattern Presses to imprint an easy-to-follow guide on cake top or sides.

Rosettes

Hold bag at 90° angle with tip slightly above surface. Squeeze and move hand to the left, up and around in a circular motion to starting point. Stop pressure and pull tip away. For a fancy effect, trim center with a star.

Spirals

Follow rosettes technique. Starting at outer edge, move tip in a clockwise direction in a continuous circular motion decreasing size of circles until center is reached. Stop pressure and pull tip away.

Drop Flower Tips

These are the easiest flowers for a beginning decorator to do. The number of openings on the end of the tip determines the number of petals the flower will have. Each drop flower tip can produce two different flower varieties—plain or swirled. Swirled drop flowers cannot be made directly on cake. Some form center holes. Small tips include numbers 107, 108, 129, 217, 220, 224, 225; medium tips are 109, 131, 135, 140, 177, 190, 191, 193, 194, 195; for large flowers, tips 1B, 1C, 1E, 1G, 2C, 2D, 2E and 2F.

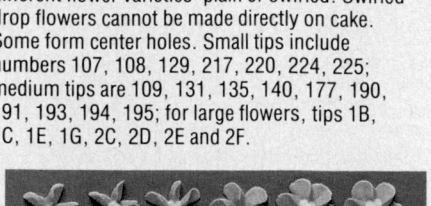

Drop Flowers

Icing consistency should be slightly stiffer. Hold bag at a 90° angle with tip touching surface and pipe as you would a star. For swirled flowers: Curve wrist around to the left and as you squeeze out icing, bring hand back to the right. Stop pressure, pull tip away. Add tip 2 or 3 dot centers.

LEAF TIPS

The v-shaped openings of these tips give leaves pointed ends. With any leaf tip you can make plain, ruffle or stand-up leaves. Make leaves with center veins from small 65s, 65-70, to large, 112-115 and 355. Other popular numbers are 71-76, 326, 349, 352.

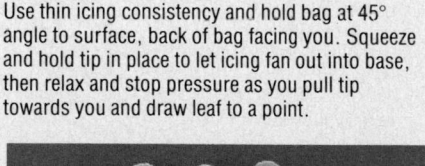

Basic Leaf

Use thin icing consistency and hold bag at 45° angle to surface, back of bag facing you. Squeeze and hold tip in place to let icing fan out into base, then relax and stop pressure as you pull tip towards you and draw leaf to a point.

Stand Up Leaf

Hold bag at a 90° angle. Touch tip lightly to surface and squeeze, holding tip in place as icing fans out to form base. Relax and stop pressure as you pull tip straight up and away, creating stand-up leaf effect.

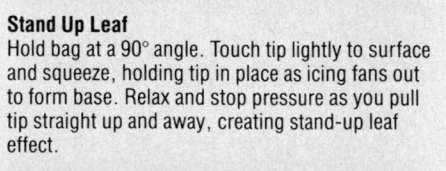

Holly Leaf

With tip 68, follow basic leaf method and use medium consistency royal icing to pipe desired size leaf. While icing is wet, pull out tiny points around edge with a dampened Decorator's Brush. Let dry on flower formers for a curved look. Do not make directly on cake.

The Techniques

Petal Tips

These tips have an opening that is wide at one end, narrow at the other. This teardrop-like shaped opening yields a variety of petals that form flowers like the rose, carnation, daisy, pansy and more (see pages 101-103). Petal tips can also make ribbons, drapes and swags; bows and streamers. Plain rose tips include numbers 101s, 101, 102, 103, 104, 124, 125, 126, 127 and giant roses, tip 127D. Swirled rose tips that make instant-curled petals are 97, 116, 118 and 119. Others include 59s, 59, 60, 61, 121, 122, 123, 62, 63, 64 and 150.

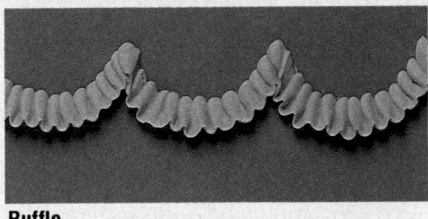

Ruffle

Use medium icing consistency. Hold bag at a 45° angle to surface, finger tips on bag facing you. Touch wide end of tip to surface, angle narrow end out about ¼-in. away from surface. As you squeeze, move hand up and down slightly to ruffle the icing. **For Stand-Up Ruffle** just turn tip so wide end is at the top.

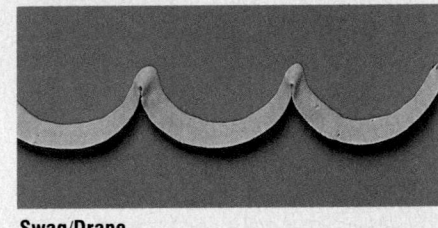

Swag/Drape

Use same procedure as for ruffle. As you squeeze, swing tip down and up to the right forming ribbon drape.

Bows

Creating bows with a petal tip is different from a round or star tip because of the shape of tip but otherwise the technique is the same. With tip 104 and medium icing consistency, hold bag at a 45° angle to surface. The wide end of the tip should touch the surface and the narrow end should point straight up. While squeezing, move the tip up and around to the starting point and continue around, making a second loop on the left. The two loops should form a figure 8. Still holding bag in the same position return to the center and squeeze out two streamers.

Stripe/Basketweave Tips

These are decorating tips with a smooth side for making smooth, wide icing stripes and/or one serrated side for making ribbed, wide icing stripes. When short ribbed horizontal stripes are interwoven in vertical rows the effect is that of a basketweave. Tips are 46 and 47. For smooth stripes, 44 and 45. For ribbed stripes, 48 and 327. Large ribbon tips include 1D, 2B and 789 (Cake Icer).

Basketweave

Use star or basketweave tips and medium consistency icing. For an interesting effect, use a round tip to make vertical lines.

● Hold bag at 45° angle to cake with serrated side of tip facing up (or use round tip). Touch tip lightly to surface and squeeze out a vertical line of icing.

● Next, hold bag at 45° angle to surface, finger tips gripping bag facing you. Touch tip, serrated side facing up, to top left side of vertical line and squeeze out a horizontal bar. Add two more horizontal bars, each about a tip width apart, to cover vertical line.

● With bag and tip at 45° angle, make another vertical line of icing to right of first one, overlapping ends of horizontal bars. Use same procedure as step two to cover this line with horizontal bars, working them in spaces of bars in first row.

● Repeat entire procedure, alternating vertical lines and horizontal bars, to create a basketweave effect. Other tips may be used for basketweave, but serrated tips 46-48 give icing a ribbed basket effect.

Violet Leaf

With tip 102, begin at center of the flower nail. Move out towards edge of nail and begin jiggling out ruffles. Gradually move hand upwards as you turn nail. After curve is formed, move hand back down to starting place. Paint veins and stems with icing color. For curved effect, place in flower former to dry.

Stripes

● This versatile technique can be made with star and ribbon tips. They can be piped straight, curved or side-by-side to fill in an area. Hold decorating bag at 45° angle to surface. As you squeeze out icing with steady, even pressure, move tip in vertical direction laying out a ribbed stripe of icing. Stop pressure and pull tip up and away. When covering an area, stripes can be slightly overlapped for added dimension.

Ribbon Stripe Bow

● To make a bow with a basketweave tip as shown, hold bag at a 45° angle with the ribbed side of tip up. Start in center and move bag up and to the right. As you bring bag down to form loop, turn tip so that the ribbed side is now down. Repeat procedure for left loop. Pipe streamers with smooth or ribbed side up.

Flutes

● A pretty effect to add between rows of shells. Hold tip 104 at 45° angle so that wide end of tip is between two shells. Squeeze and move tip up slightly as icing fills in between shell. Stop pressure, lower tip, pull away.

Making a Rose

The flower nail (p. 132) is a decorating tool used to make the most popular flower of all, the rose. It is also used to make pretty flowers, like the violet, apple blossom and daisy. Flower nails come in a variety of sizes. No. 7 and No. 9 are the popular choices for small and average size blooms. Large flowers would use a 2 or 3-in. flower nail.

The key to making any flower on the nail is to coordinate the turning of the nail with the formation of a petal. The stem of the nail is held between your left thumb and forefinger, so you can turn the flat nailhead surface at the same time you're piping a flower with your right hand. Using the flower nail takes practice, but the beautiful results are well worth the effort!

Note: Left-handed decorators should use the nail opposite of above instructions.

Make all flowers on the nail with royal or stiffened buttercream icing (see p. 93-94), and the tips specified for each flower. Air dry flowers made in royal icing, and freeze buttercream flowers (buttercream roses can also be placed directly on iced cake) until firm at least 2 hours. Then, when you're ready to decorate, remove the frozen flowers, a few at a time, and position them on the cake. (Snow White Buttercream Icing flowers can be air dried.)

For each flower you make, attach a 2-in. square of waxed paper to the nailhead with a dot of icing. Make a flower; remove waxed paper and flower together. For more about rose making, order the **Wilton Celebrates The Rose**

 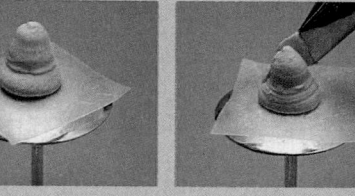 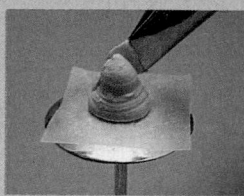  

Make The Rose Base
- Use tip 10 or 12. Hold the bag perpendicular at a 90° angle to nail with tip slightly above center of nailhead.
- Squeeze with a heavy pressure, keeping bottom of tip in icing until you've made a full, round base.
- Ease pressure as you raise tip up and away from nailhead, narrowing base to a dome head. The base is very important for successful rose-making. Be sure that it is secure to nail and can support all the petals. Practice until you feel comfortable with the technique.

The Center Bud
- Use tip 104. Hold bag at a 45° angle to nail with wide end of tip just below top of dome, and narrow end pointed in slightly. Back of bag should be pointed over your shoulder.
- Now you must do three things simultaneously...squeeze, pull tip up and out away from top of dome stretching icing into a ribbon band, as you turn the nail counterclockwise.
- Relax pressure as you bring band of icing down around dome, overlapping the point at which you started.

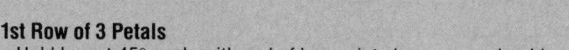

   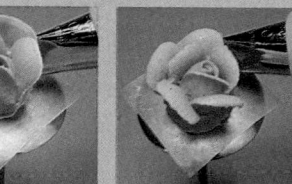

1st Row of 3 Petals
- Hold bag at 45° angle with end of bag pointed over your shoulder. Touch wide end of tip 104 to midpoint of bud base. Turn nail counterclockwise and move tip up and back down to midpoint of bud base forming first petal of rose.
- Start slightly behind end of 1st petal and squeeze out 2nd petal same as first.
- Start slightly behind end of 2nd petal and add a 3rd petal, ending this petal overlapping starting point of 1st petal. Now you have a full rosebud made on a nail to use just as you would a rosebud made on a flat surface

2nd Row of 5 Petals
- Touch wide end of tip 104 slightly below center of a petal in 1st row, angle narrow end of tip out slightly more than you did for 1st row of petals. Squeeze and turn nail counterclockwise, moving tip up, then down to form 1st petal in second row.
- Start slightly behind this last petal and make a 2nd petal. Repeat this procedure for a total of 5 petals, ending last petal overlapping the 1st petal's starting point.

3rd Row of 7 Petals
- Touch wide end of tip 104 below center of petal in 2nd row, again angling narrow end of tip out a little more. Squeeze and turn nail counterclockwise and move tip up and down forming 1st petal. Repeat for a total of 7 petals.
- Slip waxed paper and completed rose off nail. Attach another square of waxed paper and start again. Have several squares of waxed paper cut

ahead of time so you can continue rose making without stopping. HINT: An easy way to place a buttercream icing rose directly on your cake is to slide open scissors under base of rose and gently lift flower off waxed paper square and flower nail. Position flower on cake by slowly closing scissors and pushing base of flower with stem end of flower nail. Practice & watch your talent grow!

Two-Tone Roses
Create a dramatic effect by making the center petals of your rose contrast with the outer petals. You'll need to pipe the base, center bud and 1st row of petals with one color. Then in your contrasting shade, add remaining petals.

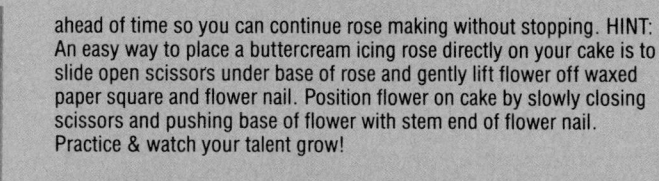

Flowers
Flat Surface Flowers:
Rosebuds, Half Roses & Sweet Peas

These are flowers you can make right on a cake, or any other flat surface. To make all these, use tip 104 and royal or stiffened buttercream icing. Attach a sheet of waxed paper to the back of a cookie sheet with dots of icing or use Wilton Practice Board.

Make your practice flowers in horizontal rows and when you've filled the entire sheet, loosen the waxed paper with a spatula to remove it and start again.

When you're decorating a cake with lots of flat-surface flowers, make all the ones you need ahead of time using the same cookie sheet method. Air dry flowers made with Royal or Snow-White Buttercream. Freeze flowers made with buttercream until hard (at least 2 hours). Remove buttercream flowers with your spatula, a few at a time as you decorate, so they stay firm. Note: When you make flowers directly on a cake, use buttercream, not royal icing.

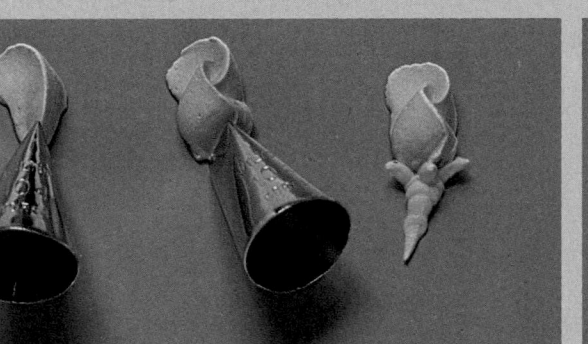

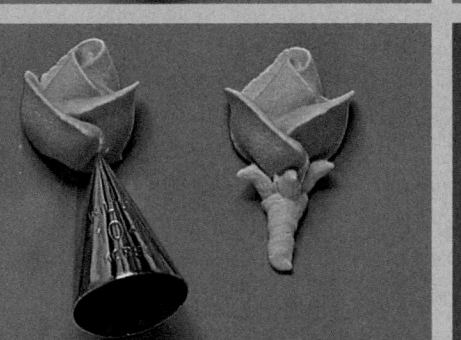

A. Rosebud
• Make base petal. Hold bag at a 45° angle so that the end of bag points over your right shoulder, finger tips gripping bag facing you. Touch wide end of tip 104 to surface, point narrow end to the right. Squeeze, move forward ¼-in.; hesitate so icing fans out, then move back as you stop pressure.
• Make overlapping center petal. Hold bag in same position as above with wide end of tip touching inside right edge of base petal, narrow end of tip pointing slightly up above base petal. Squeeze as icing catches inside edge of base petal and rolls into interlocking center bud, Stop pressure; touch large end back to surface and pull tip away.
• Make sepals and calyx directly on cake with tip 3 and thinned icing. Hold bag at a 45° angle to base of bud with end of bag pointing towards you. Touch tip to bud. Squeeze and pull tip up and away from flower, relaxing pressure as you draw calyx to a point. Add three tip 3 sepals.

B. Half Rose
• Make a rosebud without sepals and calyx. To make left petal: Hold bag at a 45° angle so the end of bag points to the right, finger tips gripping the bag should face you. Touch wide end of tip 104 to bottom left side of bud. Squeeze, move it up, around to the right and down, relaxing pressure.
• To make right petal: Hold bag in opposite position as for left petal. Touch wide end of tip to bottom right side of bud base. Squeeze, move up, around to the left and down to center of bud base. Stop pressure, pull tip away.
• Make sepals and calyxes with tip 3 and thinned icing. Follow same procedure as for step 3 of rosebud, starting at bottom center of half rose.

C. Sweet Pea
• Make center petal. Hold bag at a 45° angle to surface so that back end of bag points towards you. Touch wide end of the tip to surface with narrow end of tip straight up. Squeeze, raise tip slightly and let icing roll into center petal. Stop pressure, lower tip, pull away.
• Make side petals. Touch wide end of tip to bottom left edge of center rolled petal, point narrow end up and out to the left. Squeeze, lift tip slightly, stop pressure, lower tip, pull away. Repeat procedure for right petal, starting at bottom edge of center petal.
• Add calyx to flower base with tip 3 and thinned icing. Hold bag at 45° angle to surface so that end of bag points towards you. Insert tip into flower base and hold in place as you squeeze to build up pressure as you draw tip down, narrowing calyx to a point.

D. To Attach Flowers & Leaves To Wire Stems.
• **For flowers:** On waxed paper square, using royal icing, pipe a dot base with tip 4. Make 1/8-in. hook on one end of 4-in. florist wire and insert hook into base. With slightly moistened decorator's brush, smooth and taper icing on the wire. Push other end of wire into a piece of styrofoam to dry base. Remove waxed paper and attach flower with dots of icing. **For Leaves:** Pipe tip 3 royal icing dot on a waxed paper square and immediately push in hooked end of wire. Use tip 352 and royal icing to pipe a leaf directly on top of wire. Again, push into styrofoam to dry. Then remove waxed paper square. Entwine stems together. Note: Use only royal icing for attaching flowers to stems.

Flower Nail Flowers

For best results, use royal icing to pipe these impressive blooms. To curve petals, dry on convexed or concaved flowers formers. Instructions will indicate the number of flowers needed, so make extras to allow for breakage.

Daisy

Use royal icing and tip 103. Dot center of nail with icing as guide for flower center. Hold bag at a 45° angle with tip almost parallel to nail surface, wide end of tip pointing to nail center, narrow end pointing out. Now, starting at any point near outer edge of nail, squeeze and move tip towards center icing dot. Stop pressure, pull tip away. Repeat procedure for a total of twelve or more petals.
• Add tip 4 yellow flower center and press to flatten. For pollen-like effect, dampen your finger, press in edible glitter, then flatten center.

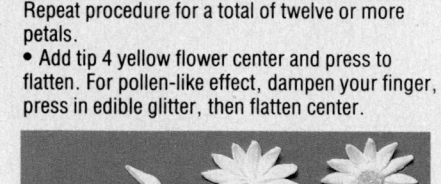

Chrysanthemum

• Hold bag at 90° angle to nail and pipe tip 6 mound of icing on nail center. Use tip 79 and very stiff royal icing for short petal effect. Hold bag at a 45° angle to outer base edge of mound, with half-moon opening of tip 79 pointing up. Squeeze row of ½-in. long cupped base petals using pull-out star technique.
• Add second row of shorter petals atop and in between those in first row. Repeat procedure making each additional row of petals shorter than the previous row. When entire mound is covered, add a few stand-up petals to top and tip 1 center dots.

Bachelor Button.

• Like the chrysanthemum, start with a tip 7 dot base. Pipe a cluster of short pull-out dots in the center with tip 1. With tip 14, cover the rest of the mound with pull-out stars.

Daffodil And Jonquil

• Use tip 104 for daffodil or tip 103 for jonquil. Hold bag at a 45° angle to nail, with large end of tip touching nail, narrow end pointed out and almost parallel to nail surface. Squeeze and as you turn nail, move tip out about ½-in. and back to center of nail to form petal. Repeat procedure for five more petals. Dip fingers in cornstarch and pinch ends of petals to form points. Pipe row-upon-row of tip 2 string circles and top with tip 1 zigzag for center.

Narcissus

• Use tip 102 and same procedure as for daffodil to make six 3/4-in. long petals. Add tip 1 coil center and tip 1 zigzag.

Apple Blossom

• Use tip 101 or 101s and hold bag at a 45° angle to flower nail with wide end of tip touching nail center, narrow end pointed out 1/8-in. away from nail surface.
• Squeeze bag and turn nail as you move tip 1/8-in. out from nail center and back, relaxing pressure as you return to starting point.
• Repeat procedure to make four more petals. Add five tip 1 dots for center.

Forget-Me Nots

• Very similar to the apple blossom. Use tip 101 and move tip out just 3/8-in. from center, curve around and return, letting the turn of the nail form petals. Dot center with tip 1. Use large flower nail No. 7 and pipe several at once!

Violet

• Use tip 59s and same procedure as for apple blossom to make three 3/4-in. long petals and two ¼-in. base petals. Add two tip 1 center dots.

Pansy

• Fit two decorating bags with tip 104. Fill one with yellow icing, the other with violet. Hold bag with yellow icing at a 45° angle to nail center, squeeze and move tip out to edge of nail. Turn nail as you squeeze, relax pressure as you return to nail center. Repeat to form second yellow petal. Use same procedure to add two shorter yellow petals atop the first two.
• Now with bag of violet icing, squeeze out a base petal that equals the width of the yellow petals, using a back and forth hand motion for a ruffled effect.
• Use a decorator's brush to add veins of violet icing color after flower has air dried. Add tip 1 string loop center.

Wild Rose

• Use tip 103 and hold bag at a 45° angle. Touch nail with wide end of tip with narrow end just slightly above nail surface. Begin at center of nail and press out first petal, turning nail as you move tip out toward edge of nail, and return to center of nail as you stop squeezing. Repeat 4 more times. Pull out tiny stamens with tip 1.

Poppy

• Hold wide end of tip 103 down, narrow end pointed out at 45° angle. Starting in center, pipe out a large, rounded, ruffled petal. Jiggle hand as you move up and out to edge of nail and down again into a point. Make four petals around nail.
• Pipe a second row of smaller, cupped petals inside first row, starting first petal between piped petals.
• Pipe tip 6 dot center and tip 14 pull-out star stamens.
• **For half poppy:** With wide end of tip 103 touching center of nail, small end pointed out at a 45° angle, squeeze out a ruffle semicircle. Overpipe with another ruffle petal.

Lily Nail Flowers

The Wilton Lily Nail Set lets you make natural-looking flowers with bell-like shapes and cupped, turned-up petals. Different lily nail sizes relate to the size of flowers you can make. The larger the nail, the larger the flowers. Always use royal icing for flowers made on the lily nail since softer icing will not hold their deeply-cupped shapes. To make any flower on the lily nail, place an aluminum foil square in bottom half of nail. Press in top half to form a foil cup. Remove the top half. Lightly spray foil with vegetable oil spray. This makes it easier to remove from foil after icing has dried and reduces breakage. Pipe a flower on the foil cup and lift out flower and foil to dry.

Petunia

• Prepare 1 5/8-in. lily nail. Then with wide end of tip 102 held down, narrow end up, start piping icing deep inside nail.
• Move up to outer edge as you turn nail, jiggling hand slightly all the while to form ruffled petal edge, then go back to starting point.
• Pipe 5 separate petals in all. Add tip 14 green star center. Push in artificial stamens.

Bluebell

• Use 1¼ in. lily nail. With tip 66, pipe three ¾ in. long petals, pulling only to top of nail. Between these petals, add three more.
• Push in three short artificial stamens.

Borders & More

Bold Stripe Border (p. 11)

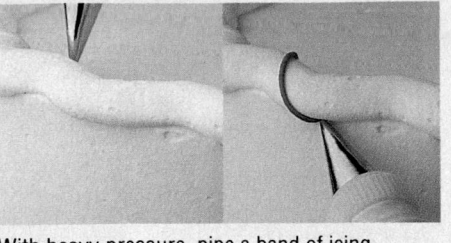

With heavy pressure, pipe a band of icing around top of cake with tip 2A. Hold bag at a 45⁰ angle and tuck tip 2 under bands. With light pressure, bring tip up and over at a slight diagonal angle. Add 2 more strings in contrasting colors. Repeat procedure at 1 in. intervals.

Upright Elongated Zigzags (p. 16)

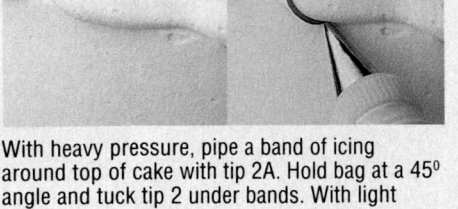

Use tip 21 and hold hand at a 45⁰ angle to side of cake. Move bag in an up and down motion, allowing tail to extend after the 3rd zigzag. Be sure to keep width of zigzags even.

Fan Border (p. 42)

Edge base with tip 18 line. Mark 2 1/2 in. wide intervals around base. Fill in intervals with tip 18 zigzag scallops. Using royal icing, pipe tip 2 strings from cake side to base. With buttercream pipe bows with tip 2. Pipe tip 18 shells above bows. Outline zigzag scallops with tip 13. Trim shells and strings with tip 2 dots.

Triple Shell Border (p.72)

With tip 18, pipe row of curved shells. Directly below first row, pipe another row of curving shells in the opposite direction. With a contrasting color, pipe a row of basic shells in center of curved pairs with tip 16.

Overlapping Shell Border (p.79)

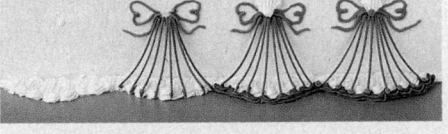

Using tip 19, slant bag and pipe an upright shell on cake side. Overlapping tail of upright shell, pipe a basic shell at base. Repeat procedure around base. With tip 3, outline basic shells with beading, if desired.

Pearl Beading

In the idea section several cakes were dripping with pearls and the effects. . .spectacular. To work with pearl beading, we suggest that the complete length (5 yds.) be used. Cut strand after wrapping around cake to insure that strand won't be too short. For safety, it is advisable to only decorate with long strands of pearl beading. Remove pearls before cutting.

Crown Border with Overlapping Drop Strings

Use tip 32 to make a row of side-by-side upright shells. Add overlapping drop strings with tip 4 following procedure below.

Overlapping Drop Strings

With toothpick, dot mark specified intervals on sides of your cake. Touch tip 3 to a mark, allow your string to skip the next mark and attach to the following one. Return to the mark that was skipped and drop string to connect the next mark. Be sure to keep depth of strings even.

Pine Cones (p. 40)

• Wrap waxed paper around Tree Former. Fold and tape under base. Ice a 2 in. area on end of cone.
• Pipe tip 97 upright petal at end of cone (turn like a flower nail).
• Add 2 more upright "center bud" petals, overlapping as you go. Pipe row of 5, then row of 6 petals below bud, turning hand out to open petals.
• Finish with row of 6, then row of 7 petals, turned out until petals lie flat.
• When dry, remove pine cone from former.

Cattails (p. 33):

• Break pieces of uncooked spaghetti into desired lengths. Fill decorating bag, fitted with tip 6, with green royal icing. Insert a piece of spaghetti into open end of tip, then as you squeeze bag, pull spaghetti out of tip coating "stem" with icing. Push end into craft block to dry.
• When dry, insert stem halfway into bag fitted with tip 10 and filled with brown icing. Let dry. Trim tops of cattails with tip 2 pull-out strings.

Cage Bars (p. 28):

Using tip 8, follow instructions for coating and drying spaghetti.

Pull-out Grass, Fur or Hair

Use tip 233 or 234 and medium icing consistency. Hold bag at a 90⁰ angle. As you squeeze out icing, pull tip up and away from surface. When icing strand is long enough (about 1/2 in.), stop pressure and pull tip away.

Lace, Ribbons, Tulle, Flower Puffs & Fabric Leaves

are easy to work with and look quite stunning. Here are a few hints to remember: Nylon lace will not absorb grease so it is the best choice. Be sure to use waterproof, satiny ribbon for the same reason. Before attaching real trims, let icing crust a bit, then anchor in place with dots of icing.

Lattice

Lattice is piped from the center of the design, outward. Use thinned icing and a tip 2 or 3; hold bag at a 45⁰ angle at the top of design with tip slightly above cake. Squeeze out a diagonal line to the right, all the way to the edge of your design. On both sides of the first line, fill in more lines, evenly spaced and going in the same direction. Return to starting point in center and pipe diagonal lines to left.

Lettering with Decorative Build-up

Using the small round tip indicated in cake instructions, on the down strokes of desired letters, hesitate an instant as you pipe, giving a short back and forth movement.

Sotas

This cornelli-like lacework is a Philippine technique. Randomly pipe tip 2 curls, V's and C's so that they touch.

Tinted Coconut or Sugar

Place shredded coconut or sugar in a plastic sandwich bag. Add a few drops of paste icing color (diluted slightly with water) or use liquid icing color. Shake bag until color is evenly distributed.

Victorian Gazebo, p. 37

For Gazebo: Using Gazebo Patterns, outline wall and roof panels with tip 3. Cover latticework lines with tip 2 strings. For stability, overpipe lattice lines once more. Since panels are extremely fragile, you may want to make extras. Allow panels to dry completely. Cut base out of cardboard, cover Fanci-Foil Wrap and ice smooth. When dry, use tip 3 to attach seams of wall panels together around base. Trim seams and base with tip 3 beads. Edge doorways and windows with tip 349 leaf garlands. Trim with tip 1 dot berries. Attach roof panels following same procedure (don't attach to walls). For support, when putting roof together, place a round craft block piece under the peak where the six roof pieces make a point.
• For trees: On prepared tree formers, (see p. 130) "paint" surface with thinned royal icing. Let dry. Cover with tip 1s sotas. When dry, remove tree from former very carefully.
• Carolers: Paint dresses with thinned royal. With tip 1, pipe puffed sleeves, zigzag fur, patterns, hats and muffs. Trim with tip 1 pull-out string leaves and dot berries. On men, add tip 1 earmuffs, tip 101s scarves, tip 4 top hats. Cut song books out of paper, fold and add titles. Attach with icing or glue.

Figure Piping

Clowns (p. 11):

Using medium consistency buttercream and tip 2A, hold bag at a 90⁰ angle and squeeze out a line of icing for body. Gently push tip 12 into body and pull out arms and legs. Pipe ball hands and shoes with tip 12. Trim suit with tip 102 ruffles and tip 3 dots. Push in Derby Clown head and add Circus Balloons.

Water Slide Kids (p. 14)

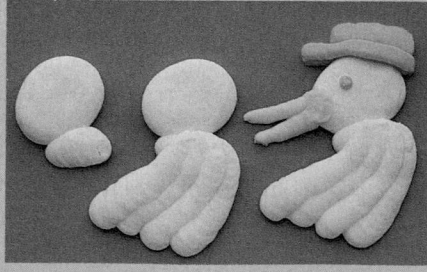

With royal icing, outline Inner Tube Pattern (one for each kid) using tip 12. Dry a few (the ones that go on water slide) on convexed flower formers. When dry, pipe kids directly on inner tubes.
For sitting kids: With medium consistency icing, hold tip 12 at a 90⁰ angle and with heavy pressure, squeeze out icing until body builds up to desired height. Use tip 7 to pipe ball heads, pull out arms and legs. For lying down kids: Use tip 12 and a 45⁰ angle. Squeeze out a line of icing for bodies. Add heads, arms and legs with tip 7. On all kids: Outline suits with tip 3, then pipe in (smooth with finger dipped in cornstarch). Add facial features, dot toes and finger and suit trims with tip 1. Pipe hair with tip 2 strings.

Stork (p. 66)

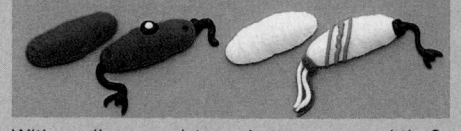

Using tip 7 and medium consistency buttercream, squeeze out ball head (flatten with finger dipped in cornstarch). With tip 7, build up body, then pipe icing with shell-motion rows (work from bottom, up). Add tip 4 hat, beak and dot eye.

Mermaid and Crabs (p. 6):

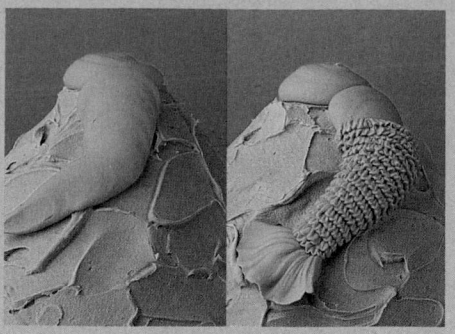

Mark Mermaid Pattern on side of cake as a guide to size. Using tip 2B and medium consistency buttercream, hold bag at a 90⁰ and build up "hip area." For tail, move tip downward at a 45⁰ angle. With a steady, even pressure, pipe in area. Decrease pressure to taper end of tail. Pipe tip 127 ruffle-motion fin. Working from the bottom, up, cover tail with rows of tip 101s.

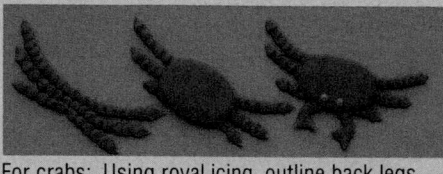

For crabs: Using royal icing, outline back legs with tip 2 on waxed paper. Pipe tip 5 ball bodies over legs (flatten with finger dipped in cornstarch). Tuck tip 2 under body and pull out front legs. Add tip 2 dot eyes. Let dry.

Carrots (p. 22)

Use tip 3. Hold bag at a 90⁰ angle to cake top; with heavy pressure, begin squeezing at top of carrot. Lift tip slightly so icing fans out. With steady even pressure, pull bag along cake top. When carrot is desired length, relax pressure and bring end to a point. Shape with fingers dipped in cornstarch.

Ghost (p. 56)

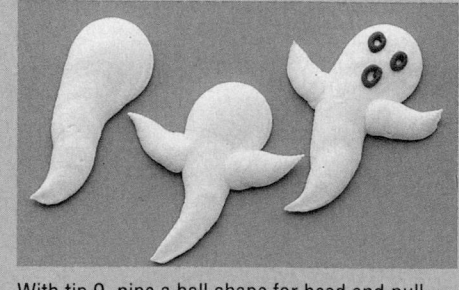

With tip 9, pipe a ball shape for head and pull out a body, tapering off the end as you gradually decrease pressure. Tuck tip into body and pull out arms. Add tip 3 dot eyes.

Gala Goodies (p.41)

- Candy Melts™*—Christmas Mix, Light Cocoa, p. 118
- Tips 1, 2, 3, 13, 349, p. 134-138
- Kelly Green, Christmas Red, Golden Yellow, Black, Orange Icing Colors, p. 124
- Meringue Powder, p. 125
- Royal Icing, p. 93

- To prevent candy from slipping, dot back with icing, then place on waxed paper surface.
- Festive Faces: Outline and pipe in (flatten with finger dipped in cornstarch) faces with tip 3. Pipe tip 3 hats. Add tip 1 facial features. Outline collars with tip 1. For hair, use tip 3 strings, e-motion or zigzags. Add tip 13 rosette pompon to Santa's cap.
- Ornaments: Tip 2 zigzags or printing.
- Snowflakes: String and dot designs done with tip 1.
- Wreaths and poinsettias: Tip 349 leaves, trimmed with tip 1 dots.
- Candy canes: Tip 3 outline (flatten down slightly with cornstarch). Add tip 1 strings for stripes.
- Stocking: Pipe with tip 3 (shape with finger dipped in cornstarch). Add tip 2 zigzag fur.
- Trees: Tip 3 zigzags, trimmed with tip 1 dots and tip 13 stars.
- Candles: Tip 3 outlines, tip 2 flames, tip 349 leaves and tip 2 dot berries.
- Gingerbread Boy: Figure pipe with tip 3. Add tip 1 details.
*brand confectionery coating

Lures (p. 27)

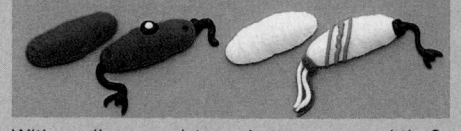

With medium consistency buttercream and tip 8, squeeze out oval bodies. Add outline hooks, lines, string and dot details with tip 2.

Color Flow

Color Flow Technique

• Tape pattern and waxed paper overlay to your work surface. (The back of a cookie pan makes a great work surface.) For curved decorations, use flower formers. Use full-strength Color Flow icing and tip 2 or 3 to outline the pattern with desired colors. If you're going to use the same color icing to fill in the outlines, let the icing outlines dry a few minutes until they "crust." If you're going to fill in with icing that differ in colors from the outlines, then let outlines dry thoroughly (1-2 hours) before filling in.

• Soften icing for filling in pattern outlines as specified in recipe. Don't use a tip for filling in outlines; instead, cut a very small opening in end of parchment bag. Begin filling in along the edges of the outlined first, squeezing gently and letting the icing flow up to the outlined almost by itself. Work quickly; filling in design from the

Color Flow Icing Recipe

(Full-Strength for Outlining)
1/4 cup water + 1 teaspoon
1 lb. sifted confectioners sugar (4 cups)
2 Tablespoons Wilton Color Flow Icing Mix

In an electric mixer, using grease-free utensils, blend all ingredients on low speed for 5 minutes. If using hand mixer, use high speed. Color Flow icing "crusts" quickly, so keep it covered with a damp cloth while using. Stir in desired icing color. In order to fill an outlined area, this recipe must be thinned with 1/2 teaspoon of water per 1/4 cup of icing (just a few drops at a time as you near proper consistency.) Color Flow is ready for filling in outlines when a small amount dropped into the mixture takes a full count of ten to disapppear. Use grease-free spoon or spatula to stir slowly.
Note: Color Flow designs take a long time to dry, so plan to do your Color Flow piece at least 2-3 days in advance.

Cookie Recipes

Grandma's Gingerbread Recipe

5 to 5 1/2 cups all-purpose flour
1 tsp. baking soda
1 tsp. salt
2 tsps. ginger
2 tsps. cinnamon
1 tsp. nutmeg
1 tsp. cloves
1 cup shortening
1 cup sugar
1 1/4 cups unsulphured molasses
2 eggs, beaten

Preheat oven to 375⁰.

Thoroughly mix flour, soda, salt and spices.

Melt shortening in large saucepan. Cool slightly. Add sugar, molasses and eggs; mix well. Add four cups dry ingredients and mix well.

Turn mixture onto lightly floured surface. Knead in remaining dry ingredients by hand. Add a little more flour, if necessary, to make a firm dough. Roll out on a lightly floured surface to 1/4 in. thickness for cut-out cookies.

If you're not going to use your gingerbread dough right away, wrap dough in plastic and refrigerate. Refrigerated dough will keep for a week, but be sure to remove it 3 hours prior to rolling so it softens and is workable. 1 recipe of this gingerbread dough will yield 40 average-size cookies.

outside edges in and from top to bottom. If you have several outlined sections, fill in one at a time.

If you're filling in a large area, have two half-full parchment bags ready, otherwise icing could "crust" before you finish filling in the patttern.

Hint: The back of a cookie pan makes a great work surface. For curved decorations, use flower formers. Since buttercream icing will break down color flow, either position color flow decoration on cake shortly before serving or place a piece of plastic wrap cut to fit on area first on set atop sugar cubes.

To pipe with piping gel:
Pour off any liquid, then tint desired color with paste icing color. Add a small amount of color at a time. (it takes color very fast). Use a cut bag to flow piping gel into desired area.

Roll-Out Cookies

1 cup butter
1 cup sugar
1 large egg
2 tsps. baking powder
1 tsp. vanilla
3 cups flour

Preheat oven to 400⁰. In a large bowl, cream butter and sugar with an electric mixer. Beat in egg and vanilla. Add baking powder and flour, one cup at a time, mixing after each addition. The dough will be very stiff; blend last flour in by hand. Do not chill dough. **Note:** Dough can be tinted with Icing Color.

Add small amounts until desired color is reached. **For chocolate cookies:** Stir in 3 ounces melted, unsweetened chocolate (if dough becomes too stiff, add water, a teaspoon at a time).

Divide dough into 2 balls. On a floured surface, roll each ball into a circle approximately 12 inches in diameter and 1/8 in. thick. Dip cutters in flour before each use. Bake cookies on an ungreased cookie sheet on top rack of oven for 6-7 minutes, or until cookies are lightly browned.

All About Tier Cakes

There are many methods of constructing tiered cakes. Here are some of the most popular.

To Prepare Cake For Assembly

Place base tier on a sturdy base plate or 3 or more thicknesses of corrugated cardboard. For heavy cakes, use masonite or plywood. Base can be covered with Fanci-Foil Wrap and trimmed with Tuk-N-Ruffle or use the Wilton Ruffle Boards™. Each tier in your cake must be on a cake circle or board cut to fit. Smear a few strokes of icing on boards to secure cake. Fill and ice layers before assembly.

To Dowel Rod Cakes For Pillar & Stacked Construction

Center a cake circle or plate one size smaller than the next tier on base tier and press it gently into icing to imprint an outline. Remove circle. Measure one dowel rod at the cake's lowest point within this circle. Using this dowel rod for measure, cut dowel rods (to fit this tier) the same size using pruning shears. If the next tier is 10-in. or less, push seven ¼-in. dowel rods into cake down to base within circle guide. Generally the larger and more numerous the upper tiers, the more dowels needed. Very large cakes need ½-in. dowels in base tier.

Stacked Construction

This method is often combined with pillar construction. Dowel rod bottom tier. Center a corrugated cake circle, one size smaller than the tier to be added, on top of the base tier. Position the following tier. Repeat procedure for each additional tier. To keep stacked tiers stable, sharpen one end of a dowel rod and push through all tiers and cardboard circles to base of bottom tier. To decorate, start at top and work down.

Pillar Construction

Dowel rod tiers. Optional: Snap pegs into separator plates to prevent slipping (never substitute pegs for dowel rods). Position separator plates on supporting tiers, making sure that pillar projections on each tier will line up with pillars below. Mark center backs of cakes. Decorate cakes. At reception, align pillar projections and assemble cakes on pillars.

Fast & Easy Push-In Leg Construction

Dowel rods are not needed because legs attached to separator plates push right through the tiers down to the plate below.

Ice cakes on cake circles. To mark where legs will go, simply center separator plate for tier above (projections down) and gently press onto the tier. Lift plate off. Repeat this procedure for each tier (except top). Position upper tiers on separator plates. Decorate cakes.

To assemble: Insert legs into cake at marks. Push straight down until legs touch cake board. Add plate with cake to legs. Be sure plates are securely fastened to legs. Continue adding tiers in this way until cake is assembled.

Dowel Rod

Stacked

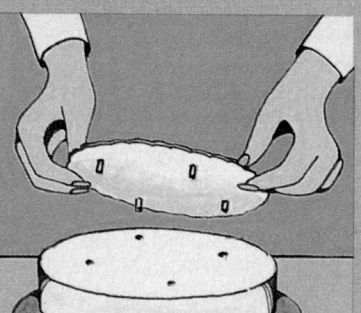

Mark Center Back

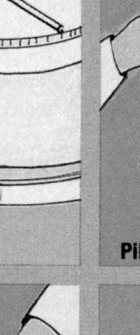

Pilla

Mark Where Legs Go

Push-In Leg

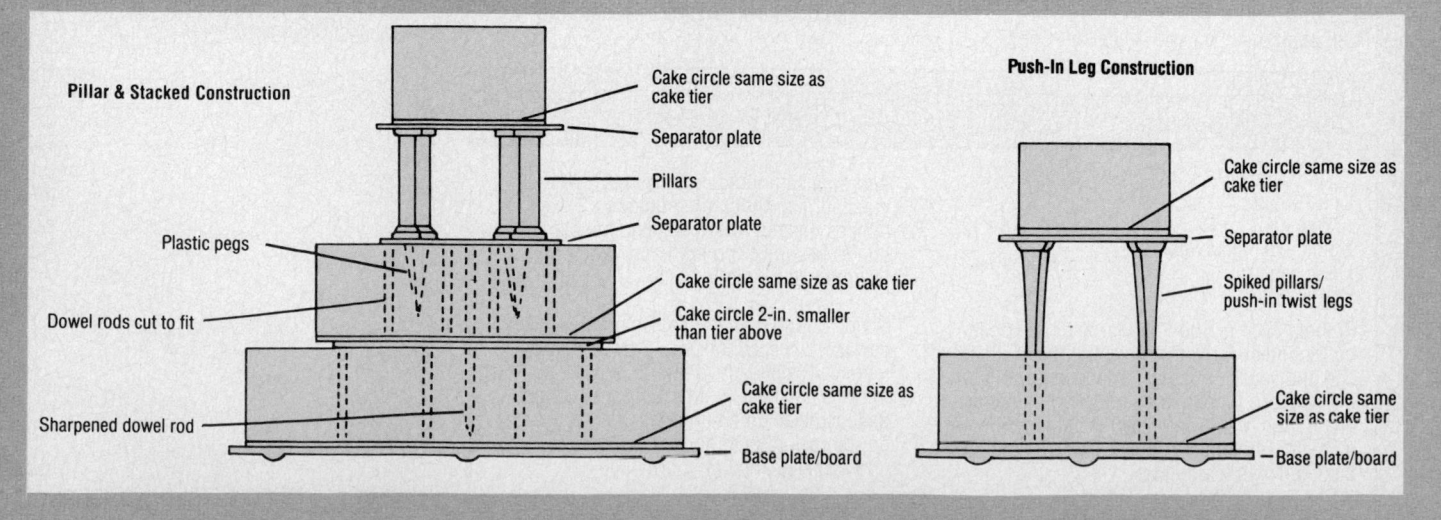

Pillar & Stacked Construction

- Cake circle same size as cake tier
- Separator plate
- Pillars
- Separator plate
- Plastic pegs
- Cake circle same size as cake tier
- Dowel rods cut to fit
- Cake circle 2-in. smaller than tier above
- Cake circle same size as cake tier
- Sharpened dowel rod
- Base plate/board

Push-In Leg Construction

- Cake circle same size as cake tier
- Separator plate
- Spiked pillars/ push-in twist legs
- Cake circle same size as cake tier
- Base plate/board

• Before placing separator plate or cake circle atop another tier, sprinkle a little confectioners sugar or coconut flakes to prevent plate or circle from sticking. Letting icing crust a bit before positioning plate on cake will also prevent sticking.

• You will have less crumbs when icing, if cakes are baked a day in advance.

• When filling or torting large layers, use less than you usually would. Your dam of icing should also be far enough from edge so filling doesn't form a bubble.

• The cake icer tip (789) is an invaluable timesaver in icing wedding tiers.

• The 16-in. bevel pan takes 1½ cake mixes. So your beveled sides bake properly, pull batter out from center to add depth to the sides.

• When transporting tiers, place cakes on damp towels or carpet foam and drive carefully.

• Some of the plates of the Tall Tier Stand will not sit level when not on the stand. Pack atop crumpled foil, tissue or towels when transporting. To decorate, set plates on pan or bowl. The column cap nut of the Tall Tier Stand attaches under the top tier cake. Therefore, this cake must be positioned after assembling the Tall Tier Stand. Place top tier on a cake circle slightly larger than the cake to make positioning easier. Add base borders after assembling the top tier.

• To keep balance, cut cakes on the Tall Tier Stand from top tier down.

• To divide tiers, use the Cake Dividing Set. The Wheel Chart makes it easy to mark 2-in. intervals on 6 to 18-in. diam. cakes. The triangle marker gives precise spacing for stringwork and garlands. The raised lines on separator plates can also be followed for easy dividing.

• When using Spiked Pillars and stacked construction, double cake boards or use separator plates between layers to prevent the weight of tiers from causing the pillars to pierce through cake.

Wedding Cake Data

One cake mix yields 4 to 6 cups of batter. Pans are usually filled ½ to ⅔ full; 3-in. deep pans should be filled only ½ full. Batter amounts on this chart are for pans two-thirds full of batter. Icing amounts are very general and will vary with consistency, thickness applied and tips used. These amounts allow for top and base borders and a side ruffled border. For large cakes, always check for doneness after they have baked for one hour.

The charts to the right show how to cut popular shaped wedding tiers into pieces approximately 1-in. x 2-in. by two layers high (about 4-in.). Even if you prefer a larger serving size, the order of cutting is still the same.

Number of servings are intended as a guide only.

Pan Shape	Size	# Servings 2 Layer	Cups Batter/ 1 Layers 2"	Baking Temps	Baking Time	Approx. Cups Icing to Frost and Decorate
Oval	7¾ x 5¾"	13	2½	350°	25	3
	10¾ x 7⅞"	30	5½	350°	30	4
	13 x 9¾"	44	8	350°	30	5½
	16 x 12¾"	70	11	325°	30	7½
Round	6"	14	2	350°	25-30	3
	8"	25	3	350°	30-35	4
	10"	39	6	350°	35-40	5
	12"	56	7½	350°	35-40	6
	14"	77	10	325°	50-55	7¼
	16"	100	15	325°	55-60	8¾
Round 3" Deep (# Servings for 1 layer)	8"	15	5	325°	60-65	2¾
	10"	24	8	325°	75-80	4¾
	12"	33	11	325°	75-80	5¾
	14"	45	15	325°	75-80	7
Half Round	18"					
2" layer		127†	9*	325°	60-65	10½
3" layer		92††	12*	325°	60-65	10½
Petal	6"	8	1½	350°	25-30	3½
	9"	20	3½	350°	35-40	6
	12"	38	7	350°	35-40	7¾
	15"	62	12	325°	50-55	11
Hexagon	6"	12	1¾	350°	30-35	2¾
	9"	22	3½	350°	35-40	4¾
	12"	50	6	350°	40-45	5¾
	15"	72	11	325°	40-45	8¾
Heart	6"	11	1½	350°	25	2½
	9"	24	3½	350°	30	4½
	12"	48	8	350°	30	5¾
	15"	76	11½	325°	40	8¾
Square	6"	18	2	350°	25-30	3½
	8"	32	4	350°	35-40	4½
	10"	50	6	350°	35-40	6
	12"	72	10	350°	40-45	7½
	14"	98	13½	350°	45-50	9½
	16"	128	15½	350°	45-50	11
	18"	162	18	350°	50-55	13

*Batter for each half round pan. †Four half rounds. ††Two half rounds.

Wedding Cake Cutting Guide

The first step in cutting is to remove the top tier, and then begin the cutting with the 2nd tier followed by 3rd, 4th and so on. The top tier is usually saved for the first anniversary so it is not figured into the serving amount.

Cutting guides for shapes not shown can be found in other Wilton publications.

The diagrams below show how to cut popular shaped wedding tiers into pieces approximately 1-in. x 2-in. by two layers high (about 4-in.). Even if you prefer a larger serving size, the order of cutting is still the same.

To cut oval tiers, move in 2-in. from the outer edge and cut across. Then slice 1-in. pieces of cake. Now move in another 2-in. and slide again until the entire tier is cut.

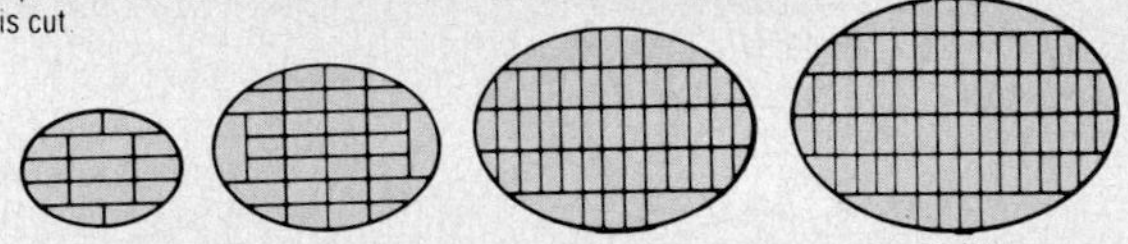

7¾x5¾ 10¾x7⅞ 13x9¾ 16x12¾

To cut round tiers, move in two inches from the tier's outer edge; cut a circle and then slice 1-in. pieces within the circle. Now move in another 2-in., cut another circle, slice 1-in. pieces and so on until the tier is completely cut. The center core of each tier and the small top tier can be cut into halves, 4ths, 6ths and 8ths, depending on size.

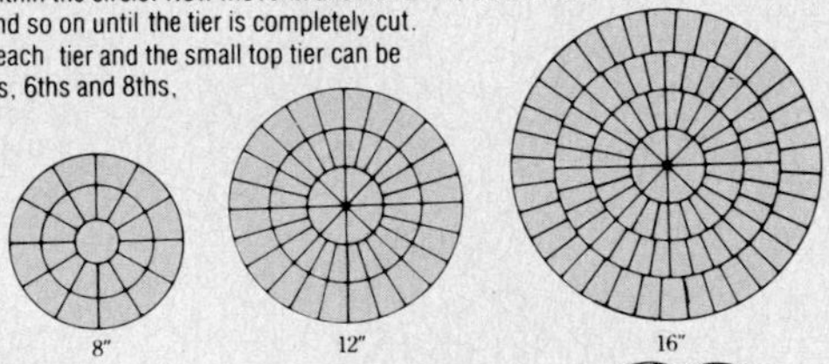

8" 12" 16"

Cut petal-shaped tiers similar to round tiers as diagram shows.

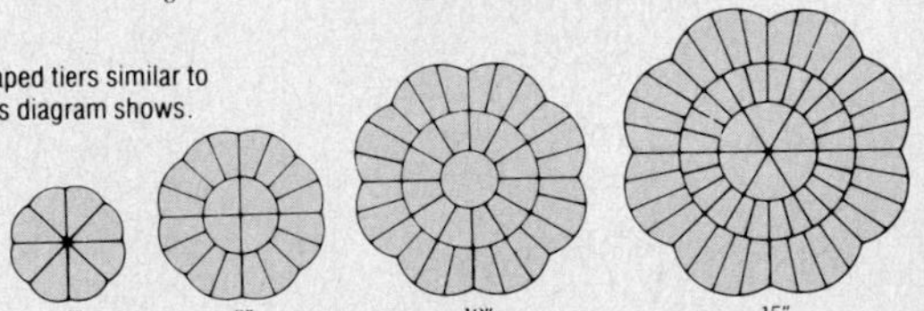

6" 9" 12" 15"

Cut hexagon tiers similar to round tiers.

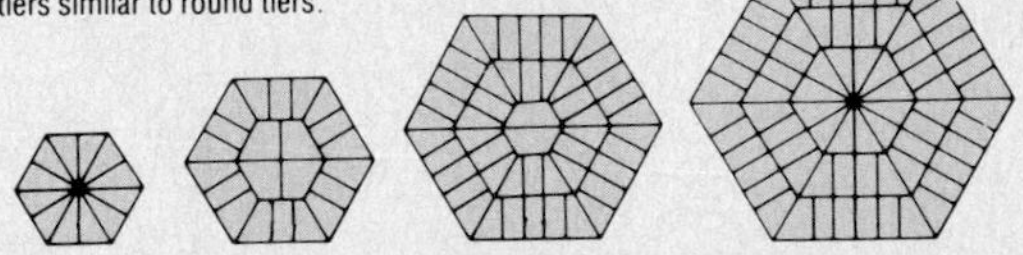

6" 9" 12" 15"

To cut heart-shaped tiers, divide the tiers vertically into halves, quarters, sixths or eighths. Within rows, slice one inch pieces of cake.

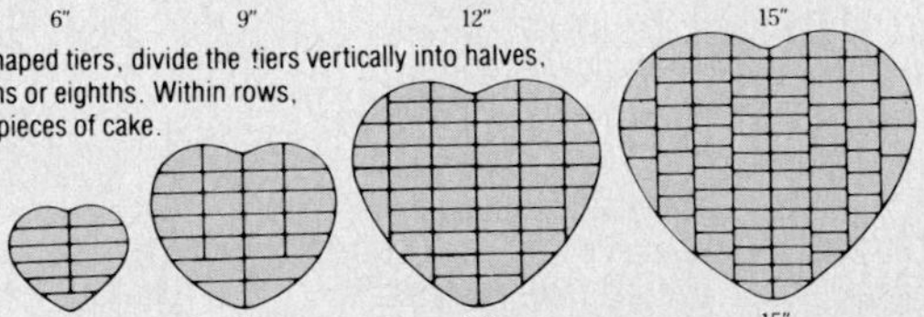

6" 9" 12" 15"

To cut square tiers, move in 2-in. from the outer edge and cut across. Then slice 1-in. pieces of cake. Now move in another 2-in. and slice again until the entire tier is cut.

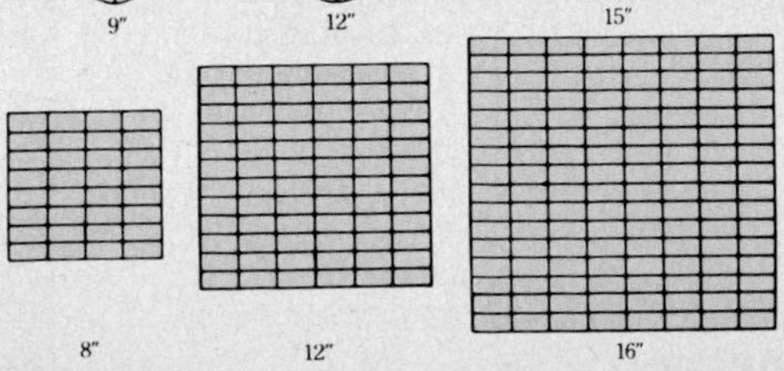

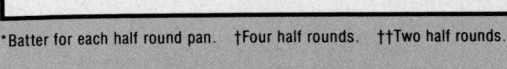

8" 12" 16"

Candy Making

Wilton Candy Melts™ brand confectionery coating take the guesswork out of making candy at home. They melt easily, right to the ideal consistency for molding and dipping, and have a creamy, rich flavor. For a change of taste, they can be flavored with Wilton Candy Flavors. See our complete collection of candy making products (p. 116-118).

Candy Melts Are So Easy To Use

For melting, molding and dipping directions, simply refer to the back of the Candy Melts package. Remember that constant stirring is very important to insure even heating, when using the double boiler method. Here's a no-mess way of melting in microwave: Fill an uncut disposable decorating bag half-full of Candy Melts. Microwave 1 minute at half power; knead candy. Repeat at 30-second intervals until candy is completely melted. Then cut the tip and squeeze melted coating out into candy molds.

To Flavor: The creamy, rich taste can be enhanced by adding approximately ¼ teaspoon Wilton oil-based Candy Flavor (p. 118) to 1 lb. of melted Candy Melts. Never use alcohol based flavorings; they will cause coatings to harden.

To Color: Add Wilton Candy Colors (p. 119) to melted Candy Melts a little at a time. Mix thoroughly before adding more color. Colors tend to deepen as they're mixed. Pastel colored candies are most appetizing, so keep this in mind when tinting.

To Mold Multi-Color Candy

"Painting" Method: Use a decorator's brush dipped in melted Candy Melts. Paint features or details desired. Let set. Fill mold. Refrigerate until set. Unmold. **"Layering" Method:** Pour melted coating into dry molds to desired height. Refrigerate until partially set. Pour contrasting color melted coating to desired height. Refrigerate until partially set. Repeat until desired numbers of layers are formed. Let candy harden in refrigerator. Unmold. Wilton Classic Candy Molds are available in a wonderful variety of unique and traditional shapes. Their generous depth makes painting and layering fun and easy. See page 121 for our outstanding Classic Candy Molds selection.

To Mold Candy Plaques

Molding a section or the entire pan out of Candy Melts is easy and impressive.

• Pour melted coating into center of pan. Tap pan gently on counter to break up bubbles and spread coating evenly over bottom (approximately ¼ in. thick). For control, use a decorating bag fitted with tip 2 or snip off a very small end off disposable bag.

• Place pan in refrigerator for approximately 5 to 10 minutes (check occasionally, if coating becomes too hard it will crack). Unmold onto hand or soft towel (tap pan gently, if necessary).

• Cookie cutters work great, too. Place cutter on waxed paper; pour in candy. Unmold when set per instructions above.

• For multi-color effect: Paint desired area with a decorator's brush, Let set. Pour in melted coating to fill remaining area.

To Make Candy Leaves

On the back of clean, thoroughly dried, grape or rose leaves, paint on melted Candy Melts with a soft pastry or decorator's brush. Pull out pointed or curved edges to resemble certain kinds of leaves such as the "oak" leaves.
Refrigerate and when completely set, carefully peel off candy.

Ganache Glaze

So easy to make with our delicious Candy Melts * brand confectionery coating. Elegantly covers cakes with a luscious, satiny-smooth finish.

Ganache Glaze Recipe

14 oz. package of Candy Melts
½ cup whipping cream

Finely chop wafers (use food processor). Heat whipping cream just to boiling point (do not boil) in a sauce pan. Add chopped wafers and stir until smooth and glossy. If mixture is too thin to pour, wait a few minutes until cool. To cover, place cake on a wire rack over a drip pan. Pour glaze into center and work towards edges.

Modeling Candy "Clay"
- 14 oz. bag of Candy Melts
- ⅓ cup light corn syrup
- Candy or Icing Color (optional)

Melt candy as directed on package. Stir in corn syrup and mix only until blended

Shape mixture onto a 6 in. square of waxed paper and let set at room temperature until dry.

Wrap well and store at room temperature until needed. Modeling candy handles best if hardened overnight.

To use: If you wish to tint candy, add candy or icing color. Knead a small portion at a time. If it gets too soft, set aside at room temperature or refrigerate briefly. Lasts for several weeks in a well-sealed container.

When rolling out candy, sprinkle surface with cornstarch to prevent sticking. Thickness of rolled-out candy should be approximately ⅛ in. Hint: Secure pieces together with dots of buttercream icing, if necessary.

MODELING A ROSE
Start with the base and mold a cone that's approximately 1½-in. high from a 3/4-in. diameter ball of modeling candy. Next, make petals. Flatten 3/8-in. ball of modeling candy into a circle that's about ¼-in. thick on one side and about the diameter of a dime. Make several petals this size.

- Wrap first petal around the point of the cone to form a bud. Now press three more petals around the base of the bud.

- Gently pinch edges of petals. Make five more petals using slightly larger balls of modeling candy. Flatten, then thin edge with finger and cup petals. Press petals under first rows of petals. Continue adding petals, placing them in between and slightly lower than previous row. For a fuller flower, continue adding petals in this manner.

To Make Flowers
Use tools and instructions included in our Gum Paste Flowers Kit for making daffodil, violet and leaves.

Make 1 recipe of Modeling Candy with white Candy Melts. Tint ½ of recipe yellow. Divide remainder into 3rds. One remains white, tint rest green and violet with icing colors.

For Daffodil: Do steps 1 through 3 (in gum paste kit instruction book), except use cornstarch instead of grease. Let petals dry on

flower formers. For trumpet or cup, roll out white modeling candy. Cut out trumpet with small carnation cutter. With a knife, cut away a triangular 4th. Dip modeling stick (included in kit) in cornstarch and form trumpet around it. Let dry. Attach trumpet to petals with royal icing. Edge top with tip 2 royal icing zigzags.

For Leaves: Roll out green modeling candy. Cut out leaves with large leaf cutter. Dip leaf mold into cornstarch, then press candy into mold. Remove leaf from mold and allow it to dry on flower former.

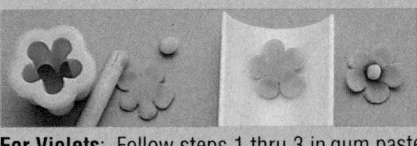

For Violets: Follow steps 1 thru 3 in gum paste kit instruction book. Let flowers dry on flower formers. For centers, make tiny balls from yellow modeling candy. Attach with dots of royal icing.

To Make Rolled Fondant Roses
Follow modeling a rose instructions (at left), using rolled fondant instead of modeling candy clay. To color fondant, add color a few drops at a time to ball of fondant and knead in with hands.

Piping Decorations With Candy
(see Christmas Trees, p. 38 or Panels p. 80).
- Trace pattern and place on a heavy board or piece of glass, cover with waxed paper and tape securely.

- Cut bag method: Fill a parchment or disposable bag with melted Candy Melts. Cut a very small opening in end of bag (approximately the size of a tip 3). If candy thickens, bag can be reheated in microwave. For thicker decorations such as panels, pipe candy using a round tip. Outline edges of pattern design and let set 5 to 10 minutes. Flow in candy (to smooth surface, skim area with end of bag immediately) and let set. Allow piece to set completely 10 to 15 minutes.

For tree: Use a cut bag or tip 2. You'll need 1 full tree and 2 half tree pieces for each 3-D tree. When set, attach a half in center of full tree with melted candy. Let set 10 to 15. Set tree upright and attach remaining half to opposite side following same procedure. Since these are very delicate, you may want to make extras, in case of breakage. For panels: Use tip 4 to outline and flow in panels. Panel should be approximately 1/8 in. thick, so allow 15 to 20 minutes for candy to set. You'll need 6 large panels and 6 small sections for each tier; 18 side sections (6 on each tier) are used. Panels positioned on sides of tiers.

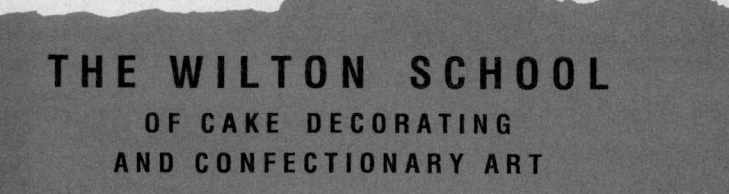

THE WILTON SCHOOL
OF CAKE DECORATING
AND CONFECTIONARY ART

Learn how to decorate from the experts! Since 1929, when Dewey McKinley Wilton first opened the Wilton School, hundreds of thousands of students have learned the fundamentals of decorating the Wilton Way. The Wilton Method of Cake Decorating stresses classic decorating– beginning with a thorough understanding of the fundamentals. Students are then encouraged to express themselves creatively.

The Wilton School has a Certificate of Approval to operate issued by the Illinois State Superintendent of Schools. Students receive instruction, supervision and guidance by expert instructors/decorators.

World renown, the Wilton School has greatly expanded its curriculum since the Wilton Method was first introduced 60 years ago. Today the basic Master Course is supplemented by courses in foreign methods, Lambeth, chocolate artistry, gum paste, pulled sugar, cakes for catering and more. The following is a summary of courses we offer:

MASTER COURSE – 2 weeks, 70 hours. Focuses on the fundamentals of cake decorating. Designed for the cake decorating shop owner, baker, caterer, chef or enthusiast.
TUITION: $550

INTRODUCTION TO GUM PASTE COURSE – 12 hours–four afternoons during the Master Course. This mini-course teaches the art of making lovely gum paste flowers, bouquets and more.
TUITION: $125

ADVANCED GUN PASTE/FOREIGN METHODS COURSE – 2 weeks, 80 hours. Designed for the more serious decorator. Covers: Nirvana, the English method of cake decorating that uses color flow panels; South African and Australian Methods, which use delicate royal icing wings and are done on rolled fondant-covered cakes; gum paste flowers and arrangements. A gum paste doll is constructed. Previous decorating experience is required.
TUITION: $550

LAMBETH CONTINENTAL COURSE – 1 week, 40 hours. Teaches intricate overpiping of borders on royal icing and rolled fondant-covered cakes. All students decorate cakes using a combination of overpiped borders. Previous decorating experience is required.
TUITION: $300

PULLED SUGAR COURSE – 9 hours, 3 afternoons during Master Course. Learn how to use pulled sugar to cover a cake, make flowers, candy dishes, ribbons, bows and more.
TUITION: $150

CHOCOLATE ARTISTRY WITH ELAINE GONZALEZ – 5 days, 30 hours. Well-known choclatier and author of *Chocolate Artistry* presents an in-depth course devoted exclusively to making and decorating candy. Professional techniques for creating fabulous candies from molded treats to delicious truffles are taught.
TUITION: $300

CAKES FOR CATERING – A 5 day, 40-hour course where students learn to ice and decorate cakes to serve large or small groups. The class covers wedding and other tiered cakes, sheet cakes, large rounds and squares and petit fours, including small cakes and cookies. Learn to design theme party cakes and get special tips for quick and easy, but spectacular designs. Decorating experience required.
TUITION: $300

The Wilton School is located in Woodridge, Illinois (a suburb of Chicago). Course enrollment is limited. Apply early. For more information, or to enroll, write to: School Secretary, Wilton School of Cake Decorating and Confectionery Art, 2240 W. 75th St., Woodridge, IL 60517. Or call 708-963-7100 for free brochure and schedule. You may charge your courses on VISA or Mastercard.

WILTON
HOME STUDY
COURSE IN
CAKE DECORATING

Even if you've never tried cake decorating before, the Wilton Home Study Course will show you how to decorate beautiful cakes for every occasion. Easy-to-follow 5-lesson course includes the specialty tools you need plus the step-by-step instructions, illustrations and photographs that make it easy!

Enroll in the Wilton Home Study Course in Cake Decorating now. The cost is only $17.99 plus $3.00 postage and handling per lesson. See details on page 128.

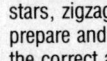

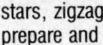

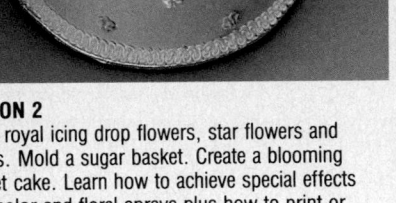
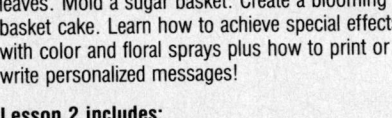

LESSON 1
Discover the easy way to pipe buttercream icing stars, zigzag borders and more! Learn how to prepare and color icing for your decorating bag, the correct angle to use, and how to control the pressure for expert results. Make a "Happy Birthday" cake.

Lesson 1 includes:
• Notebook Easel and Lesson Pages
• Decorating Tips 4, 16 and 18
• Quick-Change Plastic Coupler
• Two Jars of Paste Icing Color
• Shaped "Happy Birthday" Cake Pan
• 12" Featherweight Decorating Bag
• Pattern Sheets and Practice Board
• Cardboard Cake Circle
• *Cake Decorating Easy As 1-2-3 Book*

LESSON 2
Make royal icing drop flowers, star flowers and leaves. Mold a sugar basket. Create a blooming basket cake. Learn how to achieve special effects with color and floral sprays plus how to print or write personalized messages!

Lesson 2 includes:
• Lesson Pages
• Flower Basket Sugar Mold
• Large Stainless Steel Angled Spatula
• Decorating Tips 3, 20, 67 and 131
• 2 Jars of Paste Icing Color
• Meringue Powder (4 oz. canister)
• Pack of 50 Parchment Paper Triangles
• Cardboard Cake Circle
• 6 Pattern Sheets

LESSON 3
Learn the proper techniques for making shells, rosebuds, sweet peas ruffles, bows and more! Learn to make bouquets on a heart-shaped cake ideal for anniversaries, birthdays, Valentine's Day, weddings, showers.

Lesson 3 includes:
• Lesson Pages
• Two 9" Heart-Shaped Aluminum Pans
• Decorating Tips 22, 103 and 104
• 12" Featherweight Decorating Bag
• Quick-Change Plastic Coupler
• Cardboard Cake Circle
• Jar of Paste Icing Color
• 4 Pattern Sheets

LESSON 4
Pipe daisies and chrysanthemums using a flower nail. Weave basketweave stripes. Create symmetrical cake designs, pipe rope borders and more. Use your new cake turntable to decorate a round cake.

Lesson 4 includes:

• Lesson Pages
• Trim 'N Turn Cake Stand
• Decorating Tips 48 and 81
• Cardboard Cake Circle
• Flower Nails 7 and 9

• Jar of Paste Icing Color
• Wilton Cake Marker
• 6 Pattern Sheets

LESSON 5
Shape a magnificent icing rose! Pipe stringwork and create a mini-tiered cake using the pans and separator set we'll send. After this lesson you'll qualify for your Wilton Certificate of Completion!

Lesson 5 includes:
• Lesson Pages
• Round Mini-Tier Kit (includes 3 cake pans, separator plates and columns)
• Decorating Tips 2, 12, 87 and 102
• Cardboard Cake Circle
• 4 Pattern Sheets

You can do it!

We'll show you how. Even if you don't know a decorating bag from a coupler, by the end of this course, you'll be a pro.

Learn creative techniques on which you will constantly rely. Piping, drop flowers, shells, daisies, chrysanthemums and magnificent roses. The ideas and options are endless. You will quickly realize, with confidence, that "you can do it."

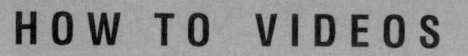

VIDEO HOME STUDY

HOW TO MAKE WEDDING CAKES
Receive invaluable lessons on how to design and assemble dramatic tier cakes for weddings, showers, anniversaries and other special occasions. Hints for transporting and serving are also included.
VHS. 901-Y-128 $19.99 each

HOW TO MAKE ICING FLOWERS
Add blooming beauty to all cakes. Learn how to make roses, Easter lilies, violets, pansies, daisies, poinsettias and more! Five lovely cake designs incorporate all the beautiful flowers included in this video.
VHS. 901-Y-119 $19.99 each

CAKE DECORATING-EASY AS 1,2,3!
Zella Junkin, Director of the Wilton School, takes you through the basics. See how to level and frost a cake perfectly, make simple borders, flowers, leaves and more.
VHS. 901-Y-115 $19.99 each

CANDY MAKING – EASY 1, 2, 3!
Have fun learning how to make truffles, candy novelties, dipped fruit, molded and filled candy. Melting candy in the microwave included.
VHS. 901-Y-125 $19.99 each

IT'S FUN AND EASY...in just three lessons, you'll learn the basic skills of cake decorating. You'll receive the home study video tapes and all the pans and tools you'll need to create six wonderful, decorated cakes for birthdays, holidays and any occasion you want to make special.

VIDEO HOME STUDY COURSE

IT'S CONVENIENT...see actual decorating techniques demonstrated right in your own home. Learn step-by-step, how to create these wonderful icing techniques yourself...then practice them on your practice board right in front of your TV. Start with the basics and build up to a beautiful rose. You'll love all the decorating fun and ease of learning it with this great new video.

IT'S A TREAT...learn from our experts. Now you can gather all the secrets of experienced cake decorators. See and hear all the hints and tips that make decorating easy. You'll be surprised at how much you can learn and accomplish with this Wilton Video Home Study Cake Decorating Course.

ENROLL IN THE WILTON VIDEO HOME STUDY COURSE NOW.
The cost is only **$29.99** plus $3.00 shipping and handling per lesson...and the videos and all the pans and tools are yours to keep. Don't delay. Return the card on page 128 with your first payment to Wilton and we'll send you Lesson I. If you are not completely satisfied, you can return the materials within 30 days for a full refund or credit.

Lesson 1
Have fun learning the fundamentals of baking and frosting shaped cakes, about icing, how to use decorating tools and more! Learn how to decorate 2 fun, shaped cakes.
Includes
Lesson I 30 minute VHS video, Lesson Plan/Guide, Huggable Bear shaped pan, 10 in. Soft Touch decorating bag, 3 disposable decorating bags, 4 metal decorating tips, 2 quick-change couplers, practice board with practice sheets, 2 jars of icing color, heavy duty cake board, Trim 'N Turn cake stand, 1992 Wilton Yearbook of Cake Decorating.

Lesson 2
Learn how to torte, how to ice a cake smooth, how to make shells, drop flowers, leaves, figure pipe. Learn how to decorate 2 cakes and a clown cupcake, using figure piping and drop flowers.
Includes
Lesson II 30 minute VHS video, Lesson Plan/Guide, 9" Round Pan Set, 3 metal decorating tips, large angled spatula, 2 jars of icing color, 3 disposable decorating bags, 30 parchment sheets, 2 cake circles, Clown Heads cake tops.

Lesson 3
Learn how to make the rose and other icing flowers, how to make bows, and how to position flower sprays on cakes. Learn how to decorate 2 heart-shaped cakes with basketweave and flowers.
Includes
Lesson III 30 minute VHS video, Lesson Plan/Guide, 9" Happiness Heart Pan Set, 3 metal decorating tips, #7 flower nail, 2 jars icing color, a container of meringue powder, 2 cake circles, a decorating comb and a Certificate of Completion.

CAKE DECORATING-EASY AS 1-2-3
Shows and explains the basics of cake decorating in simple terms. Perfect for beginners! Soft cover; 36 pages; full color; 5 1/2 x 8 1/2 in.
902-Y-1792 $1.99 each

USES OF DECORATING TIPS
Extremely valuable quick reference/idea book. Shows the versatility and range of many tips by depicting design variations. Full color; soft cover; 48 pages; 8 1/2 x 11 in.
902-Y-1375 $6.99 each

DISCOVER THE FUN OF CAKE DECORATING
Find over 100 irresistible cake ideas, from fast and easy sheet cakes to wedding cakes with complete easy-to-follow, step-by-step instructions. Includes patterns and cake serving ideas. 184 color pages; 8 1/2 x 11 in.
904-Y-206 $12.99 each

THE WILTON WAY OF CAKE DECORATING
The comprehensive cake decorating reference book for professionals and amateurs alike! Explore this must-have trilogy of techniques, tools, ideas, instructions and hints. All found in three invaluable volumes you'll be constantly consulting.

VOLUME ONE-BEGIN WITH THE BASICS!
More than 600 full-color photos portray the Wilton method of decorating. Specialty techniques, such as Color Flow, Figure Piping, Sugar Molding and Marzipan Modeling are easy to master. Includes recipes. Hard cover; 328 color pages; 8 1/2 x 11 in. Printed in Italy.
904-Y-100 $29.99 each

VOLUME TWO-ADVANCED TECHNIQUES
Our 328-page encyclopedia is brimming with Wilton-American and foreign techniques: English (Nirvana and over-piped), Australian, Continental, Mexican, Philippine and South African. Includes gum paste flowers and figures and the art of pulled sugar taught and demonstrated by Norman Wilton. Soft cover; 328 color pages; 8 1/2 x 11 in. Printed in U.S.A.
904-Y-119 $26.99 each

VOLUME THREE-USING DECORATING TIPS
More than 400 color photos highlight over 40 beautiful borders, plus dozens of flowers and other decorative motifs. Exciting figure piped and gum paste creations are demonstrated and explained. Hard cover; 328 color pages; 8 1/2 x 11 in. Printed in U.S.A.
ENGLISH VERSION
904-Y-348 $29.99 each

VOLUME THREE-SPANISH VERSION
(not shown)
Like the English version, this book is totally devoted to tips. Also features a full chapter of quinceanos cakes and easy-to-follow "pictorial dictionary."
904-Y-1348 $34.99 each

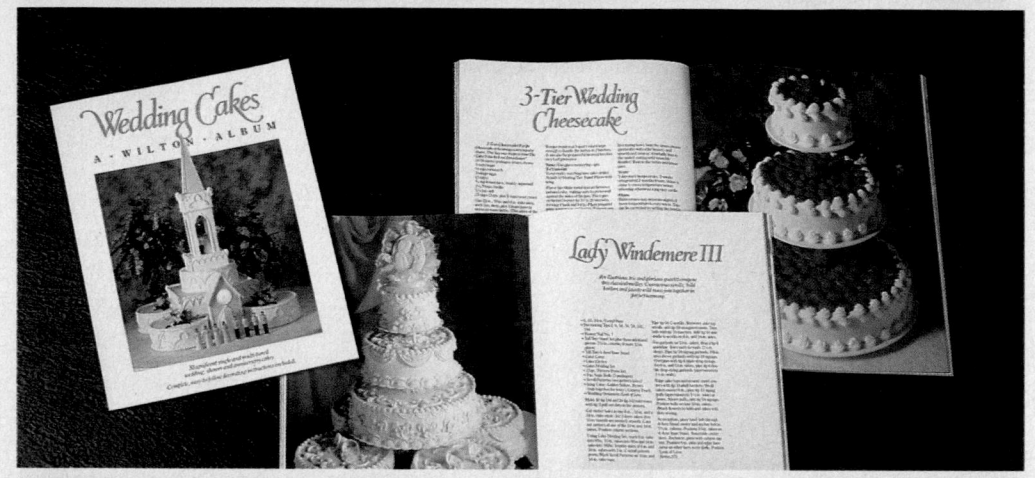

NEW! A TREASURY OF WILTON WEDDING CAKES

The newest and most exquisite collection of wedding cakes and ornaments anywhere. This book reflects more than half a century of experience Wilton has in designing wedding cakes. From Victorian to contemporary cakes and designer series porcelain ornaments. Soft cover; 96 color pages; 8 1/2 x 10 3/4 in.
908-Y-105 $6.99 each

WEDDING CAKES- A WILTON ALBUM

Mark those cherished occasions with a culinary masterpiece. Create wedding, shower and anniversary cakes-from classic to contemporary. Complete, easy-to-follow instructions, patterns, recipes and wedding cake data and cutting guide are also included. Soft cover; 82 color pages; 8 1/4 x 10 3/4 in.
908-Y-100 $6.99 each

CELEBRATE! WEDDING CAKES BY WILTON

From intricate cakes that serve hundreds to dainty creations for the most intimate gathering, this book has everything for that special bride. Scores of designs using innovative techniques including foreign methods, stairways and fountains. Instructions and patterns included. Hard cover; 192 color pages; 8 3/4 X 11 in.
916-Y-847 $12.99 each

DRAMATIC TIER CAKES

With this complete Wilton guide learn the fundamentals of constructing and decorating lavish tier cakes, from the basics of building a cake to the safest way to transport wedding tiers to the reception. Includes uses of stairways and fountains, plus tested recipes, decorating descriptions and a complete selection of products needed to make the cakes shown. A must-have for any decorator. Soft cover; 80 color pages; 8 1/2 X 11in.
902-Y-1725 $6.99 each

WILTON CELEBRATES THE ROSE

The rose. Learn all about this most popular icing flower. Includes easy-to-follow classic rose-making directions plus a quick, impressive method. Also learn how to create petal-perfect candy flowers, how to model marzipan and gum paste roses, and how to stencil cakes. Recipes and patterns included. Full-color; soft cover; 66 color pages; 8 1/2 X 11 in.
916-Y-1218 $6.99 each

NEW! 1992 YEARBOOK OF CAKE DECORATING

A great idea and resource book for the professional baker or hobbyist alike. Over 150 new cake decorating ideas in addition to cookie, candy making and wedding cake creations. Step-by-step decorating instructions and helpful hints included. Soft cover; 192 full color pages. 8 1/4 x 10 3/4 in.
1701-Y-920 $5.99 each

NEW! 1992 PATTERN BOOK

Just the helping hand you need to duplicate many cake ideas from the 1992 Yearbook. Many innovative designs. 8 1/4 x 10 3/4 in.
408-Y-920 $4.99 each

LET'S MAKE CANDY

A step-by-step guide to candy making. Kids of all ages will appreciate the expertise and caring that go into these treasures. Learn techniques for beginning and experienced candy makers. Basic candy making techniques such as molding and dipping, plus specialty ideas, such as candy clay and candi-pan are clearly explained. Soft cover; 44 full color pages, 5 1/2 X 8 1/2 in.
902-Y-2100 $1.99 each

THE COMPLETE WILTON BOOK OF CANDY

What better way to let them know you fussed. Treat family and friends to these luscious molded and dipped chocolates, dessert shells, fudge, truffles, confectionery coating candies, marzipan, hard candies. Find out just how easy it is with our delicious recipes and helpful hints. Soft cover; full color; 176 pages; 7 1/2 X 10 1/2 in.
902-Y-1243 $10.99 each

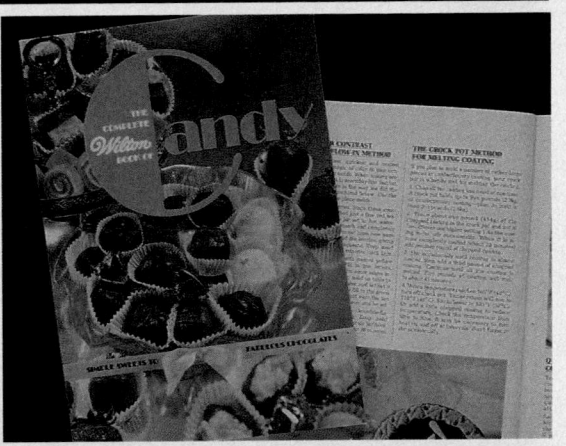

HOLIDAY

Need we say more? A complete collection of cakes, cookies, center-pieces and candy for holiday baking and making. Find dozens of unusual festive ideas you'll love to make from gingerbread, cookie dough, cakes, candy and other confections, plus unique cookie baskets. Rediscover holiday characters, trimmed orna-ments-even create you own heirlooms. Make baking and decorating a family affair with these festive designs you'll use again and again. Soft cover; 80 full color pages; 8 1/2 X 11 in.
902-Y-1225 $6.99 each

CELEBRATE WITH PARTY SPEC-TACULARS FROM A TO Z

Entertain all year 'round without making the same cake twice. Make your selections from over 150 of the most unique confections. Fun-loving cakes for children, foreign decorating methods to explore, holiday treats and much more! Even how to model Candy Melts* into flowers and figures. Soft cover; 160 color pages; 8 1/2 X 11 in.
916-Y-936 $11.99 each
*brand confectionery coating

CELEBRATE! VI

A cherished annual for cake decorators and those who love decorated cakes! A multitude of impressive designs for weddings, showers, holidays and birthdays. Methods include Australian, Philippine and English overpiped styles. Soft cover; 160 color pages; 8 7/8 x 11 1/4 in.
916-Y-618 $11.99 each

1. **NEW! CLOWNS**
8 molds; 8 designs
2114-Y-92824 $1.99 each

2. **2 PC. CREATE A FACE SET**
18 molds; 15 designs
2114-Y-97535 $3.49 set

3. **DINOSAURS**
9 molds; 4 designs per sheet.
2114-Y-98888 $1.99 each

4. **NEW! TEDDY BEARS**
8 molds; 8 designs
2114-Y-92826 $1.99 each

5. **BEARS**
4 cute designs.
2114-Y-94055 $1.99 each

6. **ALUMINUM PANDA MOLD**
Ideal for baking or molding a great treat. Sides clip together, base opens for easy filling. 5 x 5 in. Instructions, base and clips included.
518-Y-489 $4.99 each

7. **NEW! MUSICAL NOTES**
13 molds; 6 designs.
2114-Y-92832 $1.99 each

8. **TEDDY BEARS & GUMBALL MACHINES**
8 molds; 2 designs.
2114-Y-94232 $1.99 each

9. **NEW! BALLERINA LOLLIPOPS**
8 molds; 4 designs.
2114-Y-92834 $1.99 each

10. **LOLLIPOPS I**
5 molds; 5 designs.
2114-Y-90882 $1.99 each

11. **LOLLIPOPS II**
5 molds; 5 designs on sheet.
2114-Y-90861 $1.99 each

12. **NEW! FLOWERS**
10 molds; 7 designs
2114-Y-92830 $1.99 each

13. **ROSES 'N BUDS**
10 molds on sheet; 2 designs; 2 lollipops.
2114-Y-91101 $1.99 each

14. **ROSES**
10 molds; 3 designs on sheet.
2114-Y-91511 $1.99 each

15. **BABY SHOWER**
4 designs, 10 molds per sheet.
2114-Y-92816 $1.99 each

16. **MINT DISCS**
12 molds; 1 design on sheet; 1/4 in. deep.
2114-Y-91226 $1.99 each

17. **ACCORDIAN RUFFLES**
10 molds; 1 design on sheet.
2114-Y-91013 $1.99 each

18. **NEW! NEW BABY ARRIVAL**
8 molds; 7 designs
2114-Y-92822 $1.99 each

19. **BON BONS**
12 molds; 1 design on sheet.
2114-Y-91072 $1.99 each

20. **LARGE BON BONS**
8 molds; 1 design on sheet.
2114-Y-92656 $1.99 each

21. **NEW! BRIDAL TREATS**
8 molds; 5 designs.
2114-Y-92820 $1.99 each

22. **WEDDING SHOWER**
3 designs for bridal showers and weddings; 12 molds, including 2 lollipops.
2114-Y-91104 $1.99 each

23. **ROUNDS**
8 molds; 2 designs on sheet.
2114-Y-90466 $1.99 each

24. **FANCY CHOCOLATES I**
12 molds; 2 designs.
2114-Y-91269 $1.99 each

25. **LEAVES**
10 molds; 2 designs on sheet.
2114-Y-90629 $1.99 each

26. **SPORTS**
Baseball, hockey, football, basketball designs - 8 molds on sheet.
2114-Y-1102 $1.49 each

27. **GRADUATION**
4 designs, 11 molds per sheet.
2114-Y-92818 $1.99 each

28. **NEW! GARFIELD HALLOWEEN**
8 molds; 7 designs
2114-Y-92828 $1.99 each
GARFIELD Characters: ©1978 United Feature Syndicate, Inc.

29. **GARFIELD**
7 molds; 6 designs
2114-Y-90100 $1.99 each
GARFIELD Characters: ©1978 United Feature Syndicate, Inc

30. **NEW! THE SIMPSONS**
8 molds; 8 designs
2114-Y-91910 $1.99 each
MATT GROENING
TM & ©1990 Twentieth Century Fox Film Corporation, All rights reserved.

31. **BATMAN ™**
7 molds; 6 designs
2114-Y-90105 $1.99 each
TM & © 1989 DC Comics Inc.

32. **TEENAGE MUTANT NINJA TURTLES ®**
7 molds; 7 designs
2114-Y-90110 $1.99 each
© &® 1990 Mirage Studios, U.S.A. Exclusively licensed by Surge Licensing, Inc.

1. 3-D SANTA
About 4 in. tall.
2114-Y-1374 $1.99 each

2. CHRISTMAS I
8 festive molds, 7 designs.
2114-Y-94136 $1.99 each

3. CHRISTMAS II
10 molds, 9 joyful designs per sheet.
2114-Y-94152 $1.99 each

4. NEW! CHRISTMAS LOLLIPOP
8 molds; 8 designs
2114-Y-97536 $1.99 each

5. SNOWFLAKES
8 molds. 2 designs on sheet.
2114-Y-90661 $1.99 each

6. 2-PC. CHRISTMAS 6LASSICS SET
Santas, Sleigh, Reindeer and Toys. 6 designs, 18 molds.
2114-Y-1224 $2.99 set

7. 2-PC. CHRISTMAS CLASSICS II SET
Trees, trims & holiday friends. 6 designs. 18 molds.
2114-Y-1225 $2.99 set

8. CHRISTMAS TREES
14 molds on sheet.
2114-Y-91099 $1.99 each

9. HEARTS
15 classic molds on sheet.
2114-Y-90214 $1.99 each

10. NEW! I LOVE YOU LOLLIPOP
8 molds; 8 designs
2114-Y-91911 $1.99 each

11. HEARTS I
11 molds, 3 designs on sheet.
2114-Y-91030 $1.99 each

12. HEARTS II
8 molds; 2 designs on sheet.
2114-Y-90645 $1.99 each

13. BIT 'O IRISH
10 St. Pat's day molds on sheet; 4 designs.
2114-Y-91105 $1.99 each

14. 3-D BUNNY
4 1/2 in. high.
2114-Y-1390 $1.99 each

15. EGG MOLD SET
2-pc. plastic molds. Includes one each; 5 x 4in.; 4 1/2 x 3in.; 3 x 2in.
1404-Y-1040 $3.99 set

16. NEW! EASTER LOLLIPOP
8 molds; 8 designs
2114-Y-91912 $1.99 each

17. EASTER RABBITS
12 cottontails per sheet.
2114-Y-91200 $1.99 each

18. EASTER TREATS
8 designs. 8 molds.
2114-Y-91000 $1.99 each

19. 2-PC. EASTER VARIETY SET
2 sheets per set. 13 designs. 26 molds.
2114-Y-3131 $2.99 set

20. EGG CLASSIC
Each 1 x 1 1/2 in. long; 12 molds per sheet.
2114-Y-90998 $1.99 each

21. PLAYFUL BUNNIES
8 designs. 8 molds.
2114-Y-90999 $1.99 each

22. THANKSGIVING
3 traditional designs, including turkey lollipops. 9 molds. 2 lollipops.
2114-Y-91128 $1.99 each

23. 3-D PUMPKIN
About 3 in. high.
2114-Y-1447 $1.99 each

24. 2-PC. HALLOWEEN VARIETY SET
2 sheets of molds. 11 designs. 18 molds.
2114-Y-1031 $2.99 set

25. JACK-O-LANTERNS
2 1/2 in. wide. 3 jolly-faced molds on sheet.
2114-Y-91056 $1.99 each

26. PUMPKIN
12 identical smiling molds.
2114-Y-90740 $1.99 each

27. NUMBERS
18 molds per sheet.
2114-Y-92912 $1.99 each

28. SCRIPT WORDS
Best, Wishes, Congratulations.
2114-Y-92914 $1.99 each

29. SCRIPT WORDS II
Happy, Birthday, Anniversary.
2114-Y-92915 $1.99 each

30. 2-PC. ALPHABET SET
Capital letters; two of each vowel; plus two t's and s's
2114-Y-92910 $3.49 set

1.

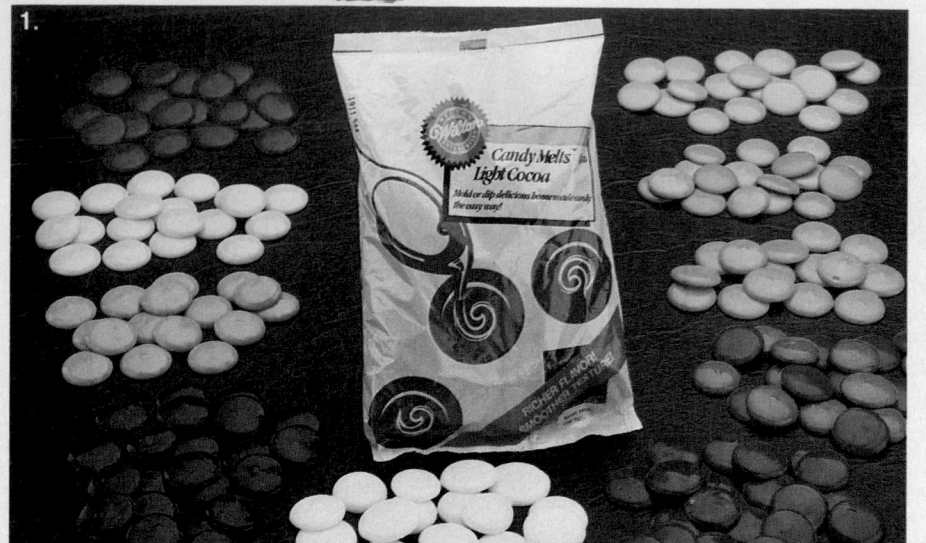

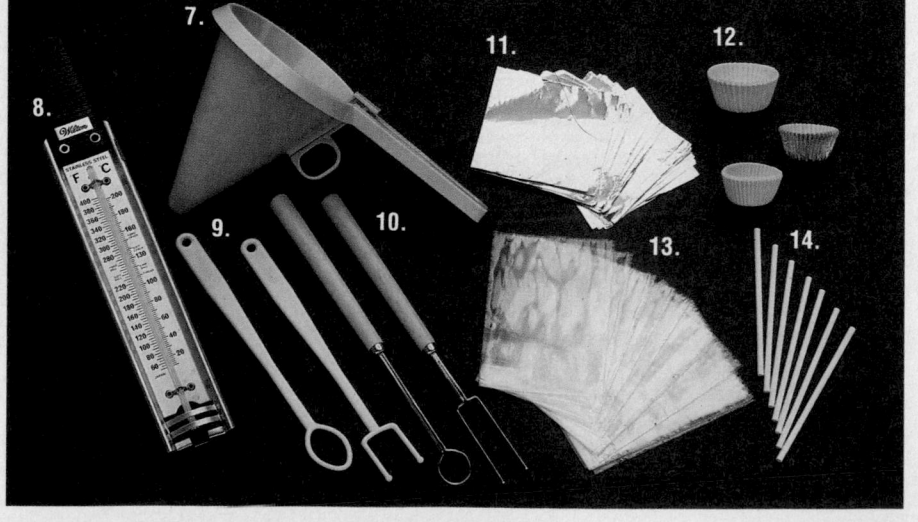

1. CANDY MELTS ™ *
The multi-talented brand confectionery coating. Creamy, easy-to-melt wafers are ideal for all your candy making—molding, dipping and coating. Delicious taste that can be varied with our Candy Flavors. 14 oz. bag. Certified Kosher. **$2.50 each**
White 1911-Y-498
Light Cocoa (All natural, cocoa flavor) 1911-Y-544
Dark Cocoa (All natural, cocoa flavor) 1911-Y-358
Pink 1911-Y-447
Yellow 1911-Y-463
Green 1911-Y-404
Christmas Mix (Red, Green)
(Available 9/4-12/15) 1911-Y-1624
Pastel Mix (Pink, Lavender, Blue)
(Available 12/1-5/31) 1911-Y-1637
Orange (Available 7/16-10/31) 1911-Y-1631
Red (Available 9/4-1/31) 1911-Y-499
All colors are vanilla flavored
*brand confectionery coating

2. CANDY COLORS KIT
Rich, concentrated oil-based color that blends beautifully into Wilton Candy Melts. Contains red, green, yellow and orange; 1/4 oz. jars. Convenient and economical.
1913-Y-1299 $3.99 kit

3. 4-PC. CANDY FLAVOR SET
It's easy to add your favorite flavor. Cinnamon, Cherry, Creme De Menthe and Peppermint. 1/4 oz. bottles.
1913-Y-1029 $3.99 set

4. CANDY WAFER AND FONDANT MIX
Great for satiny smooth candies or icing cakes creatively. 16 oz.
1911-Y-1427 $3.99 each

5. CANDY FILLINGS Delicious and ready to use.
Caramel 16 oz.	1911-Y-1400	$4.49 each
Coconut 16 oz.	1911-Y-1028	$4.49 each
Nougat 10 oz.	1911-Y-1488	$4.49 each

6. CANDY CENTER MIX
Create creamy centers that can be dipped or molded for candy favorites. 9 oz.
Creme Center Mix	1911-Y-1901	$2.49 each
Chocolate Flavored	1911-Y-1903	$2.49 each
Cherry	1911-Y-1905	$2.49 each

7. EASY-POUR FUNNEL
Push button controls the flow. 5 x 4 in. wide; nylon.
1904-Y-552 $3.99 each

8. CANDY THERMOMETER
Necessary accessory for hard candy, nougat, more.
1904-Y-1168 $15.99 each

9. 2-PC. CANDY DIPPING SET
White plastic spoon and fork, each 7 3/4 in. long.
1904-Y-800 $2.99 each

10. 2-PC. DIPPING SET
Sturdy metal with wooden handles; 9 in. long.
1904-Y-925 $8.99 each

11. FANCY CANDY WRAPPERS
Gold foil to protect and add a professional finish to your candy. 125 sheet, each 3 x 3 in.
1912-Y-2290 $3.49 pack

12. CANDY CUPS
Crisply pleated cups, just like professionals use. Choose gold foil or white glassine-coated paper in 1 in. diameter. White also available in 1 1/4 in. size. Packs of 100.
Gold Foil	415-Y-306	$1.49 pack
White	1912-Y-1243	$1.19 pack
White - 1 1/4 in. diameter	1912-Y-1245	$1.29 pack

13. LOLLIPOP BAGS
Plastic bags for lollipops and other candies. 3 x 4 in. 50 bags in a pack.
1912-Y-2347 $2.69 pack

14. LOLLIPOP STICKS
Sturdy paper sticks are easy to add to candy molds. 4 1/2 in. long. 50 sticks per pack.
1912-Y-1006 $1.69 pack

Wilton is happy to offer a new selection of fine cooking, baking and kitchen organization products. – High quality accessories created to save time in the kitchen and built to last for years.

1. COOKIE PRESS
Spritz cookie press from Italy. Complete with 12 cookie-forming discs and 8 decorating nozzles.
0000-Y-231 $38.99 set

2. SPRITZ COOKIE PRESS SET
Easy-squeeze trigger action. Includes 10 plastic disks in classic holiday shapes.
2104-Y-2303 $10.99 set

3. 5-PC. ROSETTE SET
Create light and delicate rosettes in five beautiful shapes.
0000-Y-1744 $7.79 set

4. ROLL ALONG COOKIE CUTTER SET
18 interchangeable holiday designs. Cuts 6 different designs at once.
2104-Y-2404 $6.99 set

5. *LANGUES DE CHAT PAN/MOLD*
Create this traditional French cookie, 10 at a time, in this high quality tin mold. Also great for ladyfingers or eclairs.
0000-Y-2315 $6.99 each

6. *MADELAINE MOLD*
Sophisticated baking made easy in this fine quality tinned steel mold. Recipe ideas included.
0000-Y-1289 $9.99 each

7. *SEA SHELL MOLD*
Make beautiful tea cakes of light sponge cake in this high quality tinned steel pan. Tasty topped with jam or whipped cream.
0000-Y-2318 $8.19 each

8. *MINI MADELAINE MOLD*
Bake bite-sized delicacies in an instant. Extra heavy-gauge tinned steel.
0000-Y-1317 $23.39 each

ICE CREAM SCOOPS
Small and average size, for ice cream, mashed potatoes, cookie dough, more!

9. *SMALL SIZE ICE CREAM SCOOP*
18/8 stainless steel. Smaller size creates 100 scoops from one quart of ice cream.
0000-Y-632 $10.69 each

10. *ICE CREAM SCOOP*
18/8 stainless steel. Average size creates 50 scoops from one quart of ice cream. Also use for cookie dough, mashed potatoes, more!
0000-Y-630 $11.19 each

11. *COOLING GRIDS*
Even the smallest shapes won't fall through. Chrome-plated steel.

| 10 x 16 in. | 2305-Y-128 | $4.99 each |
| 14 1/2 x 20 in. | 2305-Y-129 | $7.99 each |

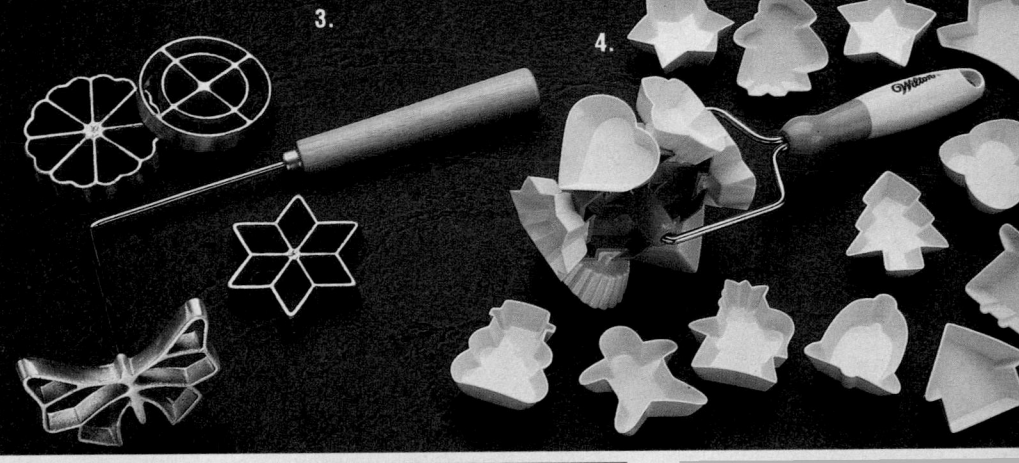

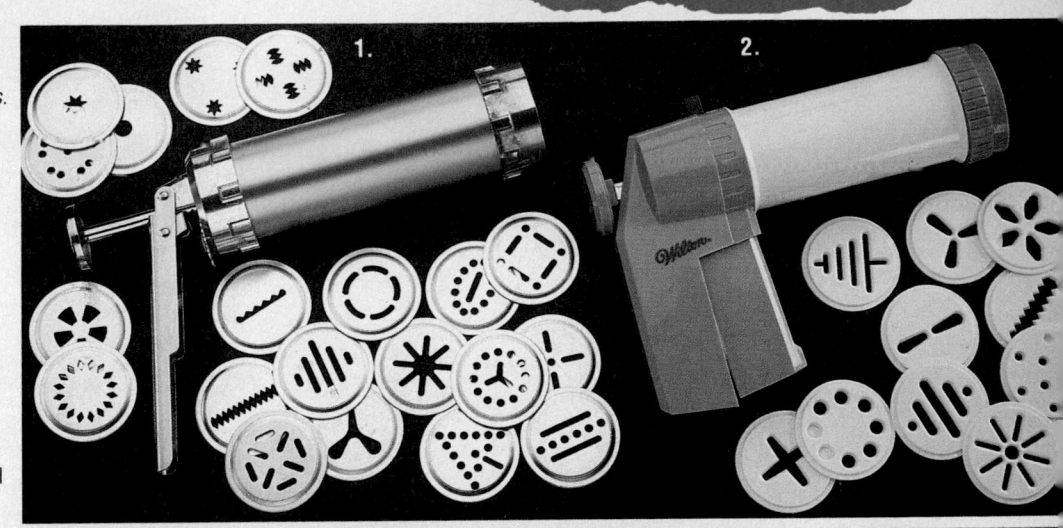

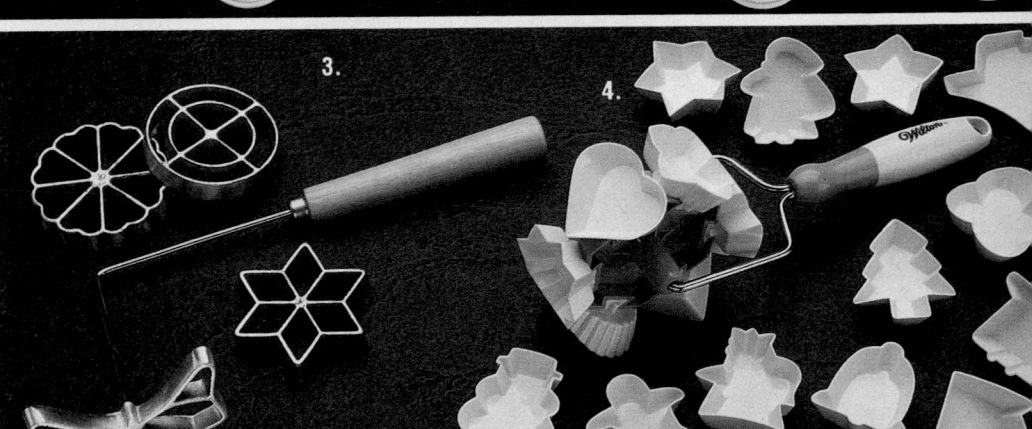

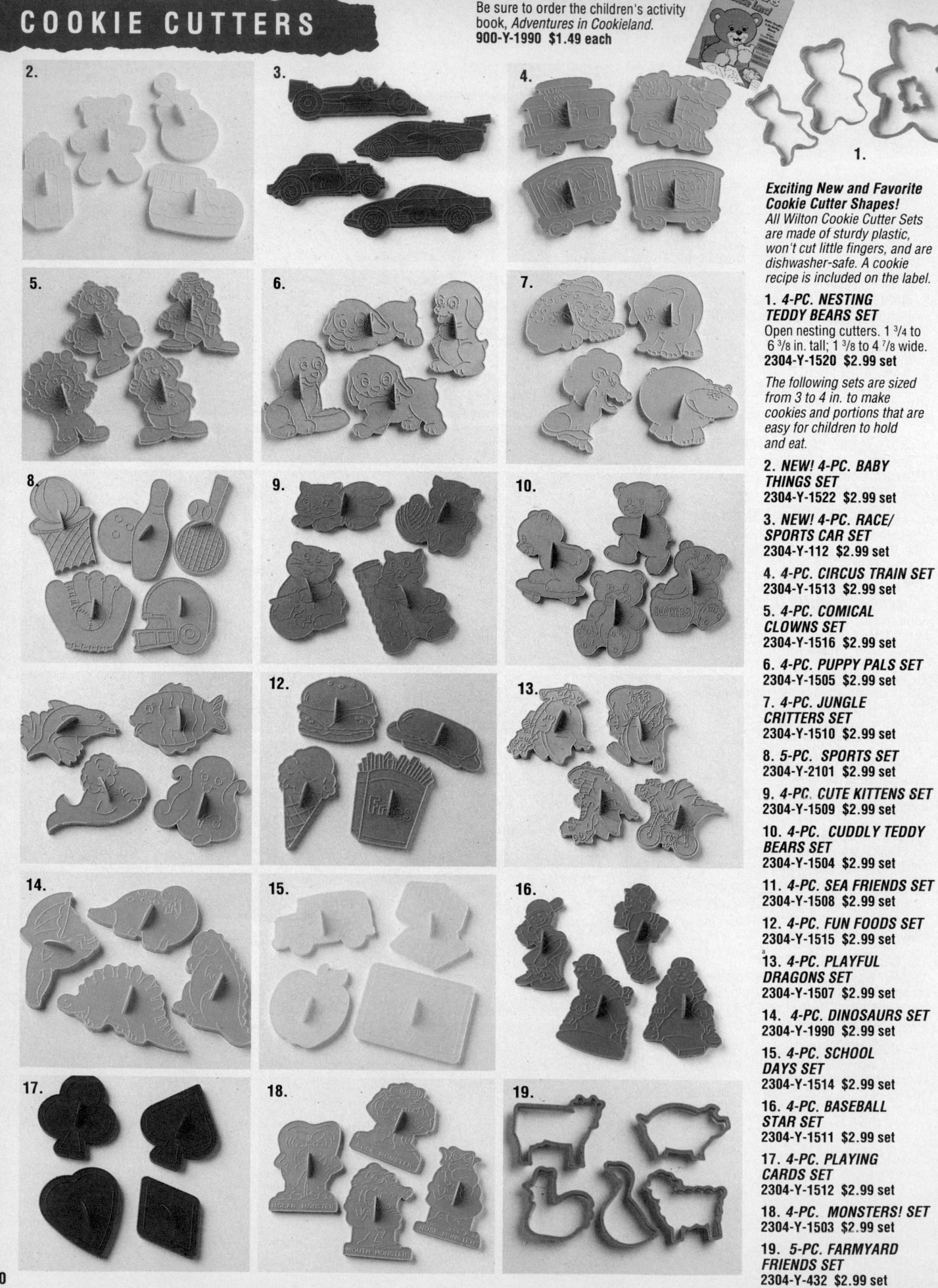

COOKIE CUTTERS

Be sure to order the children's activity book, *Adventures in Cookieland*.
900-Y-1990 $1.49 each

2.

3.

4.

1.

5.

6.

7.

8.

9.

10.

11.

12.

13.

14.

15.

16.

17.

18.

19.

Exciting New and Favorite Cookie Cutter Shapes!
All Wilton Cookie Cutter Sets are made of sturdy plastic, won't cut little fingers, and are dishwasher-safe. A cookie recipe is included on the label.

1. 4-PC. NESTING TEDDY BEARS SET
Open nesting cutters. 1 $3/4$ to 6 $3/8$ in. tall; 1 $3/8$ to 4 $7/8$ wide.
2304-Y-1520 $2.99 set

The following sets are sized from 3 to 4 in. to make cookies and portions that are easy for children to hold and eat.

2. NEW! 4-PC. BABY THINGS SET
2304-Y-1522 $2.99 set

3. NEW! 4-PC. RACE/ SPORTS CAR SET
2304-Y-112 $2.99 set

4. 4-PC. CIRCUS TRAIN SET
2304-Y-1513 $2.99 set

5. 4-PC. COMICAL CLOWNS SET
2304-Y-1516 $2.99 set

6. 4-PC. PUPPY PALS SET
2304-Y-1505 $2.99 set

7. 4-PC. JUNGLE CRITTERS SET
2304-Y-1510 $2.99 set

8. 5-PC. SPORTS SET
2304-Y-2101 $2.99 set

9. 4-PC. CUTE KITTENS SET
2304-Y-1509 $2.99 set

10. 4-PC. CUDDLY TEDDY BEARS SET
2304-Y-1504 $2.99 set

11. 4-PC. SEA FRIENDS SET
2304-Y-1508 $2.99 set

12. 4-PC. FUN FOODS SET
2304-Y-1515 $2.99 set

13. 4-PC. PLAYFUL DRAGONS SET
2304-Y-1507 $2.99 set

14. 4-PC. DINOSAURS SET
2304-Y-1990 $2.99 set

15. 4-PC. SCHOOL DAYS SET
2304-Y-1514 $2.99 set

16. 4-PC. BASEBALL STAR SET
2304-Y-1511 $2.99 set

17. 4-PC. PLAYING CARDS SET
2304-Y-1512 $2.99 set

18. 4-PC. MONSTERS! SET
2304-Y-1503 $2.99 set

19. 5-PC. FARMYARD FRIENDS SET
2304-Y-432 $2.99 set

1. 10-PC. ZANY ZOO CANISTER SET
10 plastic animal-shaped cutters in plastic storage container; cookie recipe included.
509-Y-9550 $3.99 set

2. 26-PC. CHILDREN'S A TO Z CANISTER SET
Spell out F-U-N so many ways with this educational 26-piece set. Sturdy, reusable plastic storage container. Recipe on label.
2304-Y-91 $5.99 set

3. 13-PC. NUMBERS CANISTER SET
Addition, subtraction, multiplication and equal signs included in this 13-piece set. Sturdy, reusable plastic storage container.
2304-Y-92 $5.99 set

4. 26-PC. ALPHABET SET
26-piece set. 2 X 1 1/8 in. each.
2304-Y-1521 $8.99 set

5. 4-PC. TEENAGE MUTANT NINJA TURTLES ® SET*
Raphael, Michelangelo, Leonardo, Donatello.
2304-Y-1500 $2.99 set
© & ® 1990 Mirage Studios, U.S.A., Exclusively licensed by Surge Licensing, Inc.

6. 4-PC. SUPER MARIO BROTHERS ® SET*
2304-Y-1502 $2.99 set
1989 Nintendo of America Inc.

7. 4-PC. GARFIELD™ SET*
Trouble-making duo; Garfield and Odie.
2304-Y-1501 $2.99 set
GARFIELD Character: ©1978 United Feature Syndicate, Inc.

8. 4-PC. BATMAN™ SET*
Caped-crusader and his arch rival, Joker.
2304-Y-1506 $2.99 set
TM & © 1989 DC Comics Inc.

9. 4-PC. LOONEY TUNES SET*
Bugs Bunny, Porky Pig, Sylvester, Tweety.
2304-Y-404 $2.99 set
1988 Warner Bros. Inc. Wilton Enterprises Authorized User

10. 4-PC. SESAME STREET SET*
Big Bird, Cookie Monster, Ernie, Bert.
2304-Y-129 $2.99 set
Sesame Street Characters
© Jim Henson Productions, Inc. All rights reserved.

11. 5-PC. SIMPSONS FAMILY SET
2304-Y-1517 $2.99 set
MATT GROENING
TM & ©1990 Twentieth Century Fox Film Corporation All rights reserved

12. NEW! 8-PC. "GOING PLACES" SESAME STREET CANISTER SET*
2304-Y-118 $5.99 set
Sesame Street Characters
© Jim Henson Productions, Inc. All rights reserved.

13. 6-PC. NESTING OVAL SET
3 1/4 to 7 in. long. 2 1/8 to 4 3/4 in. wide.
2304-Y-388 $2.99 set

14. 6-PC. NESTING STAR SET
From 1 5/8 to 4 5/8 in.
2304-Y-111 $2.99 set

15. 6-PC. NESTING HEART SET
1 1/2 to 4 1/8 in.
2304-Y-115 $2.99 set

16. 6-PC. NESTING ROUND SET
1 1/2 to 4 in.
2304-Y-113 $2.99 set

17. NEW! 5-PC. CRINKLE CUTTERS SET
Great for canapes and hors d'oeuvres as well as cookies.
2304-Y-109 $2.99 set
*Cookie recipes included.

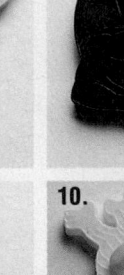

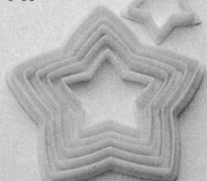
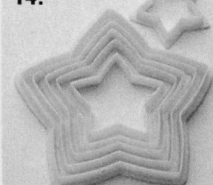

17.

CHRISTMAS COOKIES

All these fun cutters include a cookie recipe on the label.

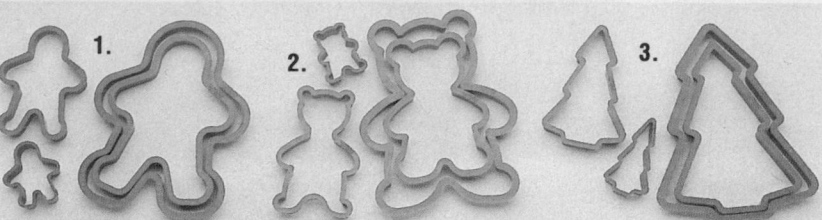

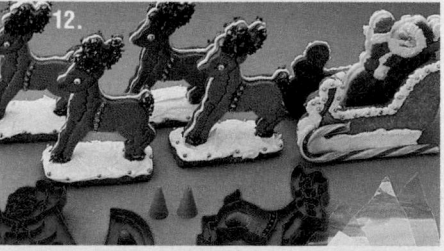

1. NEW! 4-PC. NESTING GINGERBREAD BOY SET
Fun plain or decorated. Recipe and decorating instructions. 1 3/4 to 6 3/8 in. tall; 1 3/8 to 4 3/4 in. wide.
2304-Y-1530 $2.99 set

2. NEW! 4-PC. NESTING TEDDY BEAR SET
Poppa, Mama and Baby Bear join in the holiday festivities. Recipe and decorating instructions. 1 3/4 to 6 3/8 in. tall; 1 3/8 to 4 7/8 in. wide.
2304-Y-1532 $2.99 set

3. NEW! 4-PC. NESTING CHRISTMAS TREE SET
Festive fun; easy to decorate. Recipe and decorating instructions. 2 5/8 to 6 3/8 in. tall; 1 3/8 to 4 3/4 in. wide.
2304-Y-1531 $2.99 set

4. 4-PC. GINGERBREAD FAMILY SET
Set includes two 5 1/2 X 4 in. adults and two 2 1/2 X 1 1/2 in. children.
2304-Y-121 $2.99 set

5. 5-PC. HOLIDAY SHAPES SET
Santa, angel, tree, boy and girl-3 5/8 to 6 in. high.
2304-Y-105 $2.99 set

6. 10-PC. CHRISTMAS CANISTER SET
10 festive holiday shapes. 2 1/2 to 3 1/2 in. Reusable sturdy plastic container.
509-Y-1225 $3.99 set

7. 4-PC. CHRISTMAS SET
Favorite holiday shapes. Angel, Santa, Wreath, Tree. 4 1/4 to 5 in.
2304-Y-995 $2.99 set

8. 4-PC. CHRISTMAS TREATS SET
Fun-loving Yuletide favorites. Cottage, holly, reindeer, snowman. 4 3/4 to 5 1/2 in.
2304-Y-1290 $2.99 set

9. NEW! MINI GINGERBREAD HOUSE KIT
Create a village of little houses for holiday tables and under the Christmas tree-great family fun. Kit includes patterns, disposable bags, tips and instruction booklet.
2104-Y-1528 $3.99 kit

10. NO-BAKE GINGERBREAD HOUSE KIT
Looks like real gingerbread! Just assemble and decorate house pieces provided in kit. Or cover with real graham crackers. Can also be used as a pattern for an edible gingerbread house. Candy and all necessary tools are included.
2104-Y-2990 $9.99 kit

11. NEW! GINGERBREAD HOUSE KIT
An enchanted cottage where holiday memories begin. Kit includes patterns, 3 plastic gingerbread people cutters, disposable bags, tips and instruction booklet.
2104-Y-1525 $7.49 kit

12. SANTA SLEIGH AND REINDEER COOKIE KIT
It's the jolly old man himself. Create quite a unique centerpiece or holiday ornament. Two-sided cookie cutters make flat or stand up Santas and reindeer. Kit is complete with 4 plastic cutters, disposable bags, tips and easy-to-follow instruction book.
2104-Y-1500 $7.99 kit

13. CHRISTMAS COOKIE TREE KIT
What fun holiday idea for the whole family. Ice, stack and trim cookie stars. Kit includes 10 plastic star cutters in graduated sizes, plus instruction book.
2105-Y-3424 $5.99 kit

14. SANTA'S STABLE KIT
A magical Christmas fantasy for the entire family. Recreate the reindeer's North Pole headquarters on a holiday table top. Kit includes patterns, sturdy plastic cookie cutters, liquid colors, disposable bags, tips, and easy-to-follow instructions.
2104-Y-2949 $7.99 kit

15. NEW! 4-PC. GARFIELD CHRISTMAS SET
He's festive and fun in his holiday finery. Recipe included. 3 to 3 7/8 in. tall; 2 1/4 to 4 in. wide.
2304-Y-114 $2.99 set

GARFIELD Character: ©1978 United Feature Syndicate, Inc.

15.

1. HAUNTED HOUSE KIT
Construct a gingerbread mansion to conjure up some Halloween fun. Kit includes patterns, sturdy plastic cookie cutters, 4 disposable bags, 1 round tip, liquid colors, easy-to-follow instructions, and cookie recipe.
2104-Y-1031 $7.49 each

2. 4-PC. HALLOWEEN COOKIE CUTTER SET
Four haunting shapes for little goblins. Ghost and tombstone, cat, pumpkin and witch. 5 1/4 to 5 1/2 in. Recipe on label.
2304-Y-994 $2.99 set

3. 10-PC. HALLOWEEN CANISTER SET
Ten not-so-spooky characters in a handy reusable container. 3 to 4 1/4 in. Recipe on label.
2304-Y-1031 $3.99 set

4. 4-PC. JACK-O-LANTERN CUTTER SET
This silly jack-o-lantern goes through four funny moods. 3 to 3 3/4 in. Recipe on label.
2304-Y-90 $2.99 set

5. NEW! 10-PC. I LOVE YOU COOKIE CANISTER SET
10 novelty cutters in a reusable container. 1 5/8 to 3 7/8 in. tall; 2 3/8 to 4 in. wide.
2304-Y-1105 $4.99 set

6. 6-PC. NESTING HEARTS SET
An invaluable collection of 6 different sized nesting hearts. 1 1/4 to 4 1/8 in. Recipe on label.
2304-Y-115 $2.99 set

7. NEW! 5-PC. EASTER FAVORITES SET
Open cutters for the family to decorate. 3 1/4 to 4 3/8 in. tall; 2 1/2 to 4 1/2 in. wide.
2304-Y-1519 $2.99 set

8. 4-PC. SWEETHEART COOKIE CUTTER SET
Four romantic shapes and messages; recipe on label. 4 to 4 1/2 in.
2304-Y-1214 $2.99 set

9. NEW! 10-PC. EASTER CANISTER SET
10 Easter and spring shapes all ready for munching. Recipe on label. 2 to 3 5/8 in. tall; 2 1/8 to 4 in. wide.
2304-Y-1106 $4.99 set

10. NEW! 4-PC. HEART TO HEART SET
Four ways to say "I love you." 2 1/2 to 3 1/2 in. tall; 3 3/8 to 4 in. wide.
2304-Y-1518 $2.99 set

11. 4-PC. HAPPY EASTER SET
The season's most popular quartet. Bunny, lamb, chick and egg. 3 1/4 to 3 3/4 in. Recipe on label.
2304-Y-110 $2.99 set

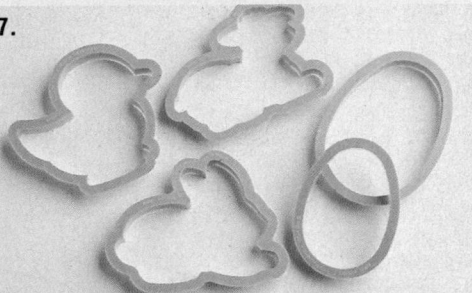

ICING COLORS

Color is vital to your decorating. With color you can add realism and vitality to all your character cakes, personalize special events cakes, highlight holiday cakes and add beauty and vibrancy to all your cakes.

Wilton Icing Colors are concentrated in a rich, creamy base, are fast-mixing and easy to use, and will not change your icing consistency. Our extensive range of icing colors makes it convenient for you to achieve the colors you need and want.

DAFFODIL YELLOW*	LEMON YELLOW	GOLDEN YELLOW	ORANGE	PINK	CHRISTMAS RED	RED-RED	RED (no taste)
IVORY	TEAL	TERRA COTTA	ROSE	COPPER	BROWN	ROSE PETAL PINK	CREAMY PEACH
VIOLET	BURGUNDY	ROYAL BLUE	CORNFLOWER BLUE	SKY BLUE	WILLOW GREEN	KELLY GREEN	LEAF GREEN
MOSS GREEN							
BLACK							

WILTON CONCENTRATED PASTE ICING COLORS are available in 1 oz. and 4 oz. jars. Specified colors are available in 20 oz. jars.

WILTON CONCENTRATED LIQUID ICING COLORS are available in 13 oz. jars. Convenient press-open cap.

WILTON CONCENTRATED AIR BRUSH COLORS are available in 8 oz. jars. Convenient press-open cap.

| ICING COLORS | CONCENTRATED LIQUID | | | | | CONCENTRATED LIQUID 13 oz. | AIR BRUSH 8 oz. |
	1 oz.		4 oz.		20 oz.		
Daffodil Yellow	610-Y-175	1.99	N/A		N/A	N/A	N/A
Lemon Yellow	610-Y-108	1.49	611-Y-1	4.99	N/A	603-Y-108 7.69	609-Y-12 3.80
Golden Yellow	610-Y-159	1.49	611-Y-2	4.99	N/A	603-Y-110 6.99	N/A
Orange	610-Y-205	1.49	611-Y-3	4.99	N/A	603-Y-109 6.99	609-Y-11 3.80
Pink	610-Y-256	1.49	611-Y-4	4.99	N/A	603-Y-105 7.69	609-Y-16 4.20
Christmas Red	610-Y-302	1.49	611-Y-5	4.99	N/A	603-Y-107 7.99	609-Y-10 4.40
Red-Red	610-Y-906	1.99	611-Y-16	5.79	612-Y-16 20.99	603-Y-102 7.99	609-Y-9 4.40
Red (no taste)	610-Y-998	1.99	611-Y-18	4.99	N/A	603-Y-101 7.99	N/A
*Ivory	610-Y-208	1.49	611-Y-23	4.99	N/A	603-Y-121 7.69	N/A
*Teal	610-Y-207	1.49	611-Y-25	4.99	N/A	603-Y-115 6.99	609-Y-2 4.20
*Terra Cotta	610-Y-206	1.49	611-Y-24	4.99	N/A	603-Y-116 7.69	609-Y-1 4.40
Rose	610-Y-401	1.49	611-Y-6	4.99	N/A	N/A	N/A
Copper	610-Y-450	1.49	611-Y-7	4.99	N/A	N/A	609-Y-6 4.20
Brown	610-Y-507	1.69	611-Y-8	5.79	612-Y-8 18.99	603-Y-103 6.99	609-Y-14 3.80
*Rose Petal Pink	610-Y-410	1.49	611-Y-20	4.99	N/A	603-Y-118 7.69	N/A
*Creamy Peach	610-Y-210	1.49	611-Y-21	4.99	N/A	603-Y-117 7.69	609-Y-5 4.40
Violet	610-Y-604	1.49	611-Y-9	4.99	N/A	603-Y-112 7.99	609-Y-13 4.40
Burgundy	610-Y-698	1.99	611-Y-11	5.79	N/A	603-Y-114 7.99	N/A
Royal Blue	610-Y-655	1.49	611-Y-10	4.99	612-Y-10 16.99	603-Y-106 7.69	609-Y-4 4.40
*Cornflower Blue	610-Y-710	1.49	611-Y-19	4.99	N/A	603-Y-119 7.69	609-Y-3 4.20
Sky Blue	610-Y-700	1.49	611-Y-12	4.99	N/A	603-Y-111 7.69	609-Y-17 3.80
*Willow Green	610-Y-855	1.49	611-Y-22	4.99	N/A	603-Y-120 7.69	N/A
Kelly Green	610-Y-752	1.49	611-Y-13	4.99	N/A	603-Y-113 6.99	609-Y-7 3.80
Leaf Green	610-Y-809	1.49	611-Y-14	4.99	612-Y-14 16.99	603-Y-104 6.99	609-Y-8 3.80
Moss Green	610-Y-851	1.49	611-Y-15	4.99	N/A	N/A	N/A
Black	610-Y-981	1.69	611-Y-17	5.79	612-Y-17 18.99	603-Y-100 7.99	609-Y-15 4.40

*Special Blend Color

AIR BRUSH

1. AIR BRUSH AND HOSE
Create colorful special effects on your cakes with this superior quality single action air brush. Perfect way to add beautiful color backgrounds, highlight your borders and tint your flowers. Nickel-plated solid brass. Generous capacity angled color-holder cup. Includes 6-ft. PVC hose and airbrush holder.
415-Y-4000 $117.99 air brush with hose and holder

2. AIR BRUSH COMPRESSOR
Professional quality, piston-type compressor for maximum dependability. 1/12 horsepower provides maximum pressure of 40 lbs. per square inch. Easy to control; on/off switch.
415-Y-4001 $199.99 each

3. TWO-BRUSH MANIFOLD ADAPTER
Allows two air brushes to be used with just one compressor.
415-Y-4100 $59.99 each

1. 10-ICING COLORS KIT
1 oz. jars of icing colors. Violet, Leaf Green, Royal Blue, Brown, Black, Pink, Watermelon, Moss Green, Orange, and Lemon Yellow.
601-Y-5569 $12.99 kit

2. 8-ICING COLORS KIT
1/2 oz. jars of colors. Christmas Red, Lemon Yellow, Leaf Green, Sky Blue, Brown, Orange, Pink, and Violet.
601-Y-5577 $8.99 kit

3. 4-ICING COLORS KIT
(SOFT PASTEL COLORS) 1/2 oz jars of paste colors. Petal Pink, Creamy Peach, Willow Green, Cornflower Blue.
601-Y-5588 $3.29 kit

4. WHITE-WHITE ICING COLOR
Just stir into icing to make icing made with butter or margarine white. Perfect for wedding cakes. 2 oz. plastic bottle.
603-Y-1236 $2.99 each

5. CAKE AND PASTRY FILLING
Luscious and delicious, chunky real fruit filling ready to use from the 10 oz. resealable glass jar. Perfect to fill and torte up to 10" round cake, a real treat in tarts, pies and fancy pastries! 10 oz.

Filling	Stock No.	Price
Cherry	709-Y-3	$1.99
Strawberry	709-Y-1	$1.99
Raspberry	709-Y-2	$1.99

6. READY-TO-USE DECORATOR ICING
Perfect for decorating and frosting. Use for borders, flowers, writing, etc. Just stir and use! Delicious homemade taste! 16 oz.
710-Y-117 $1.99 each

7. CREAMY WHITE ICING MIX
Convenient mix that provides rich, homemade taste. Just add butter and milk. Ideal for frosting as well as decorating. Yields 2 cups.
710-Y-112 $2.19 each

8. PIPING GEL
Clear gel. Can be tinted with paste color. Use for glazing, writing, more. 10 oz.
704-Y-105 $3.29 each

9. GLYCERIN †
A few drops stirred into dried-out icing color restores consistency. 2 oz.
708-Y-14 $1.99 each

10. BUTTER FLAVOR †
Gives a rich, buttery taste to icing, cakes, cookies. Adds no color! 2 oz.
604-Y-2040 $1.79 each

11. CLEAR VANILLA EXTRACT †
Perfect for decorating because it won't change the color of you icing. 2 oz. Great for baking, too!
604-Y-2237 $1.79 each

12. ALMOND EXTRACT †
Delicious almond flavor for icing, cookies, cakes. 2 oz.
604-Y-2126 $1.79 each

13. COLOR FLOW MIX
Add water and confectioners sugar for smooth icing for color flow designs. 4 oz. can yields about ten 1 1/2 cup batches.
701-Y-47 $6.99 each

14. MERINGUE POWDER MIX
For Royal icing, meringue, boiled icing,
4 OZ. CAN 702-Y-6007 $4.49 each
8 OZ. CAN 702-Y-6015 $6.99 each

†Certified Kosher

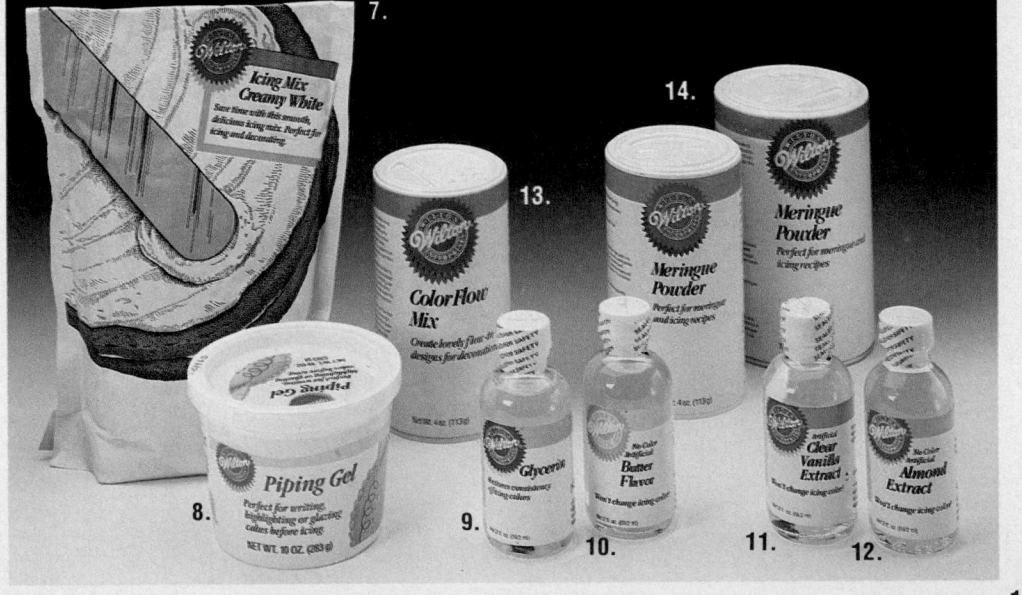

BAKING PAPERS

BAKING CUPS
Introducing the newest assortment from Wilton. Exclusive designs. Cups are made of grease-resistant paper that is microwave-safe. Great for baking or using as candy and nut cups.

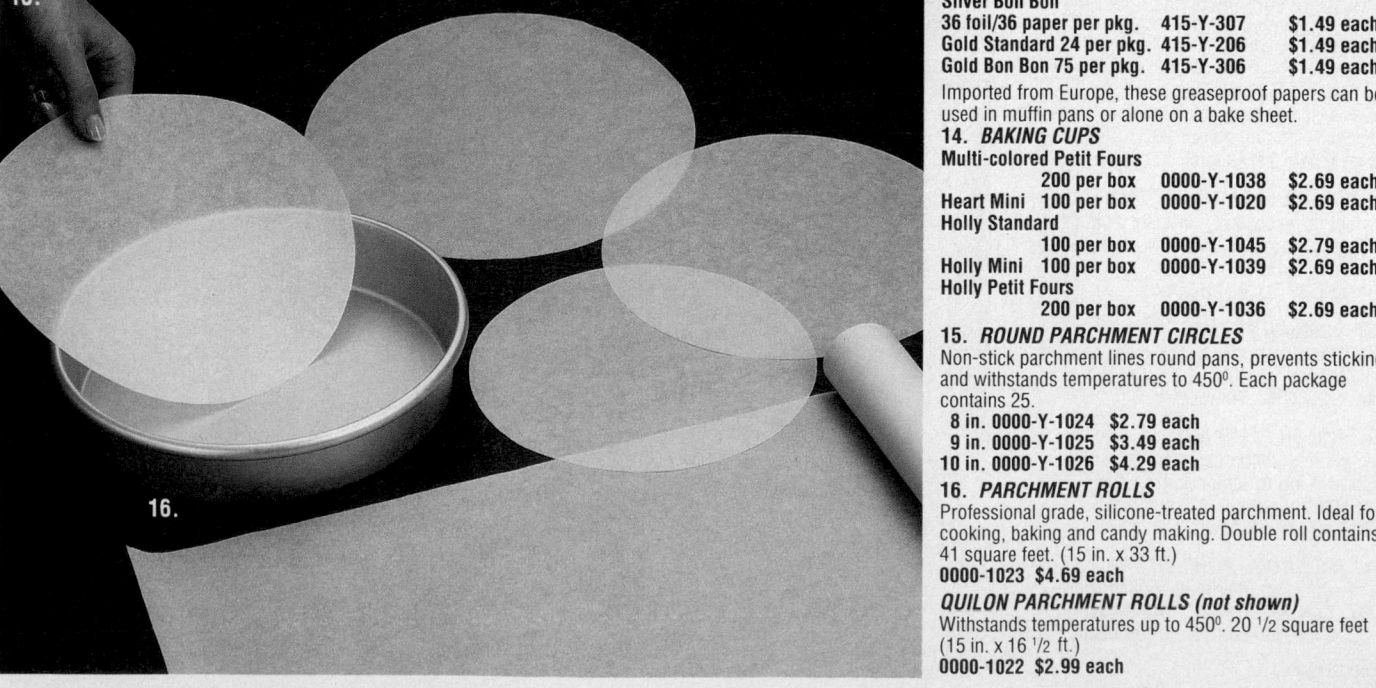

1. WHITE BAKING CUPS
Jumbo	50 per box	415-Y-1113	$1.49 each
Standard	75 per box	415-Y-1115	$1.49 each
Mini	100 per box	415-Y-1117	$1.49 each

2. BALLOONS BAKING CUPS
Jumbo	40 per pkg.	415-Y-101	$1.49 each
Standard	50 per pkg.	415-Y-201	$1.49 each
Mini	75 per pkg.	415-Y-301	$1.49 each

3. TEDDY BEARS BAKING CUPS
Jumbo	40 per pkg.	415-Y-102	$1.49 each
Standard	50 per pkg.	415-Y-202	$1.49 each
Mini	75 per pkg.	415-Y-302	$1.49 each

4. PARTY! PARTY! BAKING CUPS
Jumbo	40 per pkg.	415-Y-103	$1.49 each
Standard	50 per pkg.	415-Y-203	$1.49 each
Mini	75 per pkg.	415-Y-303	$1.49 each

5. CLOWNS BAKING CUPS
Jumbo	40 per pkg.	415-Y-104	$1.49 each
Standard	50 per pkg.	415-Y-204	$1.49 each
Mini	75 per pkg.	415-Y-304	$1.49 each

6. BELLS AND RIBBONS BAKING CUPS
Standard	50 per pkg.	415-Y-205	$1.49 each

7. HEARTS BAKING CUPS
Standard	50 per pkg.	415-Y-210	$1.49 each

8. SANTA CLAUS BAKING CUPS
Standard	50 per pkg.	415-Y-208	$1.49 each

9. CHRISTMAS TREES BAKING CUPS
Standard	50 per pkg.	415-Y-209	$1.49 each

10. RED BAKING CUPS (GLASSINE PAPER)
Standard	50 per pkg.	415-Y-211	$1.49 each

11. CANDY AND PARTY CUPS
Glassine-coated for complete grease-proof confidence. Sized to fit small and large Wilton candy mold shapes.
White (1 in.)
Bon Bon	100 per pkg.	1912-Y-1243	$1.19 each

White (1 1/4 in.)
Mini	75 per pkg.	1912-Y-1245	$1.29 each

Red and Green (1 1/4 in.)
Mini 36 ea. col. per pkg.		1912-Y-1247	$1.19 each

12. NUT AND PARTY CUPS
Fine-quality, grease resistant cups perfect to hold nuts, mints and candies for shower favors.
White (3 1/4 oz.)
Standard	24 per pkg.	415-Y-400	$1.49 each

White (1 1/4 oz.)
Mini	36 per pkg.	415-Y-500	$1.49 each

13. FOIL BAKING AND PARTY CUPS
Silver foil package contains both pure aluminum foil cups and paper cups; gold foil cups are wax-laminated paper on foil. Both silver and gold foil can be used with or without muffin pan. Pure foil provides the best muffin release.
Silver Standard
24 foil/24 paper per pkg.	415-Y-207	$1.49 each

Silver Bon Bon
36 foil/36 paper per pkg.	415-Y-307	$1.49 each
Gold Standard 24 per pkg.	415-Y-206	$1.49 each
Gold Bon Bon 75 per pkg.	415-Y-306	$1.49 each

Imported from Europe, these greaseproof papers can be used in muffin pans or alone on a bake sheet.

14. BAKING CUPS
Multi-colored Petit Fours
	200 per box	0000-Y-1038	$2.69 each
Heart Mini	100 per box	0000-Y-1020	$2.69 each

Holly Standard
	100 per box	0000-Y-1045	$2.79 each
Holly Mini	100 per box	0000-Y-1039	$2.69 each

Holly Petit Fours
	200 per box	0000-Y-1036	$2.69 each

15. ROUND PARCHMENT CIRCLES
Non-stick parchment lines round pans, prevents sticking and withstands temperatures to 450°. Each package contains 25.
8 in.	0000-Y-1024	$2.79 each
9 in.	0000-Y-1025	$3.49 each
10 in.	0000-Y-1026	$4.29 each

16. PARCHMENT ROLLS
Professional grade, silicone-treated parchment. Ideal for cooking, baking and candy making. Double roll contains 41 square feet. (15 in. x 33 ft.)
0000-1023 $4.69 each

QUILON PARCHMENT ROLLS (not shown)
Withstands temperatures up to 450°. 20 1/2 square feet (15 in. x 16 1/2 ft.)
0000-1022 $2.99 each

Wilton is pleased to offer an expanded assortment of basic kitchen tools. You can attain first-class results in your own kitchen with these successful performers.

BAKING TOOLS

PROFESSIONAL-QUALITY ROLLINGS PINS
Many great pastries begin with a great rolling pin. This collection offers many styles and options. All made of rock maple with nylon bearings. The perfect weight for home or professional use.

1. 15 x 3 in.
0000-Y-561 $29.29 each

2. 12 1/2 x 2 in.
0000-Y-564 $14.89 each

3. 10 1/2 x 2 in.
0000-Y-560 $12.59 each

4. MARBLE ROLLING PIN/CRADLE
Stay-cool surface provides for easy rolling.
10 in. 0000-Y-580 $13.19 each

ROLLING PIN COVERS
Handy cover prevents dough from sticking to pin. Stretches to fit any size rolling pin. Each package contains two covers.

5. 20 inches long 0000-Y-194 $1.99 each
6. 14 inches long 0000-Y-193 $1.89 each

7. PASTRY CLOTH AND ROLLING PIN COVER
Contains one heavyweight pastry cloth, 20 x 24 in., and one 14 in. stretch rolling pin cover.
0000-Y-196 $4.99 each

8. 3-CUP SIFTER
Easy-turn crank provides uniform sifting. Stainless steel.
0000-Y-736 $17.39 each

9. MEASURING SPOONS
Stainless steel set of 4 includes 1/4, 1/2 and 1 teaspoons and 1 tablespoon.
0000-Y-363 $4.09 each

STAINLESS STEEL WHISKS
Two versatile 10 in. versions.

10. Ridged wires make it sturdy enough to mix batters, sauces and cream.
0000-Y-814 $5.39 each.

11. Delicate wires ideal for whipping egg white and light liquids.
0000-Y-796 $2.49 each

12. PASTRY BLENDER
Sturdy wooden handle with sleek metal blades.
0000-Y-349 $5.99 each

13. BLENDING/MASHING FORK
Back bladed tines make it easy to mash, cut and blend.
0000-Y-176 $2.89 each

14. 1 IN. PASTRY AND PAINTING BRUSH
100% natural bristles. Ideal for pastry buttering, basting sauces and glazing breads.
0000-Y-1190 $2.19 each

15. FEATHER PASTRY BRUSH
A natural for brushing egg whites, butter and more. Leaves no marks and doesn't shred.
0000-Y-110 $1.69 each

16. CAKE TESTER
Cake is done when it comes out clean! Neat and money-saving. Great shower favors.
0000-Y-387 $1.89 each

17. DUAL PASTRY WHEEL
Sturdy metal wheels cut exact plain or scalloped edges.
0000-Y-139 $4.49 each

18. PASTRY CRIMPER
Crimps, seals and cuts. Great for canapes, cookies and ravioli.
0000-Y-1205 $3.79 each

19. MRS. T's TART TAMPER
Makes two sizes of tarts. Place rolled-out dough gently over mold. Press end of tart maker into center of dough. Trim away excess dough.
0000-Y-837 $4.49 each

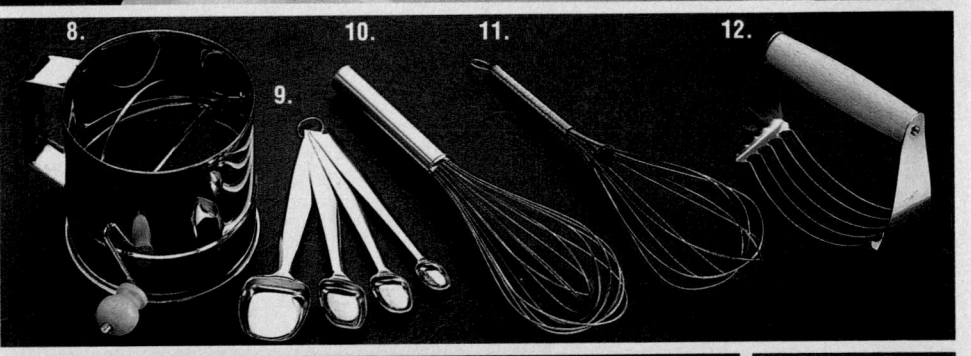
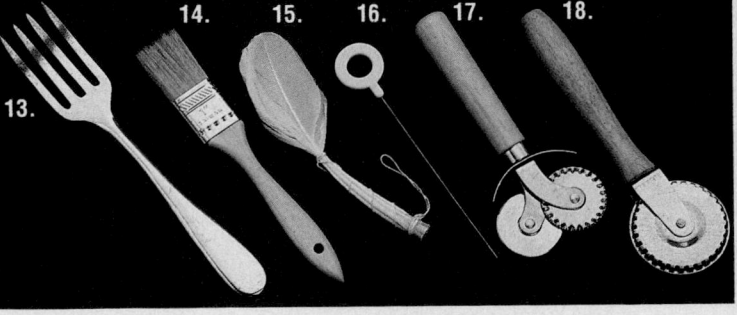
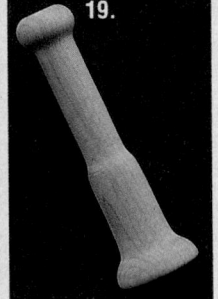

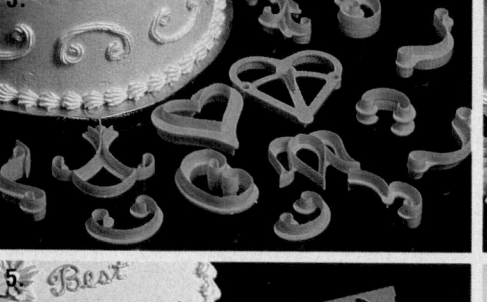

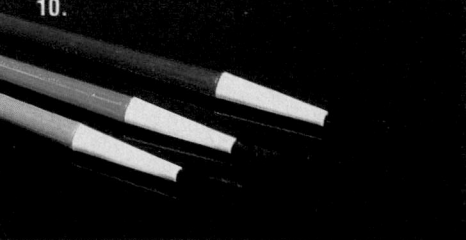

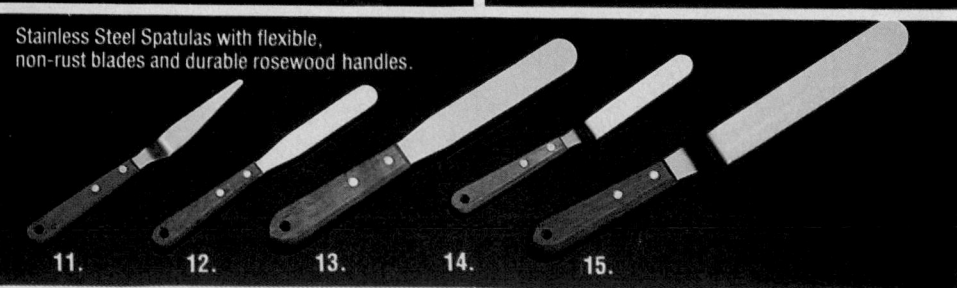

1. NEW! MAKE ANY MESSAGE LETTER PRESS SET
Now you can customize that perfect message, right down to the letter. 56 piece interchangeable set.
2104-Y-0010 $7.99 set

2. ALL-OCCASION SCRIPT PATTERN PRESS SET
Press and pipe messages easily with all-occasion and seasonal words and phrases: Merry Christmas, Happy New Year, Easter, Thanksgiving, God Bless You, I Love You and Good Luck.
2104-Y-2090 $3.99 set

3. 15-PC. DECORATOR PATTERN PRESS SET
Traditional designs ready to solo or use in combination. Many can also be reversed for symmetrical designs.
2104-Y-2172 $4.99 set

4. 9-PC. PATTERN PRESS SET
Discover fancy florals; classic curves make any occasion so special.
2104-Y-3101 $4.49 set

5. SCRIPT PATTERN PRESS MESSAGE SET
Lets you put it into words so beautifully. Combine the words Happy, Birthday, Best, Wishes, Anniversary, Congratulations and make a lasting impression.
2104-Y-2061 $3.49 set

6. MESSAGE BLOCK LETTER PATTERN PRESS SET
Have just the right words at your fingertips. Includes the same six words as the Script Set. 2 x 6 3/4 x 3/4 in. high.
2104-Y-2077 $3.49 set

7. CAKE DIVIDING SET
Handy when chart marks 2-in. intervals on 6 to 18-in. diameter cakes. Triangle marker for precise spacing for stringwork, garlands, more. Includes instructions.
409-Y-800 $8.99 set

8. DECORATING COMB
An easy technique that makes it look like you fussed. Makes ridges in icing. 12-in. long, plastic.
409-Y-8259 $1.29 each

9. DECORATING TRIANGLE
Each side adds a different contoured effect to icing. 5 X 5-in. plastic.
409-Y-990 99¢ each

10. DECORATOR'S BRUSHES SET
Perfect for smoothing icing, painting candy molds and colorful touches. Set of 3.
2104-Y-846 $1.49 set

STAINLESS STEEL & ROSEWOOD SPATULAS

11. 8 IN. TAPERED
409-Y-517 $2.69 each

12. 8 IN. SPATULA
409-Y-6043 $2.69 each

13. 11 IN. SPATULA
409-Y-7694 $4.59 each

14. 8 IN. ANGLED SPATULA
409-Y-738 $2.69 each

15. 12 IN. ANGLED SPATULA
409-Y-134 $4.99 each

Stainless Steel Spatulas with flexible, non-rust blades and durable rosewood handles.

Attend Wilton Method Cake Decorating Classes near your home!

Convenient Wilton Method of Cake Decorating Classes are now being held in area department and craft stores and cake decorating specialty shops close to your home. You'll learn exciting basic decorating techniques in 4 easy lessons.* For a complete list of the classes nearest you, send us this coupon right away or call toll free 1-800-323-1717, Operator 440. (In Illinois, call 1-800-942-8881, Operator 440.)

Name_____

Address_____

City _____ State_____ Zip _____

Daytime Phone No. ( ) _____
　　　　　　　　　area code

*Four 2-hour lessons include course book and personalized instruction.
　Class program available in continental United States only

Wilton Home Study Course CAKE DECORATING!

$17.99 Per Lesson* Learn cake decorating the easy Wilton way! Order Lesson 1 today! Just fill in and mail this card.

☐ Yes! Send me Lesson One of the Wilton Home Study Course of Cake Decorating for only $17.99 plus $3.00 for shipping and handling. I understand that if I'm not completely satisfied, I can return both the instruction manual and materials within 30 days for a full refund or credit. I understand that the other four lessons will be sent to me for the same low price of $17.99 plus $3.00 for shipping and handling. Any lesson can be returned within 30 days for a full refund or credit if I'm not completely satisfied.

Enclosed is a check or money order payable to Wilton Home Study Course or charge my Visa or Master Card account:

☐ Visa
☐ MasterCard
(Circle one)　　　　　　　(card number)　　　　　　　　　(Exp. date)

Name _____ _____
　　　　　　　　　(Please print)　　　　　Signature　(for credit card only)

Address_____

City _____ State_____ Zip_____

Daytime Phone No. ( ) _____
　　　　　　　area code　　　　*Plus shipping and handling　　　Dept. No. LH

Wilton Home Study Course VIDEO CAKE DECORATING

$29.99 Per Lesson* ☐ Yes! Send me Lesson One of the Wilton Video Home Study Course of Cake Decorating for only $29.99 plus $3.00 for shipping and handling. I understand that if I'm not completely satisfied, I can return the video, instruction manual and materials within 30 days for a full refund or credit. I understand that the other two lessons will be sent to me-one each month through Lesson 3---for the same low price of $29.99 plus $3.00 for shipping and handling.

Enclosed is a check or money order payable to Wilton Home Study Course or charge my Visa or Master Card account:

☐ Visa
☐ MasterCard
(Circle one)　　　　　　　(card number)　　　　　　　　　(Exp. date)

Name _____ _____
　　　　　　　　　(Please print)　　　　　Signature　(for credit card only)

Address_____

City _____ State_____ Zip_____

Daytime Phone No. ( ) _____
　　　　　　　area code　　　　*Plus shipping and handling　　　Dept. No. LI

||||| |||

BUSINESS REPLY MAIL
FIRST-CLASS MAIL   PERMIT NO. 305   DOWNERS GROVE, IL

POSTAGE WILL BE PAID BY ADDRESSEE

2240 W. 75th Street
Woodridge, IL 60517

Attention: Retail CS, MS #9C

Enclose in envelope provided on Order Form or call (708) 963-7100

Enclose in envelope provided on Order Form or call (708) 963-7100

1. FEATHERWEIGHT DECORATING BAGS

Lightweight, strong, flexible polyester bags are easy to handle, soft, workable and never get stiff. Specially coated so grease won't go through. May be boiled. Dishwasher safe. Instructions included.

Size	Stock No.	Each
8 in.	404-Y-5087	$2.29
10 in.	404-Y-5109	$3.49
12 in.	404-Y-5125	$4.49
14 in.	404-Y-5140	$5.89
16 in.	404-Y-5168	$6.99
18 in.	404-Y-5184	$7.49

2. DISPOSABLE DECORATING BAGS

Use and toss-no fuss, no muss. Perfect for melting Candy Melts* in the microwave, too. Strong, flexible, and easy-to-handle plastic. 12 in. size fits standard tips and couplers.
*brand confectionery coating

2104-Y-358   **$3.99 pack of 12**
24-Count Value Pack
2104-Y-1358   **$6.29 pack of 24**

3. PARCHMENT TRIANGLES

Make your own disposable decorating bags with our quality, grease-resistant vegetable parchment paper.

12in. 2104-Y-1206   **$4.49 pack of 100**
15in. 2104-Y-1508   **$5.49 pack of 100**

4. TIP SAVER

Reshape bent tips. Molded plastic.
414-Y-909 $2.79 each

5. TIP SAVER BOXES

Keep decorating tips clean and organized,
A. 26-Tip Capacity 405-Y-8773 **$4.99 each**
B. 52-Tip Capacity 405-Y-7777 **$6.99 each**

PLASTIC COUPLERS

Use to change tips without changing bags when using the same color icing.

6. LARGE COUPLER

Fits 14 in. to 18 in. Featherweight bags. Use with large decorating tips.
411-Y-1006 $1.19 each

7. ANGLED COUPLER

Reaches around sharp angles. Fits all bags and standard decorating tips.
411-Y-7365 79¢ each

8. STANDARD COUPLER

Fits all decorating bags, standard tips.
411-Y-1987 59¢ each

9. TIP COVER

Slip over tip and save to take filled bags of icing along for touch-ups. Plastic.
414-Y-915 Package of 4 99¢ pkg.

10. MAXI TIP BRUSH

Gets out every bit of icing fast and easy.
414-Y-1010 $1.69 each

11. TIP BRUSH

Plastic bristles clean tips thoroughly.
418-Y-1123 $1.19 each

12. DESSERT DECORATOR

Easy-to-control lever lets you decorate cakes, pastries, cookies with one hand. Includes 5 easy-to-change decorating nozzles.
415-Y-825 $10.99 each

13. CAKE LEVELER

Levels and tortes cakes up to 10 in. wide and 2 in. high.
415-Y-815 $2.99 each

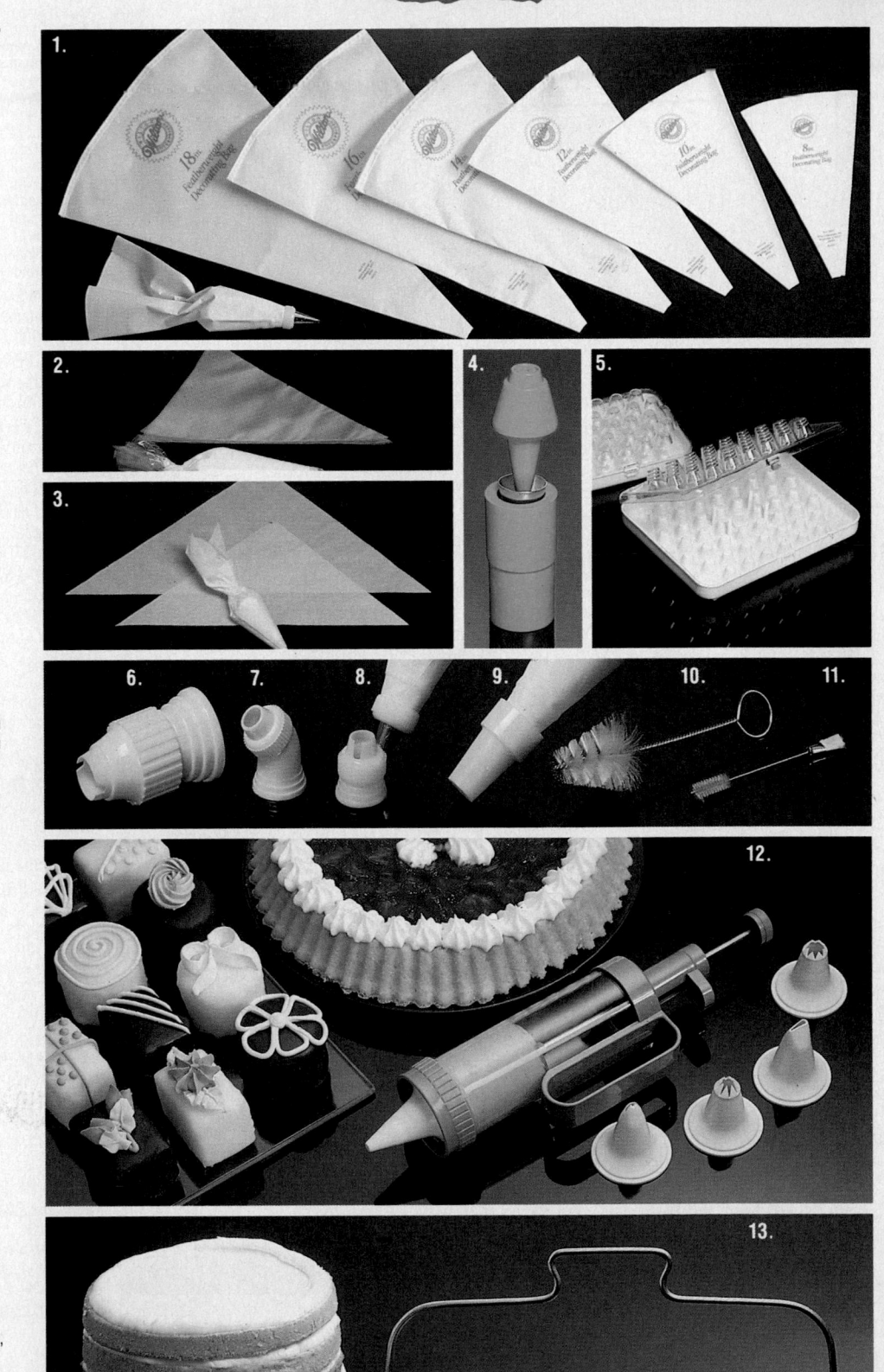

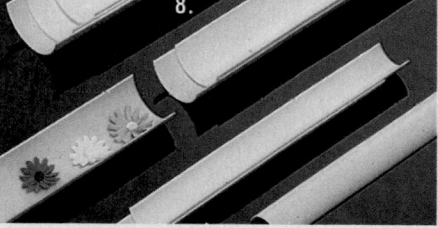

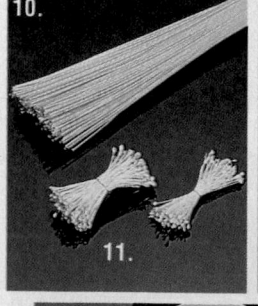

1. READY-TO-USE ICING ROSES

Save decorating time! Stock up on all colors and sizes for your next cake.

Color	Size		Stock No.	Price
White	Large	1 1/2 in.	710-Y-411	$3.99 for 9
White	Medium	1 1/4 in.	710-Y-311	$3.99 doz.
White	Small	1 in.	710-Y-211	$2.99 doz.
Red	Large	1 1/2 in.	710-Y-412	$3.99 for 9
Red	Medium	1 1/4 in.	710-Y-312	$3.99 doz.
Red	Small	1 in.	710-Y-212	$2.99 doz.
Pink	Large	1 1/2 in.	710-Y-413	$3.99 for 9
Pink	Medium	1 1/4 in.	710-Y-313	$3.99 doz.
Pink	Small	1 in.	710-Y-213	$2.99 doz.
Yellow	Large	1 1/2 in.	710-Y-414	$3.99 for 9
Yellow	Medium	1 1/4 in.	710-Y-314	$3.99 doz.
Yellow	Small	1 in.	710-Y-214	$2.99 doz.
Peach	Large	1 1/2 in.	710-Y-415	$3.99 for 9
Peach	Medium	1 1/4 in.	710-Y-315	$3.99 doz.
Peach	Small	1 in.	710-Y-215	$2.99 doz.

2. FLOWER NAIL NO. 9

1 1/4 in. diameter.
402-Y-3009 69¢ each

3. FLOWER NAIL NO. 7

1 1/2 in. diameter.
402-Y-3007 89¢ each

4. 2 IN. FLOWER NAIL

Use with curved and swirled petal tips, 116-123, to make large blooms.
402-Y-3002 $1.09 each

5. 3 IN. FLOWER NAIL

Has extra large surface, ideal with large petal tips.
402-Y-3003 $1.19 each

6. 1-PC. LILY NAIL

1 5/8 in. diameter.
402-Y-3012 89¢ each

7. LILY NAIL SET

Essential for making cup flowers, such as poinsettias and lilies. To use 2 pc. nails: Place aluminum foil in bottom half of nail and press top half in to form cup. Pipe flower petals. Set includes 1/2, 1 1/4 and 2 1/2 in. diam. cups. Sturdy white plastic.
403-Y-9444 $1.99 8-pc. set

8. FLOWER FORMER SET

Plastic stands used to dry icing leaves and flowers in a convex or concave shape. Set of nine (11 in. long) in three widths: 1 1/2, 2, 2 1/2 in. (3 of each size.)
417-Y-9500 $5.99 set

9. TREE FORMER SET

Use to make icing pine trees and to dry royal icing or gum paste decorations. Set of four, 6 1/2 in. high.
417-Y-1150 $1.99 set

10. FLORIST WIRE

Medium weight for a multitude of projects. 175 white wires (18 in. long) per pack.
409-Y-622 $8.99 pack

11. STAMENS

Make flowers more realistic. 144 per pack.
Pearl White 1005-Y-102 $1.49 pack
Yellow 1005-Y-7875 $1.49 pack

12. EDIBLE GLITTER

Sprinkles sparkle on scores of things. 1/4 oz. plastic jar.
White 703-Y-1204 $2.29 each

13. GUM PASTE MIX

East to use! Just add water and knead. Results in a workable, pliable dough-like mixture to mold into beautiful flowers and figures. 1 lb. can.
707-Y-124 $4.99 each

14. GLUCOSE

Essential ingredient for making gum paste. 24 oz. plastic jar.
707-Y-109 $4.29 each

15. GUM-TEX™ KARAYA

Makes gum paste pliable, elastic, easy to shape. 6 oz. can.
707-Y-117 $6.49 each

16. GUM PASTE FLOWERS KIT

Make lifelike, beautiful gum paste flowers. Create bouquets or single blooms for cakes, centerpieces, favors and more. Full color how-to book contains lots of ideas and step-by-step instructions. Kit includes 24 plastic cutters, 1 leaf mold, 3 wooden modeling tools and 2 squares of foam for modeling. 30-pc. kit.
1907-Y-117 $14.99 kit

1. STARTER CAKE DECORATING SET
- 4 metal decorating tips
- Instruction booklet
- Six 12-in. disposable decorating bags
- Two tip couplers
- Five liquid color packets

2104-Y-2530   **$6.99 set**

2. BASIC CAKE DECORATING SET
- 5 professional quality metal tips
- Twelve 12-in. disposable bags
- Two tip couplers
- Flowers nail no. 7
- Four 1/2 oz. icing colors
- Instruction booklet

2104-Y-2536   **$9.99 set**

3. DELUXE CAKE DECORATING SET
Contains 36 essentials!
- 10 nickel-plated metal tips
- Four 1/2 oz. icing colors
- Plastic storage tray
- Eighteen 12-in. disposable bags
- Two tip couplers
- No. 7 flower nail
- Cake Decorating, Easy as 1,2,3 book.

2104-Y-2540   **$18.99 set**

4. SUPREME CAKE DECORATING SET
52 tools in all!
- 18 metal tips
- Two tip couplers
- Five 1/2 oz. icing colors
- 8-in. angled spatula
- No. 9 flower nail
- Twenty-four disposable 12 in. bags
- Cake Decorating Easy as 1,2,3 book
- Storage Tray

2104-Y-2546   **$26.99 set**

5. TOOL CADDY
You can take it with you and keep it all beautifully organized. (Tools not included.) Holds 38 tips, 10 icing color jars, couplers, spatulas, books and more. Lightweight, stain-resistant molded polyethylene.
16 5/8 x 11 1/2 x 3 in.

2104-Y-2237   **$17.99 each**

6. DELUXE TIP SET
- 26 decorating tips
- Tip coupler
- 2 flower nails
- Tipsaver plastic box

2104-Y-6666   **$18.99 set**

7. MASTER TIP SET
- 52 metal tips
- Tipsaver box
- Two flower nails
- Two couplers

2104-Y-7778   **$34.99 set**

8. PRACTICE BOARD WITH PATTERNS
Practice is a must for decorating that gets an A+. Slip practice pattern onto board under wipe-clean vinyl overlay and trace in icing. Includes stand and patterns for flowers, leaves, borders and lettering-31 designs included.

406-Y-9464   **$6.99 each**

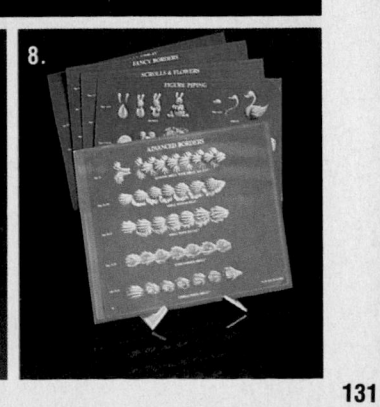
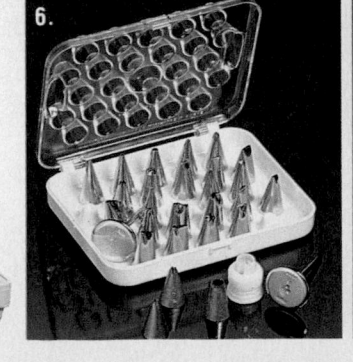

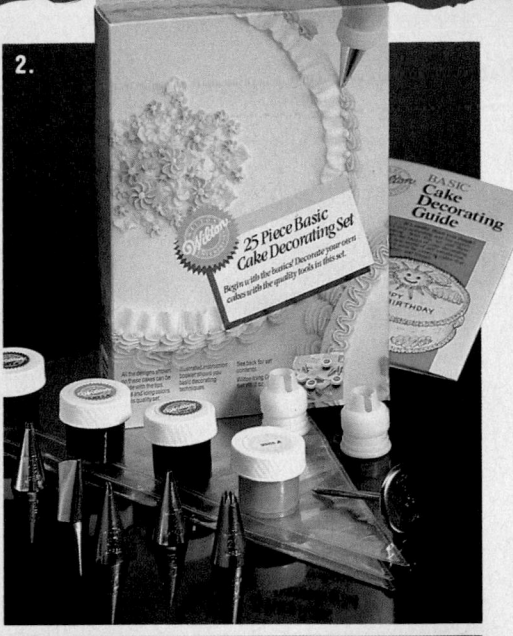

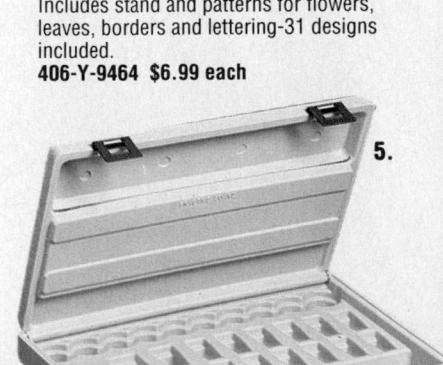
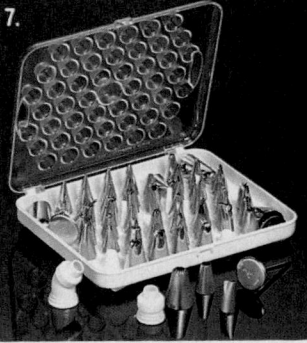

NEW!

All white board
. . . no brown edges!

8" 10" 12" 14" 16" 18"

1. NEW! RUFFLE BOARDS ™
Convenient, timesaving and ready to use. It's a cake board and ruffle in one. The Ruffle Board™ line features bleached white cake boards with all-white ruffling already attached. Creates an all-in-one, elegant presentation.

8" Ruffle Board™ 415-Y-950	**$1.99 each**	
(for 6 in. round cake)		
10" Ruffle Board™ 415-Y-960	**$2.49 each**	
(for 8 in. round cake)		
12" Ruffle Board™ 415-Y-970	**$2.99 each**	
(for 10 in. round cake)		
14" Ruffle Board™ 415-Y-980	**$3.49 each**	
(for 12 in. round cake)		
16" Ruffle Board™ 415-Y-990	**$4.39 each**	
(for 14 in. round cake)		
18" Ruffle Board™ 415-Y-1000	**$5.99 each**	
(for 16 in. round cake)		

2. TUK-N-RUFFLE
Attach to serving tray or board with royal icing or tape. 60 ft. bolts only.

Pink	802-Y-702	**$13.99**
Blue	802-Y-206	**$13.99**
White	802-Y-1008	**$13.99**

3. SHOW 'N SERVE CAKE BOARDS
Scalloped edge. Protected with food-safe, grease-resistant coating.

8 in.	2104-Y-1125	**$3.99 Pack of 10**
10 in.	2104-Y-1168	**$4.49 Pack of 10**
12 in.	2104-Y-1176	**$4.99 Pack of 8**
14 in.	2104-Y-1184	**$5.49 Pack of 6**
14 X 20 in. Rectangle		
	2104-Y-1230	**$5.99 Pack of 6**

4. FANCI-FOIL WRAP
Serving side has a non-toxic grease-resistant surface. FDA approved for use with food. Continuous roll: 20 in. x 15 ft.

Rose	804-Y-124	**$6.99 each**
Gold	804-Y-183	
Silver	804-Y-167	
Blue	804-Y-140	
White	804-Y-191	

4.

1. NEW! PARTY TRAYS

Add an elegant and professional look to your buffet table with mirror-finish look party trays. Perfectly designed for cakes, appetizers, canapes. Divided tray holds relishes and dips.

6 ½ in. Party Bowl	415-Y-1015	$1.29 ea.
14 in. Chip 'n' Dip Tray	415-Y-1016	$2.99 ea.
8x20 in. Div. Oval Party Tray	415-Y-1017	$2.49 ea.
12 ⅜ x 18 in. Div. Rec. Party Tray	415-Y-1018	$2.99 ea.
10 ½ x 16 ⅛ in. Oval Party Tray	415-Y-1020	$2.49 ea.
12 ⅛ x 18 in. Oval Party Tray	415-Y-1019	$2.99 ea.

2. SERVING TRAYS

Elegant, reusable trays in sturdy laminated plastic. Perfect for decorated cakes and desserts. Inner recessed area designed to securely fit round or rectangular cake circles and boards.

Description	Stock No.	
10 ⅛ in. holds 8-in. cake circle	415-Y-0908	$1.99 ea.
12 ⅛ in. holds 10-in. cake circle	415-Y-0910	$2.49 ea.
14 ⅜ in. holds 12-in. cake circle	415-Y-0912	$2.99 ea.
16 ¾ in. holds 14-in. cake circle	415-Y-0914	$3.49 ea.
12 ⅛ in. x 16 ⅛ in. holds 10 x 14 in.cake board	415-Y-0916	$3.49 ea.

3. DOILIES

Grease-resistant, glassine-coated paper doilies are ideal for iced cakes. Round and rectangular shapes have lace borders sized to fit around your decorated cakes. Ideal for serving cookies and canapes, too!

8 in. Round	2104-Y-90004	$1.99 Pack of 16
10 in. Round	2104-Y-90000	$1.99 Pack of 12
12 in. Round	2104-Y-90001	$1.99 Pack of 8
14 in. Round	2104-Y-90002	$1.99 Pack of 8
10 x 14 in. Rectangle	2104-Y-90003	$1.99 Pack of 8

4. CAKE CIRCLES & BOARDS

Sturdy corrugated cardboard.

6 in.	2104-Y-64	$2.39 Pack of 10
8 in.	2104-Y-80	$3.49 Pack of 12
10 in.	2104-Y-102	$4.29 Pack of 12
12 in.	2104-Y-129	$4.29 Pack of 8
14 in.	2104-Y-145	$4.29 Pack of 6
16 in.	2104-Y-160	$5.19 Pack of 6
18. in.	2104-Y-180	$ .85 Pack of 1
10 x 14 in.	2104-Y-554	$3.99 Pack of 6
13 x 19 in.	2104-Y-552	$4.49 Pack of 6

5. PROFESSIONAL CAKE STAND

Heavy-duty aluminum stand is 4 ⅝ in. high with 12 in. rotating plate. Super strong; essential for decorating tiered wedding cakes.
307-Y-2501 $49.99 each

6. LAZY DAISY SERVER

Stationary stand. Sturdy white plastic with scalloped edges. 5 in. high with 12 in. plate.
307-Y-700 $8.99 each

7. TRIM 'N TURN CAKE STAND

Flute-edged. Plate turns smoothly on hidden ball bearings. Just turn as you decorate. White molded plastic; holds up to 100 lbs. 12 in. plate.
2103-Y-2518 $7.99 each

8. REVOLVING CAKE STAND

Now with easy, rotating ball bearings! Plate turns smoothly in either direction for easy decorating and serving; 3 in. high with 11 in. diameter plate in molded white plastic.
415-Y-900 $9.99 each

DECORATING TIPS GUIDE

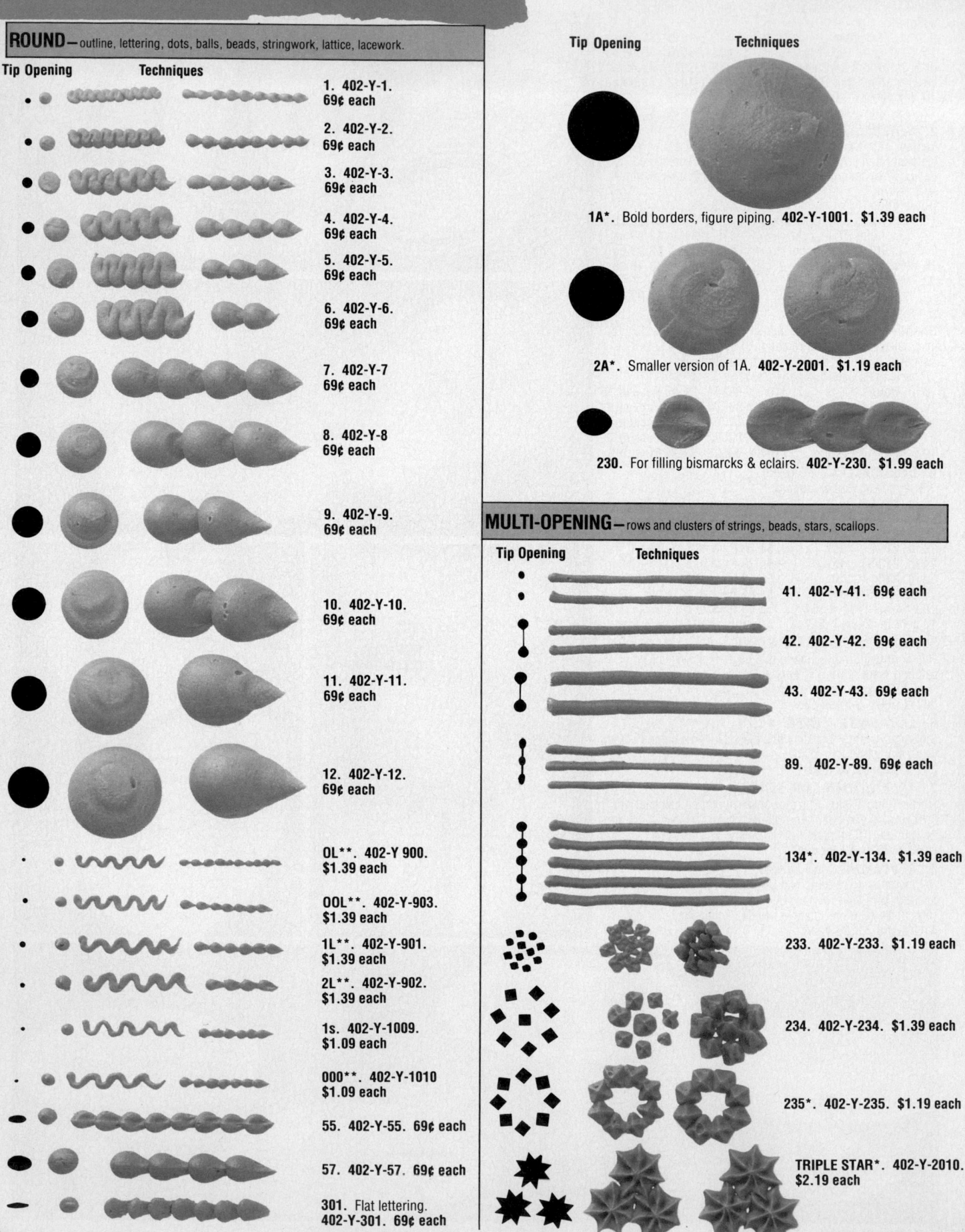

ROUND—outline, lettering, dots, balls, beads, stringwork, lattice, lacework.

Tip Opening　　**Techniques**

1. 402-Y-1. 69¢ each

2. 402-Y-2. 69¢ each

3. 402-Y-3. 69¢ each

4. 402-Y-4. 69¢ each

5. 402-Y-5. 69¢ each

6. 402-Y-6. 69¢ each

7. 402-Y-7 69¢ each

8. 402-Y-8 69¢ each

9. 402-Y-9. 69¢ each

10. 402-Y-10. 69¢ each

11. 402-Y-11. 69¢ each

12. 402-Y-12. 69¢ each

OL**. 402-Y 900. $1.39 each

OOL**. 402-Y-903. $1.39 each

1L**. 402-Y-901. $1.39 each

2L**. 402-Y-902. $1.39 each

1s. 402-Y-1009. $1.09 each

000**. 402-Y-1010 $1.09 each

55. 402-Y-55. 69¢ each

57. 402-Y-57. 69¢ each

301. Flat lettering. 402-Y-301. 69¢ each

Tip Opening　　**Techniques**

1A*. Bold borders, figure piping. 402-Y-1001. $1.39 each

2A*. Smaller version of 1A. 402-Y-2001. $1.19 each

230. For filling bismarcks & eclairs. 402-Y-230. $1.99 each

MULTI-OPENING—rows and clusters of strings, beads, stars, scallops.

Tip Opening　　**Techniques**

41. 402-Y-41. 69¢ each

42. 402-Y-42. 69¢ each

43. 402-Y-43. 69¢ each

89. 402-Y-89. 69¢ each

134*. 402-Y-134. $1.39 each

233. 402-Y-233. $1.19 each

234. 402-Y-234. $1.39 each

235*. 402-Y-235. $1.19 each

TRIPLE STAR*. 402-Y-2010. $2.19 each

**Use with parchment bags.

*Fits large coupler.

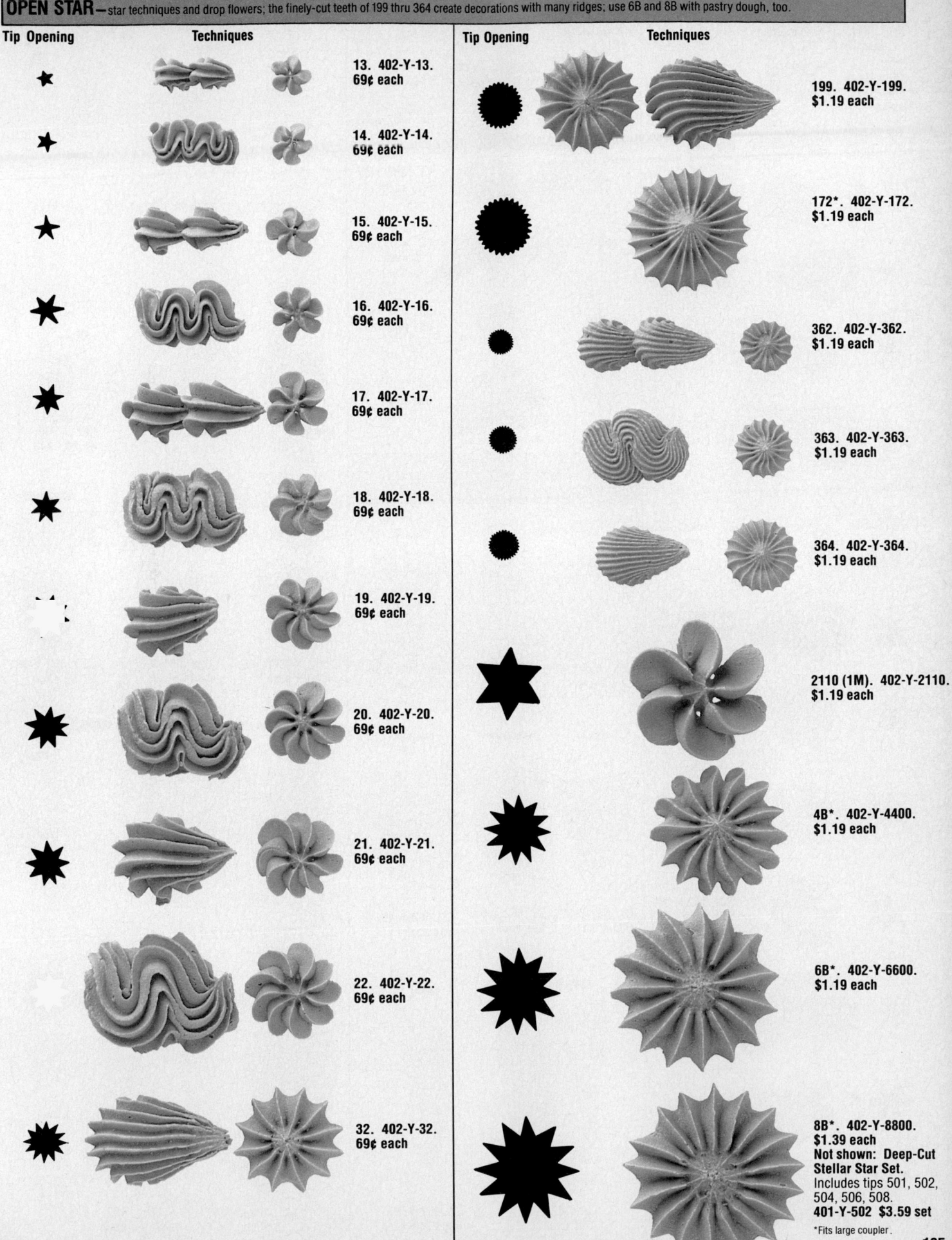

Tip Opening	Techniques	
★		13. 402-Y-13. 69¢ each
★		14. 402-Y-14. 69¢ each
★		15. 402-Y-15. 69¢ each
✶		16. 402-Y-16. 69¢ each
✶		17. 402-Y-17. 69¢ each
✶		18. 402-Y-18. 69¢ each
✶		19. 402-Y-19. 69¢ each
✴		20. 402-Y-20. 69¢ each
✴		21. 402-Y-21. 69¢ each
✴		22. 402-Y-22. 69¢ each
✴		32. 402-Y-32. 69¢ each

Tip Opening	Techniques	
●		199. 402-Y-199. $1.19 each
●		172*. 402-Y-172. $1.19 each
●		362. 402-Y-362. $1.19 each
●		363. 402-Y-363. $1.19 each
●		364. 402-Y-364. $1.19 each
✶		2110 (1M). 402-Y-2110. $1.19 each
✴		4B*. 402-Y-4400. $1.19 each
✴		6B*. 402-Y-6600. $1.19 each
✴		8B*. 402-Y-8800. $1.39 each **Not shown: Deep-Cut Stellar Star Set.** Includes tips 501, 502, 504, 506, 508. **401-Y-502 $3.59 set**

*Fits large coupler.

135

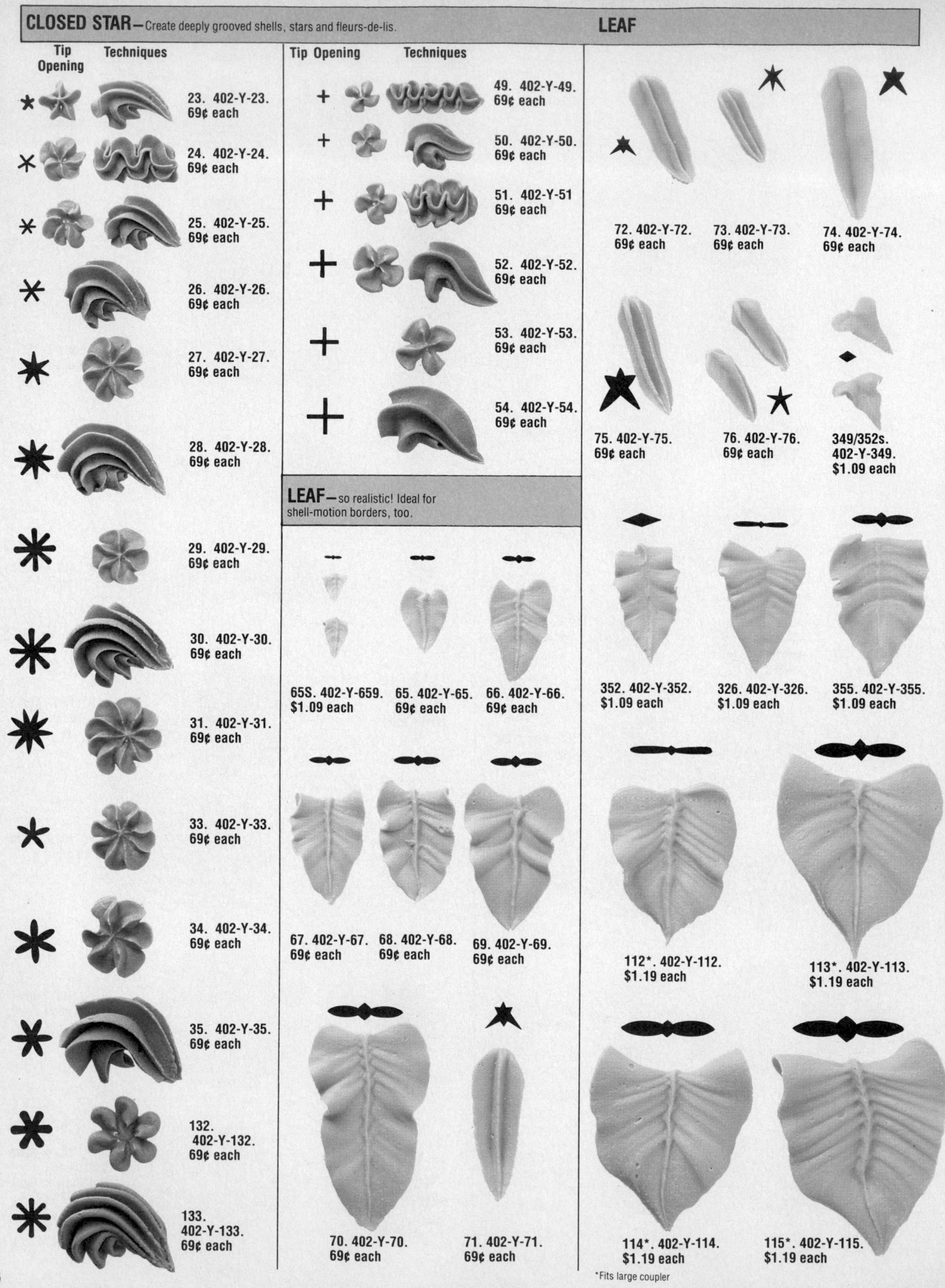

CLOSED STAR—Create deeply grooved shells, stars and fleurs-de-lis.

Tip Opening	Techniques	
		23. 402-Y-23. 69¢ each
		24. 402-Y-24. 69¢ each
		25. 402-Y-25. 69¢ each
		26. 402-Y-26. 69¢ each
		27. 402-Y-27. 69¢ each
		28. 402-Y-28. 69¢ each
		29. 402-Y-29. 69¢ each
		30. 402-Y-30. 69¢ each
		31. 402-Y-31. 69¢ each
		33. 402-Y-33. 69¢ each
		34. 402-Y-34. 69¢ each
		35. 402-Y-35. 69¢ each
		132. 402-Y-132. 69¢ each
		133. 402-Y-133. 69¢ each

Tip Opening	Techniques	
		49. 402-Y-49. 69¢ each
		50. 402-Y-50. 69¢ each
		51. 402-Y-51. 69¢ each
		52. 402-Y-52. 69¢ each
		53. 402-Y-53. 69¢ each
		54. 402-Y-54. 69¢ each

LEAF—so realistic! Ideal for shell-motion borders, too.

65S. 402-Y-659. $1.09 each

65. 402-Y-65. 69¢ each

66. 402-Y-66. 69¢ each

67. 402-Y-67. 69¢ each

68. 402-Y-68. 69¢ each

69. 402-Y-69. 69¢ each

70. 402-Y-70. 69¢ each

71. 402-Y-71. 69¢ each

LEAF

72. 402-Y-72. 69¢ each

73. 402-Y-73. 69¢ each

74. 402-Y-74. 69¢ each

75. 402-Y-75. 69¢ each

76. 402-Y-76. 69¢ each

349/352s. 402-Y-349. $1.09 each

352. 402-Y-352. $1.09 each

326. 402-Y-326. $1.09 each

355. 402-Y-355. $1.09 each

112*. 402-Y-112. $1.19 each

113*. 402-Y-113. $1.19 each

114*. 402-Y-114. $1.19 each

115*. 402-Y-115. $1.19 each

*Fits large coupler

Tip Opening   Techniques

106. 402-Y-106. $1.19 each

107. 402-Y-107. $1.19 each

108**. 402-Y-108. $1.19 each

109**. 402-Y-109. $1.39 each

129. 402-Y-129. $1.19 each

217. 402-Y-217. $1.19 each

220. 402-Y-220. $1.19 each

224. 402-Y-224. $1.19 each

225. 402-Y-225. $1.19 each

131. 402-Y-131. $1.19 each

177. 402-Y-177. $1.19 each

*Fits large coupler
**Use with parchment bags

Tip Opening

190**. 402-Y-190. $1.39 each

191. 402-Y-191. $1.19 each

193. 402-Y-193. $1.19 each

194**. 402-Y-194. $1.39 each

135**. 402-Y-135. $1.39 each

140. 402-Y-140. $1.39 each

195**. 402-Y-195. $1.19 each

2C*. 402-Y-2003. $1.19 each

2D*. 402-Y-2004. $1.19 each

*Fits large coupler
**Use with parchment bags

Tip Opening

2E*. 402-Y-2005. $1.19 each

2F*. 402-Y-2006. $1.19 each

1B*. 402-Y-1002. $1.39 each

1C. 402-Y-1003. $1.39 each

1E*. 402-Y-1005. $1.39 each

1F*. 402-Y-1006. $1.39 each

1G*. 402-Y-1007. $1.39 each

*Fits large coupler
**Use with parchment bags

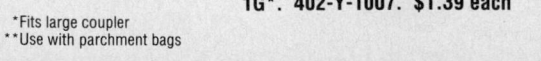

PETAL — realistic flower petals, dramatic ruffles, drapes, swags and bows.

Tip Opening | Techniques

127D (Giant Rose).
402-Y-1274. $1.39 each

101S. 402-Y-1019.
$1.09 each

101. 402-Y-101.
69¢ each

102. 402-Y-102.
69¢ each

103. 402-Y-103.
69¢ each

104. 402-Y-104.
69¢ each

124*. 402-Y-124.
$1.19 each

125*. 402-Y-125.
$1.19 each

126*. 402-Y-126.
$1.19 each

127*. 402-Y-127.
$1.19 each

59s/59⁰. 402-Y-594.
69¢ each

59. 402-Y-59.
69¢ each

Tip Opening | Techniques

60. 402-Y-60.
69¢ each

61. 402-Y-61.
69¢ each

121*. 402-Y-121.
$1.19 each

122*. 402-Y-122.
$1.19 each

123*. 402-Y-123.
$1.19 each

97. 402-Y-97.
69¢ each

116*. 402-Y-116.
$1.19 each

118*. 402-Y-118.
$1.19 each

119*. 402-Y-119.
$1.19 each

150. 402-Y-150.
$1.19 each

62. 402-Y-62.
69¢ each

63. 402-Y-63.
69¢ each

64. 402-Y-64.
69¢ each

RUFFLE — plain, fluted, shell-border, special effects.

Tip Opening | Techniques

99. 402-Y-99.
69¢ each

100. 402-Y-100.
69¢ each

339. 402-Y-339.
$1.09 each

340. 402-Y-340.
$1.09 each

86.
(right-handers).
402-Y-86.
69¢ each

87 (lefties).
402-Y-87.
69¢ each

88 (lefties).
402-Y-88.
69¢ each

353. 402-Y-353.
$1.09 each

401. 402-Y-401.
89¢ each

402*. 402-Y-402. $1.19 each

*Use with large coupler

403. 402-Y-403. $1.39 each

138

BASKETWEAVE—44, 45 make smooth stripes; rest of basketweave tips make both smooth and ribbed stripes.

Tip Opening	Techniques	Tip Opening	Techniques	Tip Opening	Techniques

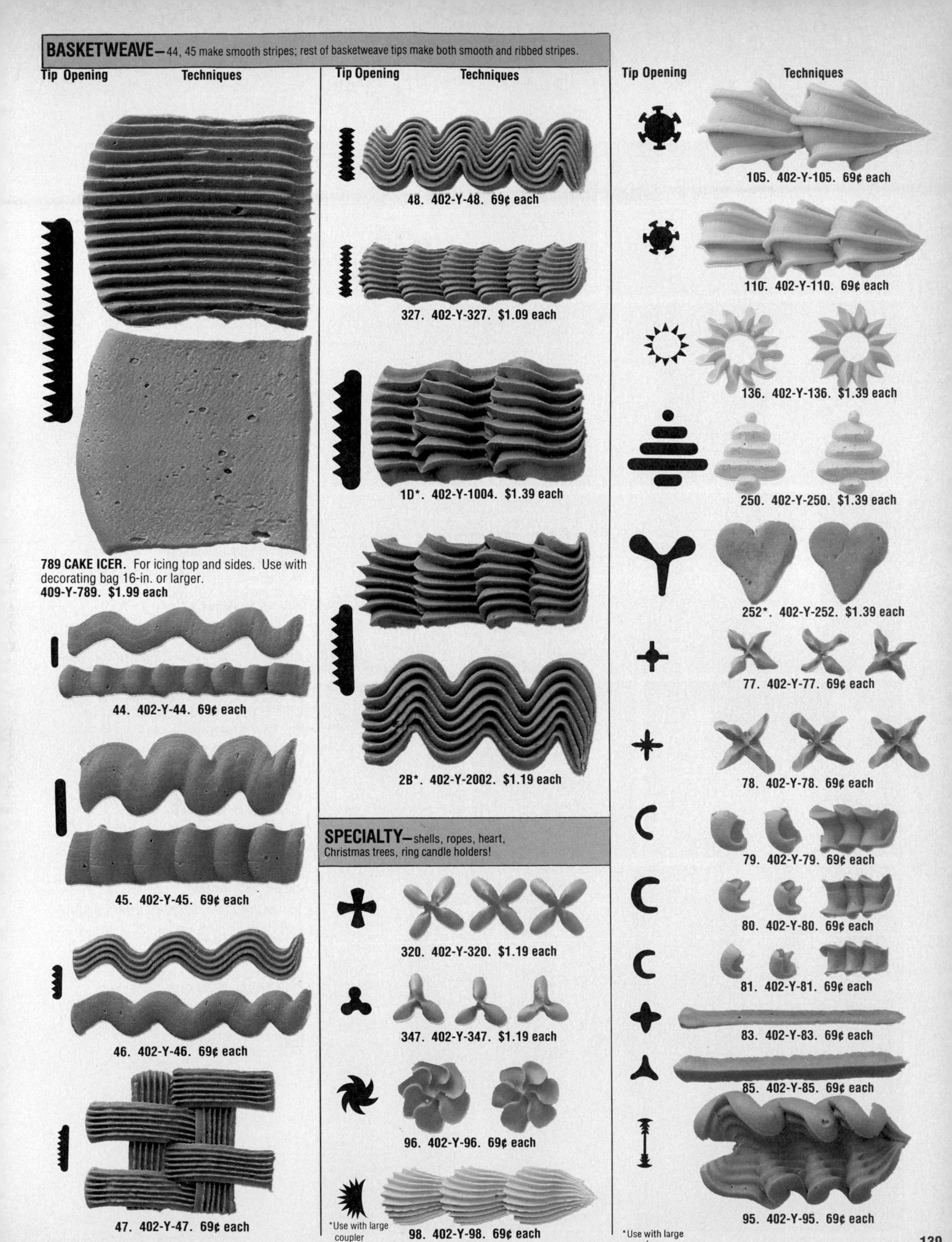

789 CAKE ICER. For icing top and sides. Use with decorating bag 16-in. or larger.
409-Y-789. $1.99 each

48. 402-Y-48. 69¢ each

327. 402-Y-327. $1.09 each

1D*. 402-Y-1004. $1.39 each

2B*. 402-Y-2002. $1.19 each

44. 402-Y-44. 69¢ each

45. 402-Y-45. 69¢ each

46. 402-Y-46. 69¢ each

47. 402-Y-47. 69¢ each

105. 402-Y-105. 69¢ each

110. 402-Y-110. 69¢ each

136. 402-Y-136. $1.39 each

250. 402-Y-250. $1.39 each

252*. 402-Y-252. $1.39 each

77. 402-Y-77. 69¢ each

78. 402-Y-78. 69¢ each

79. 402-Y-79. 69¢ each

80. 402-Y-80. 69¢ each

81. 402-Y-81. 69¢ each

83. 402-Y-83. 69¢ each

85. 402-Y-85. 69¢ each

95. 402-Y-95. 69¢ each

SPECIALTY—shells, ropes, heart, Christmas trees, ring candle holders!

320. 402-Y-320. $1.19 each

347. 402-Y-347. $1.19 each

96. 402-Y-96. 69¢ each

98. 402-Y-98. 69¢ each

*Use with large coupler

*Use with large coupler

139

1.

1. CIRCUS BALLOONS SET
12 in a bunch. 3 bunches per set. 6 ½ in. high.
2113-Y-2366 $2.49 set

2. NEW! CLOWNS SET
2¼ to 2¼ in. high
2113-Y-9003 $2.99 set

3. JUGGLER CLOWN
Jolly fellow in action. 4 in. high.
2113-Y-2252 $2.19 each

4. COUNTDOWN CLOWN
Can adjust from age 1 to 6. 4¾ x 4 in. high.
2113-Y-2341 $1.39 each

5. COMICAL CLOWNS SET
Varied expressions. 2 in. to 3 in.
2113-Y-2635 $3.29 set of 4

6. DERBY CLOWNS SET
A quartet of gigglers. On picks. 2 in. high.
2113-Y-2333 $2.49 set of 4

7. SMALL DERBY CLOWNS SET
Miniatures! Perfect for cupcakes. 2 in. high with pick.
2113-Y-2759 $1.99 pack of 6

8. CLOWN SEPARATOR SET
Two big-footed clowns balance a 6 in. round cake on top plate. Perfect to set atop a large base cake (be sure to dowel rod). They can stand on their hands or feet. Set includes two 7 in. scalloped-edge plates and two snap-on clown supports. 4-in. high.
301-Y-909 $6.99 set

9. CAROUSEL SEPARATOR SET
Galloping ponies will add excitement for that special little one. Contains: 2 brown and 2 white snap-on pony pillars, two 10 in. round plates-one clear acrylic, one plastic. Two 10 in. cardboard circles to protect plates. 9 in. high.
2103-Y-1139 $10.49 set

10. LI'L COWPOKE
Wee buckaroo; 5¼ in. high.
2113-Y-2406 $2.69 each

11. DOLLY DRESS UP
High style; 4 ½ in. high.
2113-Y-1485 $2.69 each

12. 3-PC. SPACESHIP CANDLEHOLDERS SET
3 pieces, 1¼ to 3¾ in. high. Holds standard candles.
2111-Y-2008 $3.69

13. APPALOOSA ROCKING HORSES SET
Four painted ponies; 2½ in. high.
2113-Y-2015 $3.49 set

14. HONEY BEAR
Hand-painted. 3¾ in. high.
2113-Y-2031 $2.69 each

15. CAROUSEL CAKE TOP SET
A fast, easy, circus in seconds for 10 in. or larger cakes. 9 in. high.
1305-Y-9302 $4.99 set

1. NUMERAL PICKS SET
Numbers 2 in. high. With picks, about 3½ in. high, 10 numbers and ? in set.
1106-Y-7406 **$1.39 set**

2. TEEN DOLL PICK
6 ½ in. high without pick.
2815-Y-101 **$2.99 each**

3. FRECKLE-FACED DOLL PICK
4 in. high without pick.
2113-Y-2317 **$2.99 each**

4. MINI DOLL PICK SET
4 picks, 4 ¼ in. high with pick.
1511-Y-1019 **$5.29 set**

5. TELEPHONE TEENS SET
Get in on the conversation track with these teens. 6 pieces - 3 girls, 3 boys, 1³/8 to 2 in. high.
1301-Y-706 **$3.69 set**

6. COMMUNION ALTAR
Tulle veil on girl. Each, 3 ½ in. high.
Boy 1105-Y-7886 **$2.09 each**
Girl 1105-Y-7878 **$2.09 each**

7. SHINING CROSS
Detachable pick. 3 ¾ in. high.
1105-Y-7320 **$1.09 each**

8. SLEEPING ANGELS SET
1½ in. high x 3 in. long.
2113-Y-2325 **$1.99 set**

9. 3 A.M. FEEDING
5 in. high.
2113-Y-3333 **$3.99 each**

10. CRYSTAL-CLEAR BOOTIES SET
Add ribbon laces.
2 in. high x 4 ¼ in. long.
1103-Y-9332 **$1.69 set**

11. BABY SHOES CAKE PICKS
3 in. high.
2113-Y-3811 **$1.39 pack of 6**

12. STORK CAKE PICKS
3 ¼ in. high.
2113-Y-3805 **$1.39 pack of 6**

13. DAINTY BASSINETTE
Fill with surprises. 3 ½ in. high.
2111-Y-9381 **$1.09 each**

14. MAMA STORK
4 in. high.
1305-Y-6303 **$1.69 each**

15. MR. STORK
115-Y-1502 **$6.00 each**

16. PETITE LULLABY
115-Y-1987 **$8.00 each**

17. BABY BRACELETS
1 in. diameter.
2111-Y-72 **$1.69 pack of 4**

18. TINY TODDLER
4 ³/4 in. high.
Blue 1103-Y-7429 **$2.09 each**
Pink 1103-Y-7437 **$2.09 each**

19. BABY RATTLES
Great as gift trimmers, too! 3 ½ in. long,
2113-Y-3283 **$1.09 pack of 2**

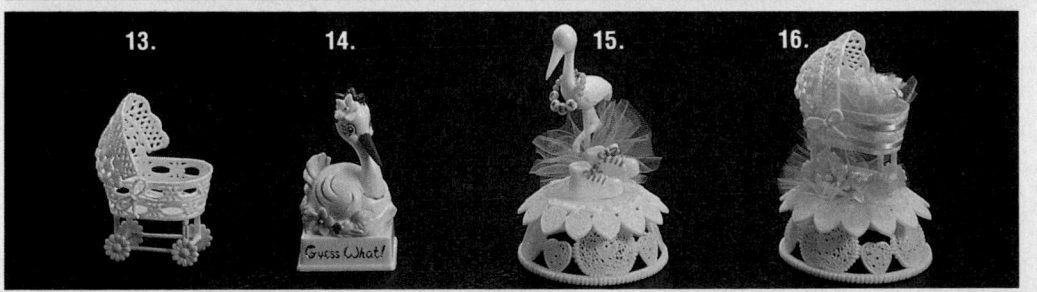

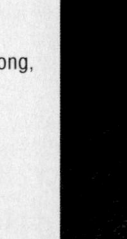

TOPPERS

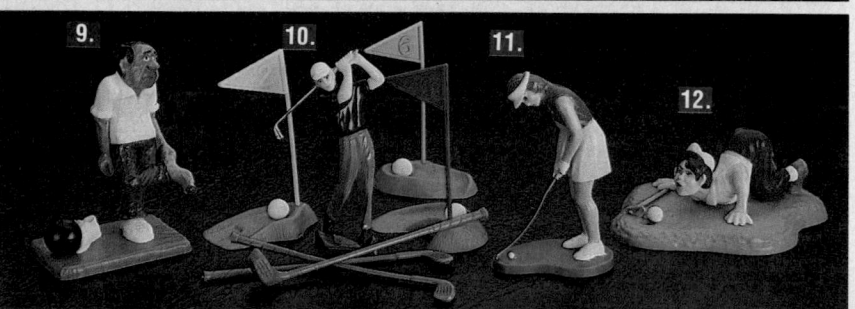

1. *NEW! SOCCER CAKE TOP SET*
9 pieces, 1³/₄ to 2 in. high.
2113-Y-9002 $2.49 9-pc. set

2. *SOFTBALL PLAYER*
4³/₈ in. high
2113-Y-3705 $3.29 each

3. *BASEBALL SET*
Batter, catcher, pitcher and 3 basemen. Handpainted. Each
2¹/₈-2³/₄ in. high.
2113-Y-2155 $2.99 6-pc. set

4. *"NICE PLAY" BASEBALL SET*
3 pieces, 1¹/₂ to 3 ¹/₈ in.high.
2113-Y-2473 $2.99 3-pc. set

5. *GOOD SPORTS COACH*
4 ¹/₂ in. high,
2113-Y-4140 $2.69 each

6. *CAMPUS CHEERLEADER*
5¹/₈ in. high
2113-Y-2708 $1.69 each

7. *BASKETBALL PLAYER*
3 ³/₄ in. high
2113-Y-9354 $1.99 each

8. *FOOTBALL SET*
Eight 1¹/₂-2 in. high players and two 4¹/₂ in. high goal posts.
2113-Y-2236 $2.99 10-pc. set

9. *BUMBLING BOWLER*
4¹/₂ in. high.
2113-Y-2783 $2.69 each

10. *GOLF SET* *
Includes 4¹/₂ in. high golfer plus 3 each: 2¹/₂ in. wide greens,
4 in. high flags, 5 in. clubs and golf balls.
1306-Y-7274 $2.09 13-pc. set

11. *NEW! FEMALE GOLFER* 4 ¹/₈ in. high.
2113-Y-9000 $1.79 each

12. *COMICAL GOLFER*
2 in. high, 4 ¹/₄ in. wide, 5 ¹/₈ in. long.
2113-Y-2554 $2.09 each

13. *FISHY SITUATION*
5 ¹/₄ in. high.   2113-Y-2074 $2.69 each

14. *END OF DOCK FISHERMAN*
Just swirl icing to resemble water: set on top. 5 in. high.
2113-Y-4832 $2.69 each

15. *FRUSTRATED FISHERMAN*   4¹/₂ in. high.
2113-Y-2384 $3.29 each

16. *MESSAGE CAKE PICKS*
Pipe on icing message. 4 ¹/₂ in. high.
1008-Y-726 $1.39 pack of 2

17. *SHARP SHOOTER* 5 ⁷/₈ in. high.
2113-Y-2422 $2.99 each

18. *JAUNTY JOGGER* 4 in. high.
2113-Y-2066 $2.69 each

19. *ARMCHAIR QUARTERBACK*
Man 3 ¹/₂ in. high; TV 2 ¹/₄ in. high
2113-Y-1302 $2.69 2-pc. set

20. *LAZY BONES*
3 in. high x 5¹/₂ in. long.
2113-Y-2414 $2.69 each

21. *PARTY GUY* 3 x 3 ³/₄ in. high.
2113-Y-3739 $2.69 each

22. *BACKYARD GARDENER* 4 ³/₈ in. high.
2113-Y-1973 $2.09 each

23. *ALL THUMBS* 5 in. high.
2113-Y-2686 $2.09 each

24. *OL' SMOKY*
Man 5 ¹/₈ in. tall; grill 2 ³/₈ in. tall.
2113-Y-2694 $2.09 2-pc. set

25. *BIG BOSS*
3 ¹/₂ in high x 2 ¹/₂ in. long.
2113-Y-3798 $2.69 each

*CAUTION: Contains small parts.
Not recommended for use by children 3 years and under.

1. *BATMAN™ CAKE TOP* 3½ in. high.
2113-Y-2902 **$1.99 set**
TM & © 1989 DC Comics Inc.

2. *NEW! GARFIELD™ PICKS*
3 ½ to 3 ⅞ in. high.
2113-Y-9007 **$1.99 set of 6**
GARFIELD Characters: ©1978 United Feature Syndicate, Inc.

3. *SESAME STREET SET**
Big Bird 3 in., Oscar the Grouch 2 in., Cookie
Monster 2¼ in., Bert 2¼ in., Ernie 2 in. high.
2113-Y-1728 **$2.99 5-pc. set**

4. *BIG BIRD PICK** 3 ½ in. high.
2113-Y-3815 **$1.99 pkg. of 6**

5. *COOKIE MONSTER PICK** 3 ¼ in. high.
2113-Y-3813 **$1.99 pkg. of 6**

6. *BIG BIRD WITH AGE**
Age indicator 1-6, 4 in. high.
2113-Y-1430 **$2.09 each**

Sesame Street Characters
© Jim Henson Productions, Inc. All rights reserved.

7. *NEW! THE SIMPSONS
BIRTHDAY TOPPER* 5 ⅜ in. diameter.
2113-Y-9005 **$1.99 each**

MATT GROENING
TM & ©1990 Twentieth Century Fox Film Corporation
All rights reserved

8. *WACKY WITCH* 5¼ in. high.
2113-Y-6118 **$2.09 each**

9. *HAPPY GHOST*
4 ⅜ in. high; 2 ¾ in. diameter.
2113-Y-3356 **$1.09 each**

10. *JACK-O-LANTERNS* 2 in.
2113-Y-3135 **$1.69 set of 4**

11. *BLACK CAT PICK* 3 in. high.
2113-Y-4301 **$1.39 pack of 6**

12. *JACK-O-LANTERN PICK* 3 ½ in. high.
2113-Y-4328 **$1.39 pack of 6**

13. *SANTA 'N TREE SET*
Santa 2 ⅝ in tall; tree 3 ⅜ in. high.
2113-Y-1647 **$1.69 2-pc. set**

14. *CHRISTMAS TREE PICK*
Festive fir. 3 ⅜ in. high.
2113-Y-4344 **$1.39 pack of 6**

15. *SNOWMAN PICK*
Favorite roly poly. 3 ⅝ in. high.
2113-Y-4360 **$1.39 pack of 6**

16. *HEART CAKE PICK* 2 in. high.
1502-Y-1011 **$1.39 pack of 12**

17. *SHAMROCK PICK* 3 ¼ in. high.
2113-Y-4387 **$1.39 pack of 6**

18. *EASTER BUNNY PICK* 3 ⅞ in. high.
2113-Y-4476 **$1.39 pack of 6**

19. *GOOD LUCK KEY PICK* 3 ¼ in. high.
2113-Y-3801 **$1.39 pack of 6**

20. *GRADUATION CAKE PICKS* 3 in. high.
1½ in. on 1¾ in. pick.
2113-Y-3803 **$1.39 pack of 6**

21. *SUCCESSFUL GRAD* 4 ¼ in. tall.
2113-Y-4549 **$1.69 each**

22. *GLOWING GRAD* 4 ½ in. tall.
2113-Y-1833 **$1.69 each**

23. *GLAD GRADUATE* 4 ½ in. tall.
2113-Y-1817 **$2.09 each**

24. *HAPPY GRADUATE* 5 in. tall.
2113-Y-1818 **$2.09 each**

*CAUTION: Contains small parts.
Not recommended for use by children 3 years and under.

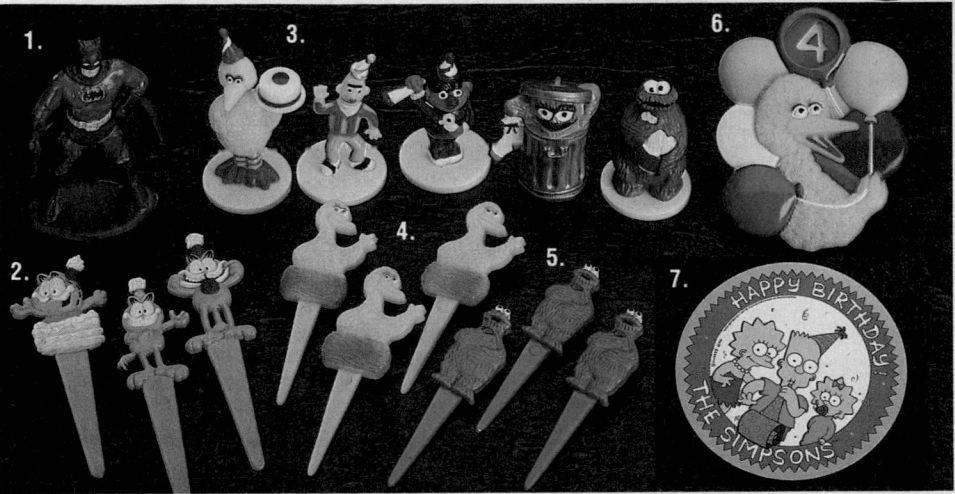

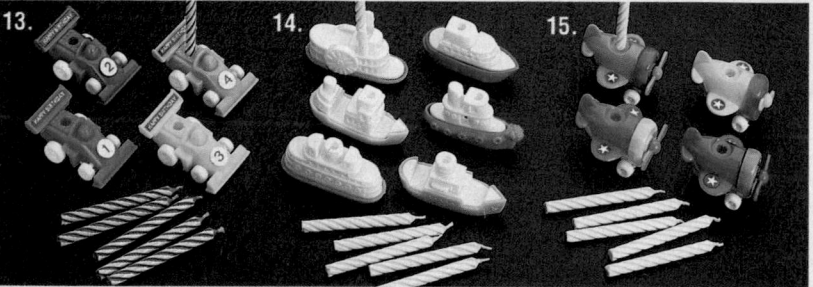

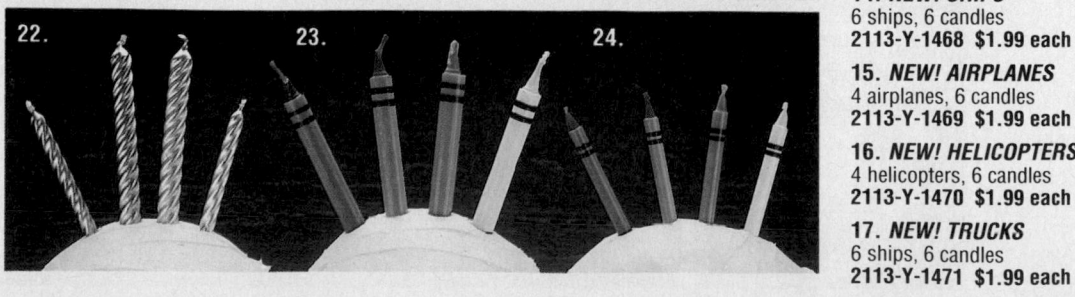

Fun and festive cake top sets for fast and easy decorating. Sets are designed to be used on 8 or 9" round or 9 x 13" sheet cakes. Each set includes 5 theme-oriented decorations that are food-safe, washable and reusable, plus 6 color - coordinating candles.

1. NEW! BASEBALL STAR
2113-Y-2819 $2.49 each

2. NEW! SOCCER STAR
2113-Y-2815 $2.49 each

3. NEW! DINOSAUR PARTY
2113-Y-2825 $2.49 each

4. NEW! BIRTHDAY BEARS
2113-Y-2823 $2.49 each

5. NEW! PARTY! PARTY!
2113-Y-2821 $2.49 each

6. NEW! ROCK & ROLL PARTY
2113-Y-2814 $2.49 each

7. NEW! KING FOR A DAY
2113-Y-2822 $2.49 each

8. NEW! VICTORIAN HEARTS
2113-Y-2820 $2.49 each

9. NEW! BALLERINA BUNNY
2113-Y-2824 $2.49 each

10. NEW! LITTLE LOCOMOTIVE
2113-Y-2818 $2.49 each

11. NEW! CIRCUS FRIENDS
2113-Y-2816 $2.49 each

12. NEW! HAPPY CLOWNS
2113-Y-2817 $2.49 each

Candle holder sets turn any cake into a party cake quickly. Sets include theme coordinating candle holders and candles.

13. NEW! RACE CARS
4 cars, 6 candles
2113-Y-1467 $1.99 each

14. NEW! SHIPS
6 ships, 6 candles
2113-Y-1468 $1.99 each

15. NEW! AIRPLANES
4 airplanes, 6 candles
2113-Y-1469 $1.99 each

16. NEW! HELICOPTERS
4 helicopters, 6 candles
2113-Y-1470 $1.99 each

17. NEW! TRUCKS
6 ships, 6 candles
2113-Y-1471 $1.99 each

18. TRAIN CAKE TOP SET
All aboard this 12-piece set. Train 1 1/4 in. to 1 5/8 in. high, 6 candles 2 1/2 in. high.
2113-Y-9004 $2.49 set

19. NEW! BALLERINAS
6 ballerinas, 6 candles.
2113-Y-1472 $2.49 each

20. CELEBRATION CANDLES 2 1/2 in. high. 24 in pkg. 59¢ per pkg.

Asst.	2811-Y-215
White	2811-Y-207
Yellow	2811-Y-208
Red	2811-Y-209
Blue	2811-Y-210
Green	2811-Y-211
Pink	2811-Y-213
Black	2811-Y-224
Neon	69¢ per pkg.
	2811-Y-225

21. CELEBRATION JUMBO CANDLES
3 1/4 in. high.
10 in pkg. 59¢ per pkg.

Asst.	2811-Y-222
Red	2811-Y-201
White	2811-Y-202
Green	2811-Y-203
Pink	2811-Y-204
Blue	2811-Y-205
Yellow	2811-Y-206
Black	2811-Y-223
Neon	69¢ per pkg.

Ass't-Pink, Green, Yellow, Orange 2811-Y-221

22. NEW! GOLD AND SILVER CANDLES
10 gold candles for special celebrations.
2811-Y-9122 $1.49 pkg.
8 jumbo gold candles mark those formal occasions.
2811-Y-9124 $1.49 pkg.
10 silver candles perfect for anniversaries.
2811-Y-9123 $1.49 pkg.
8 jumbo silver candles cause for rememberence.
2811-Y-9125 $1.49 pkg.

23. NEW! JUMBO CRAYON CANDLES
8 candles color their birthday happy.
2811-Y-226 $1.49 pkg.

24. NEW! CRAYON CANDLES
10 candles for a big time party.
2811-Y-227 $1.49 pkg.

Note: For safety reasons, these candles are fit with a short wick and will self-extinguish before burning completely.

1. NEW! BIG BIRD CANDLES
$2.79 each 3 in. high.
2811-Y-911 Big Bird #1
2811-Y-912 Big Bird #2
2811-Y-913 Big Bird #3
2811-Y-914 Big Bird #4

2. NEW! BIG BIRD HAPPY BIRTHDAY CANDLES
2811-Y-910 $2.79 each
Sesame Street Characters
© Jim Henson Productions, Inc.
All rights reserved.

3. NEW! 5-PC. SIMPSON CANDLE SET 2 to 3 ½ in.
Everyone's wacky favorite.
2811-Y-1990 $3.49 set

4. NEW! MAGGIE SIMPSON #1
Bart's little sister. 3 in. high.
2811-Y-1991 $2.49 each

MATT GROENING
TM & ©1990 Twentieth Century Fox Film Corporation All rights reserved

5. NEW! NUMERAL CANDLES
Number 0 thru 9 and ? Green confetti designs. All 3 in. high. **59¢ each**
Number 0 2811-Y-9100
Number 1 2811-Y-9101
Number 2 2811-Y-9102
Number 3 2811-Y-9103
Number 4 2811-Y-9104
Number 5 2811-Y-9105
Number 6 2811-Y-9106
Number 7 2811-Y-9107
Number 8 2811-Y-9108
Number 9 2811-Y-9109
       ? 2811-Y-9110

6. NEW! HAPPY ANNIVERSARY
Reusable. 2 ¼ x 3 ⅞ in.
2811-Y-495 $1.99 each

7. NEW! HAPPY BIRTHDAY
Decorate quickly. 3 ⅞ x 2 ⅛ in.
2811-Y-490 $1.99 each

8. NEW! TWO HEARTS
Perfect for romantic occasions.
2 ½ x 3 ½ in.
2811-Y-1214 $1.99 each

9. NEW! TEDDY BEAR #1
Kid's favorite. 3 in. high.
2811-Y-100 $2.49 each

10. NEW! TEDDY BEAR HAPPY BIRTHDAY
2 ¼ x 2 ¾ in.
2811-Y-110 $2.49 each

11. NEW! OVER THE HILL-30
Has it been that long!
2 ⅞ x 2 ¼ in.
2811-Y-9111 $1.99 each

12. NEW! OVER THE HILL-40
Say it isn't so. 2 ⅞ x 2 ¼ in.
2811-Y-9112 $1.99 each

13. NEW! RELIGHTING CANDLES 2 ½ in. high.
Have the last laugh. 10 in box.
2811-Y-220 99¢

14. SLENDERS
24 long, slender candles for all occasions. 6 ½ in. high.
2811-Y-1188 79¢

15. NEW! SPARKLERS
Do it with flare. 6½ high, 24 per box.
2811-Y-1230 99¢

16. NEW! CANDLE HOLDERS
Multi-color - 12 per set.
2811-Y-150 79¢ set

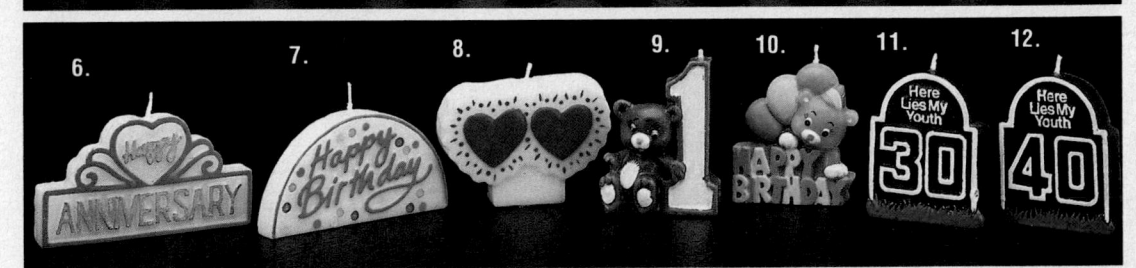

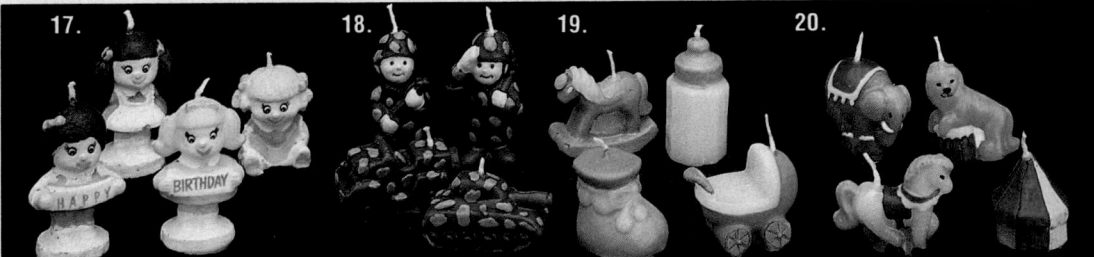

17. NEW! 4-PC. DARLING DOLLS SET
Birthday playmates.
1 ½ to 2 ¼ in. high.
2811-Y-9131 $2.99 set

18. NEW! 4-PC. ARMY SET
Just like the big guys.
1 to 2 in. high.
2811-Y-9130 $2.99 set

19. NEW! 4-PC. NEW ARRIVAL SET
Joyous bundles.
1 ¼ to 2 in. high.
2811-Y-9132 $2.99 set

20. NEW! 4-PC. BIG TOP SET
Circus time ahead.
1 ½ to 2 in. high.
2811-Y-9133 $2.99 set

21. NEW! 4-PC. PLAY BALL SET
Boys of summer. 2 in. high.
2811-Y-9134 $2.99 set

22. 4-PC. PARTY TEDDY BEAR CANDLE SET
1 ¾ in. high. 4 cuddly party favorites.
2811-Y-214 $2.99 set

23. 4-PC. LITTLE DINOSAUR CANDLE SET
Birthday playmates.
1 ¾ in. high.
2811-Y-216 $2.99 set

24. 4-PC. BIRTHDAY TRAIN CANDLE SET
4-piece set
1 in. to 1 ½ in. high.
2811-Y-218 $2.99 set

Note: For safety reasons, these candles are fit with a short wick and will self-extinguish before burning completely.

Introducing an incomparable treasury of keepsake ornaments exquisitely created by noted giftware designer, Ellen Williams. A cherished collection of fine bisque porcelain figurines accented with flowers, satin ribbons and "pearls".

For an inspiring bridal cake, coordinate these magnificent ornaments with Tier Tops and Mini-Bouquets featured on page 152. Designed to accent the lower cake tiers, these charming cake tops match or mix perfectly with the ornaments shown on these pages.

1. NEW! HEAVENLY

A lovely African-American couple beneath a lattice arch of "pearls" on an accordion-pleated base of lace. Hand-painted and hand-crafted porcelain bisque couple. 10 1/2 in. high.

Grey Tux	118-Y-603 $85.00 each
Black Tux	118-Y-604 $85.00 each

2. NEW! SWEETHEARTS

Graceful hand-painted porcelain bisque couple under an arched lace heart trimmed with "pearl" sprays. Hyacinths bloom atop lace-edged base. 9 1/4 in. high.

Grey Tux	118-Y-605 $85.00 each
Black Tux	118-Y-606 $85.00 each

3. GLORIOUS

Charming porcelain bisque figurine afloat on a lace-veiled base punctuated with floral bouquet. Lucite-look backdrop holds a spray of softly cascading lily of the valley. 12 1/2 in. high.

Grey Tux	118-Y-425 $60.00 each
Black Tux	118-Y-420 $60.00 each

4. CLASSIQUE

Timeless romantic porcelain bisque couple between two Gothic pillars edged with soft blooms, "pearls" and crisp pleats of lace. 11 in. high.

Grey Tux	118-Y-410 $50.00 each
Black Tux	118-Y-415 $50.00 each

5. DREAMS COME TRUE

Graceful arch of ribbons, lace and "pearl" dotted posies frame our loving porcelain bisque couple. Lace-edged base is trimmed with flowers and ribbons. 10 1/2 in. high.

Grey Tux	118-Y-400 $60.00 each
Black Tux	118-Y-405 $60.00 each

6. ROSE GARDEN
A glorious floral arch of roses, ribbons and "pearl" sprays frame a loving porcelain bisque couple. 11in. high; includes 6 ½ in. high couple.

White Setting/Grey Tux	118-Y-470	$75.00 each
White Setting/Black Tux	118-Y-475	$75.00 each
Ivory Setting/Grey Tux	118-Y-460	$75.00 each
Ivory Setting/Black Tux	118-Y-465	$75.00 each

7. BEAUTIFUL
Joyous porcelain couple in a mist of tulle, "pearl" leaves, flowers and lace. On a base of leaves trimmed in "pearls". 7 ½ in. high; includes 6 ½ in. high couple.

Grey Tux	118-Y-440	$70.00 each
Black Tux	118-Y 445	$70.00 each

8. TIMELESS
A radiant porcelain bisque couple under a lattice arch of "pearls". Adorned with lovely floral and "pearl" bursts on a lace and "pearl"-trimmed base. 10 in. high; includes 6 ½ in. high couple.

Grey Tux	118-Y-450	$75.00 each
Black Tux	118-Y-455	$75.00 each

9. DELICATE JOY
Solitary tiny porcelain couple on a lacy ruffled base dotted with lovely floral blooms and streamers. 6 in. high; includes 4 ½ in. in. high couple.

Grey Tux	108-Y-640	$40.00 each
Black Tux	108-Y-645	$40.00 each

10. SWEET BEGINNINGS
Lacy heart frames a tiny, joyous porcelain couple. Lace and rose-dotted base is edged with a soft blossom. 9 in. high; includes 4 ½ in. high couple.

Grey Tux	118-Y-495	$60.00 each
Black Tux	118-Y-490	$60.00 each

11. EVERLASTING
A dramatic gazebo is the setting for this glorious tiny porcelain couple. Tulle sprays tied with ribbons and flowing lily of the valley. 11½ in. high; includes 4 ½ in. high couple.

Grey Tux	118-Y-500	$60.00 each
Black Tux	118-Y-505	$60.00 each

Designer Series by Ellen Williams

1. NEW! ALLURE
An enchanting gazebo adorned with a profusion of tulle and satin bows enhances this lovely wedding setting. 11 in. high. Exquisitely detailed matte resin Lasting Love and Happiest Day couples.

White/Ivory	White Couple/Grey Tux	101-Y- 1782
White/Ivory	White Couple/Black Tux	101-Y- 1783
White/Ivory	Black Couple/Grey Tux	101-Y- 1784
White/Ivory	Black Couple/Black Tux	101-Y- 1785

$45.00 each

2. TRUE LOVE
Pearl-adorned swooning doves rest on a pair of "pearl" studded wedding bands. Tufts of tulle and soft roses. 8 1/4 in. high.
103-Y-410 $40.00 each

3. CROWNING GLORY
Two fluttering doves in flight on a lace and "pearl" trimmed heart and satiny bell. Lace also underscores base. 9 1/2 in. high.
103-Y-405 $40.00 each

4. NEW! HEART'S DESIRE
Delicate lace, flowers and ribbons encircle a sweetheart backdrop for a happy beautifully detailed matte resin Sweethearts couple. 8 in. high.

White Couple/Grey Tux	101-Y-1790	$22.00 each
White Couple/Black Tux	101-Y-1791	$22.00 each

5. NEW! LOVE'S DELIGHT
Flowers, ribbons and lace provide a lovely setting for a radiant, finely detailed matte resin Sweethearts couple. 8 1/2 in. high.

White Couple/Grey Tux	101-Y-1786	$22.00 each
White Couple/Black Tux	101-Y-1787	$22.00 each

6. NEW! I DO
Double lucite-look hearts and bells highlighted with blossoms, satin ribbons and "pearls" witness this blessed exchange. Features painstakingly detailed matte resin Lasting Love and Happiest Day couples. 9 in. high.

White/Ivory	White Couple/Grey Tux	101-Y-1778
White/Ivory	White Couple/Black Tux	101-Y-1779
White/Ivory	Black Couple/Grey Tux	101-Y-1780
White/Ivory	Black Couple/Black Tux	101-Y-1781

7. NEW! GARDEN DELIGHT
Breathtaking spiral holds a topiary of blooms and long streamers of ribbons and "pearls" accenting lovely detailed matte resin Lasting Love and Happiest Day couples. Lucite-look backdrop adds drama to the scene. 10 in. high.

White Couple/Grey Tux	101-Y-1774	$40.00 each
White Couple/Black Tux	101-Y-1775	$40.00 each
Black Couple/Grey Tux	101-Y-1776	$40.00 each
Black Couple/Black Tux	101-Y-1777	$40.00 each

8. NEW! WEDDING DREAM
A lacy-adorned arch, golden rings and ribbon bows for a sweet, gorgeously detailed matte resin Sweethearts couple. 9 in. high.

White Couple/Grey Tux	101-Y-1788	$22.00 each
White Couple/Black Tux	101-Y-1789	$22.00 each

9. BLESSED EVENT
Two satin and "pearl" trimmed bells toll this most sacred union. "Gold" cross crowns with bloom-filled ornament. 9 in. high.
103-Y-845 $40.00 each

10. INSPIRATION
The gilded cross is highlighted on a petal base flowing with tulle bursts. A soft bouquet of posies drapes cross and base. 6 1/2 in. high.
106-Y-355 $16.00 each

11. MAGICAL
Ringing in this romantic event are satin bells wrapped with a shimmery gold or silver-edged ribbon. All under a lucite-look heart. A wonderful accent for wedding or anniversary cakes. 9 in. high.
Gold 103-Y-1473 $40.00 each
Silver 103-Y-1474 $40.00 each

12. OPULENCE
"Pearl"-adorned wedding bands shimmer on a base of "pearl" leaves and accordion-pleated lace. 6 1/2 in. high.
103-Y-420 $40.00 each

13. EXUBERANCE
Two graceful swans float on a lace-trimmed base. Both glide under a shower of flowing tulle and "pearl" decked buds. 7 in. high.
103-Y-440 $25.00 each

14. LOVE FOREVER
A pair of elegant swans carrying bouquets of blossoms on a base of lace ruffles. Open-heart backdrop is treated with lace and pearl stamens. 6 1/4 in. high.
103-Y-435 $25.00 each

15. REJOICE
Our beautiful bells toll the joyous message of love and wedding good wishes. Decked with bows, blooms and pearl sprays. 7 1/2 in. high.
103-Y-415 $35.00 each

16. MASTERPIECE
Ornately-trimmed bells toll out the happiest of wedding messages. Tied with ribbon and set in a lace-trimmed heart. 9 1/2 in. high.
Ivory 103-Y-425 $40.00 each
White 103-Y-430 $40.00 each

Designer Series by Ellen Williams

Introducing the most life-like collection of wedding musicals and figurines in sturdy, matte-finished plastic. Delicately detailed with tulle veiling, hand-painted facial features, and softly-blooming flowers. A keepsake-quality collection from noted giftware designer, Ellen Williams.

1. HAPPIEST DAY COUPLE
Sweetly poised African-American couple ready to exchange vows; with lifelike resin bouquets and headpiece. 4 1/2 in. high.

White Tux	202-Y-305
Black Tux	202-Y-306
Grey Tux	202-Y-304 $6.99 each

2. SWEETHEARTS WHITE COUPLE
Soft tulle veil on modern bride flows over lacy dress. Plastic. 4 1/2 in. high.

Grey Tux	202-Y-307
Black Tux	202-Y-308
White Coat	202-Y-309 $4.99 each

3. LASTING LOVE WHITE COUPLE
Wreath of flowers on bride holds flowing tulle veil. Plastic, with lifelike resin bouquets and headpiece. 4 1/2 in. high.

White Tux	202-Y-303
Black Tux	202-Y-302
Grey Tux	202-Y-301 $6.99 each

4. SWEET SYMPHONY*
A delightful musical couple. Plays "The Wedding March". Hand-painted detail adds life-like quality to this delicately hand-crafted and hand-painted resin piece. This material allows for striking, lifelike detail. 7 3/4 in. high.

Grey Tux	215-Y-775
Black Tux	215-Y-776 $50.00 each

5. DESIGNER BRIDESMAID
So many beautiful jewel and soft tones available to match many bridal color themes; plastic. 4 1/2 in. high. Packaged in sets of 2.

Pink	203-Y-9103
Emerald	203-Y-9104
Light Mauve	203-Y-9105
Light Blue	203-Y-9106
Amethyst	203-Y-9107
Raspberry	203-Y-9108
Sapphire	203-Y-9109
Black	203-Y-9110 $3.69 set of 2

6. DESIGNER GROOMSMAN
Handsome groomsman. In attractive matte finish; plastic. 4 1/2 in. high. Packaged in sets of 2.

White Tux	203-Y-9100
Black Tux	203-Y-9101
Grey Tux	203-Y-9102 $3.69 set of 2

*musical

Why not add to the magic of that wonderful day with enchanted figurines and musical ornaments? Hand-crafted and hand-painted fine porcelain bisque figurines of keepsake quality, often with "pearl" accents.

7. MARY AND CHARLES*
This musical creation echoes fond memories of the past. Turn-of-the-century couple stands on a base of bells and flowers. Plays "Clair de Lune." 8 in. high.
215-Y-772 $75.00

8. ASHLEY AND STEVEN*
Lovely musical ornament makes a perfect wedding keepsake. Modern couple on a base of bells and flowers. Plays "Through the Eyes of Love".
8 1/2 in. high.
215-Y-773 $75.00

9. PERFECT HARMONY*
Engaging modern African-American couple created with a keen eye for detail. Bride radiates with "pearl" necklace and beautiful handcrafted rose bouquet. Plays "The Wedding March". 8 in. high.
215-Y-771 $110.00

10. TOGETHER FOREVER*
Traditional wedding couple. "Pearl"-accented bride has graceful tulle veil and bouquet with] satin and "pearl" ribbons. Plays "The Wedding March". 8 in. high.
215-Y-770 $110.00

11. ONE DREAM COUPLE
Loving Ellen Williams couple stands ready to exchange wedding vows. In fine porcelain.
6 in. high.
214-Y-420 Grey Tuxedo $25.00
214-Y-425 Black Tuxedo $25.00

12. TOGETHER FOREVER COUPLE
Romantic Ellen Williams porcelain couple in a traditional bridal pose. 6 1/2 in. high.
214-Y-400 Grey Tuxedo $35.00
214-Y-405 Black Tuxedo $35.00

13. PERFECT HARMONY COUPLE
Avant garde couple in fine porcelain from Ellen Williams. African-American pair hold hands while exchanging vows. 6 1/2 in. high.
214-Y-603 Grey Tuxedo $39.50
214-Y-604 Black Tuxedo $39.50

14. ADORING COUPLE
Dainty Ellen Williams pair dance their all-important first waltz with stars in their eyes. 5 7/8 in. high.
214-Y-605 Grey Tuxedo $45.00
214-Y-606 Black Tuxedo $45.00

15. PETITE TOGETHER FOREVER COUPLE
Petite Ellen Williams porcelain figure is perfect for cakes and table settings. 4 1/2 in. high.
214-Y-437 Grey Tuxedo $30.00
214-Y-439 Black Tuxedo $30.00

*musical

© 1991 EHW Enterprises, Inc
Licensee Wilton Enterprises
Porcelain Figurines Crafted by *Roman, Inc.*

The Ellen Williams Tier Top Collection provides many designs to mix and match with any of her wedding ornaments. These delicate poufs complement a cake beautifully when used between the tiers and on side cakes. Lovely as party favors and table decorations, too.

1. *NEW! MINI-BOUQUET*
Soft floral bouquet set on field of cameo lace. Base diameter 4 inches. Exciting look attached to pillars or cakes as well as placed between tiers.
211-Y-604 pack of 3 $18.00 pack of 3

2. *SHIMMERING RIBBON TIER TOP*
Satin-striped ribbon bows; blooming flowers touched with "pearl" sprays. Base diameter 4$^7/8$ inches. Lovely complements for Rejoice and Rose Garden.
211-Y-1993 $12.50 each

3. *BLOSSOM TIER TOP*
Contemporary spray with tulle and "pearl"-decked flowers. Base diameter 4$^7/8$ inches. Beautiful with Masterpiece, Dreams Come True and Glorious.
211-Y-1991 $7.50 each

4. *PEARL LEAVES TIER TOP*
Delicate pearl leaves peek through tufts of tulle and "pearl"-trimmed blossoms. Base diameter 4$^7/8$ inches. An exciting match for Opulence, Beautiful and True Love.
211-Y-1994 $15.00 each

5. *PEARL TIER TOP*
"Pearl" wisps decorate blooms and flower sprays. Base diameter 4 inches. For a dramatic cake use with Crowning Glory, Timeless and Classique.
211-Y-1992 $12.50 each

Loving TRADITIONS™

1-3. RING BEARER'S PILLOW
Choose from tailored look with classic or embellished treatments. Square pillows approximately 10 1/2 x 10 1/2 in .

Lacy Square-Ivory	120-Y-107	$20.00 each
Lacy Square-White	120-Y-106	$20.00 each
Pearl Heart-White	120-Y-100	$16.00 each
Floral Square-White	120-Y-104	$16.00 each

4. BRIDE'S PURSE
Dainty satin drawstring bag punctuated with fabric flowers and pearl trim. 11 x 13 in.
120-Y-601 $15.00 each

5. BRIDE'S GARTER
Traditional feminine accessory. Delicate and lacy garter is trimmed with satin band, ribbons.

Pink	120-Y-400
Blue	120-Y-402
White	120-Y-401
Ivory	120-Y-403
Black	120-Y-404 $5.00 each

6. BRIDE'S HANDKERCHIEF
Lacy cotton handkerchief to tuck into handbag.

White	120-Y-500	$5.00 each
Blue	120-Y-502	$5.00 each
Ivory	120-Y-501	$5.00 each

7. CHAMPAGNE GLASSES SET
Leaded crystal, for that memorable toast. Sold in sets of 2 glasses. Saucer set. Embossed with our exclusive Loving Traditions design. 4 3/4 high.

Bride and Groom	120-Y-210	$24.00 set
Anniversary Wishes	120-Y-211	$24.00 set

8. SHERBET GLASSES SET
Enhanced with satin ribbons. 4 1/2" high.

Bride and Groom	120-Y-203	$14.00 set
Anniversary Wishes	120-Y-205	$14.00 set

9. TOASTING GLASSES SET
Fluted leaded crystal glasses etched with beautiful roses. 8 3/8" high.

Bride & Groom Set	120-Y-200	$24.00 set
Anniversary Set	120-Y-202	$24.00 set

10. WEDDING BELL
Leaded crystal etched with traditional bridal couple design. Trimmed with satin ribbon bow and crystal-look clapper. 6" high.
120-Y-900 $17.50 each

11. CAKE & KNIFE SERVERS
Shining stainless with beautifully detailed handles. Tied with sprays of flowers, ribbons and "pearls".

Cake Knife	120-Y-701	$13.50 each
Cake Server	120-Y-702	$13.50 each
Knife & Server Set	120-Y-700	$24.00 set

153

1. FIRST WALTZ
A tender moment immortalized in glazed porcelain by *Roman, Inc.* A time to cherish forever. Gothic arched windows reflect their love. Delicate lace and tulle encircle the lovely pair. 7 1/4 in. high.
118-Y-435 $55.00 each

2. MOONLIGHT SERENADE
Romantic couple share an embrace under a flowery archway on a lace-veiled base. Glazed porcelain figurine crafted by *Roman, Inc.* 8 3/4 in. high.
118-Y-430 $55.00 each
©1988 *Roman, Inc.*

3. SOPHISTICATION
Beautiful porcelain bride and groom under a burst of lily of the valley and soft tulle. Dotted with dramatic shimmery "pearls". 8 1/2 in. high.
White Coat 117-Y-202 $45.00 each
Black Coat 117-Y-201 $45.00 each

4. NEW! WEDDING BLISS
Lacy double-ring archway surrounds a beautiful porcelain pair as they exchange vows. Lovely blooms and lace abound. 10 1/2 in. high.
White Coat 117-Y-7331 $28.00 each
Black Coat 117-Y-7332 $28.00 each

5. BRIDAL WALTZ
Making that all-important commitment in perfect unison. Charming arched windows share a view of our porcelain couple gliding in graceful harmony. Ruffles of lace and tulle decorate the bead-embossed base and outline windows. 7 1/2 in. high.

Coat	Ornament	Stock No.	Price
White	White	117-Y-321	$40.00 each
Black	White	117-Y-322	$40.00 each
White	Ivory	117-Y-329	$40.00 each
Black	Ivory	117-Y-330	$40.00 each

6. LOVE'S FANFARE
Lavish flourish and flair. Full fan and ruffly pouf of lace lavish our exquisitely detailed porcelain couple. A wreath of flowers and pearl strands float on lacy waves. Scalloped base not included. 8 in. high.
White Coat 117-Y-401 $50.00 each
Black Coat 117-Y-402 $50.00 each

7. NEW! ORCHID CASCADE
Embracing porcelain couple dancing beneath a soft canopy of blooming orchids. 9 in. high.
White Coat 117-Y-7333 $33.00 each
Black Coat 117-Y-7334 $33.00 each

8. LUSTROUS LOVE
A burst of tulle peaks from behind lace leaves; dotted with forget-me-nots and rimmed with gleaming "pearls". Satiny roses bloom while "pearls" are suspended on transparent strings around the happy glazed porcelain couple. 8 in. high.
White   117-Y-621 $35.00 each
Pink   117-Y-623 $35.00 each

9. SPLENDID
Sweeping curve of lucite-look surrounds adoring glazed porcelain pair. Cylindrical vase holds a matching spray of flowers that accents base. Add real flowers if you wish. 10 1/2 in. high.
White   117-Y-506 $28.00 each
Pink   117-Y-507 $28.00 each
Peach   117-Y-450 $28.00 each

10. GARDEN ROMANCE
Charming porcelain couple stands in a gazebo decked with flowery vines. Clusters of tulle and ribbons complete this romantic hideaway. 10 1/2 in. high.
White Iridescent 117-Y-711 $30.00 each

11. RHAPSODY
Contemporary belled arch is dotted with flowers and tulle. Stylized porcelain couple stands on crystal-look base, trimmed with tulle puff and floral spray. 9 1/2 in. high.
Pink   117-Y-305 $25.00 each
White   117-Y-301 $25.00 each

12. REFLECTIONS
Sleek, stream-lined and sophisticated. Dramatic lucite-look backdrop reflects porcelain couple, tulle burst, "pearl" sprays and florals. 8 in. high.
Blue   117-Y-130 $25.00 each
White   117-Y-268 $25.00 each
Pink   117-Y-297 $25.00 each

13. ECSTASY
Sprays of flowers and leaves surround the romantic porcelain pair. Delicate tulle forms a lovely base. 9 1/2 in. high.
White   117-Y-831 $40.00 each

14. PROMISE
Simple beauty. Dramatic lucite-look heart frames dainty white porcelain couple. Crystal-look base is covered with tulle, ribbons and fabric flowers. 9 5/8 in. high.
White   117-Y-315 $25.00 each
Pink   117-Y-311 $25.00 each

15. DEVOTION
Lucite-look arch is framed with gathered tulle and lace. Glazed porcelain couple stands on pedestal base in burst of tulle, blooms and pearl strands. 9 1/2 in. high.
White   117-Y-425 $25.00 each

8. 9.

10. 11. 12.

13. 14. 15.

1. NEW! TENDER LOVE
Tulle spray sets the backdrop for couple exchanging vows. 8 1/2 in. high.

Coat	Couple	Stock No.	Each
White	White	114-Y-402	$17.00
Black	White	114-Y-403	$17.00
Grey	White	114-Y-401	$17.00

2. NEW! CASCADE OF LOVE
Loving couple under a half arch of leaves and tulle. 9 1/2 in. high.

Coat	Couple	Stock No.	Each
White	White	114-Y-410	$20.00
Black	White	114-Y-411	$20.00
Grey	White	114-Y-412	$20.00
White	Black	116-Y-404	$20.00
Black	Black	116-Y-405	$20.00
Grey	Black	116-Y-406	$20.00

3. NEW! SIMPLICITY
Embracing couple stands in front of filigree heart. Petal base is trimmed with budding rose and tulle. 8 3/4 in. high.

Coat	Couple	Stock No.	Each
White	White	114-Y-407	$14.00
Black	White	114-Y-408	$14.00
Grey	White	114-Y-409	$14.00
White	Black	116-Y-402	$14.00
Black	Black	116-Y-401	$14.00
Grey	Black	116-Y-403	$14.00

4. NEW! MAGIC MOMENT
Gazing couple is encircled by open filigree heart. Soft blooms open on base. 11 in. high.

White Coat 114-Y-404 $20.00 each
Black Coat 114-Y-405 $20.00 each
Grey Coat   114-Y-406 $20.00 each

5. MOONLIT SNOW
Circle of blooms and "pearl" clusters surround gazing couple. On a lace-adorned base. 9 in. high.

Coat	Couple	Stock No.	Each
White	White	114-Y-201	$25.00
Black	White	114-Y-202	$25.00
White	Black	114-Y-207	$25.00
Black	Black	114-Y-208	$25.00
Grey	Black	114-Y-210	$25.00
Grey	White	114-Y-209	$25.00

6. PETITE DOUBLE RING COUPLE
Fluttering birds rest on double rings to witness this blessed event. 5 1/2 in. high.
Black Coat 104-Y-42413 $7.00 each
White Coat 104-Y-42420 $7.00 each

7. SWEET CEREMONY
Seed pearl hearts frame glistening bell. Bride and heart frame are accented with tulle. 10 in. high.
White Coat 101-Y-22028 $14.00 each
Black Coat 101-Y-22011 $14.00 each
Grey Coat   101-Y-22045 $14.00 each

8. PETITE LOVERS IN LACE
It says it all. Glowing couple beneath a double arch of lace. 7 in. high.

Coat	Couple	Stock No.	Each
Grey	Black	104-Y-842	$10.00
Grey	White	104-Y-834	$10.00
Black	Black	104-Y-302	$10.00
White	Black	104-Y-301	$10.00
Black	White	104-Y-818	$10.00
White	White	104-Y-826	$10.00

9. MORNING ROSEBUD
Doves in flight above open gate. Soft fabric flowers dot landscape. 8 in. high.
White Coat 101-Y-44020 $10.00 each
Black Coat 101-Y-44013 $10.00 each

10. EVERLASTING LOVE
Graceful arches of lace and filigree heart, dotted with tulle and wedding bands, surround floral filled bell. 10 in. high.
103-Y-236 $16.00 each

11. SPRING SONG
Perching lovebirds sing their romantic love songs in a garden of posies and tulle. 9 1/2 in. high.
111-Y-2802 $16.00 each

12. VICTORIAN CHARM
Graceful ribbon loops and fantasy florals layer over romantic satin five-bell cluster. 7 1/2 in. high.

Ivory	103-Y-1586	$20.00 each
White	103-Y-1587	$20.00 each

13. CIRCLES OF LOVE
Symbolic double rings and doves in a hideaway of flowers and "pearl" sprays. 10 in. high.

White	103-Y-9004	$25.00 each

14. HEARTS TAKE WING
Romantic beak-to-beak birds perched on a setting of heart-shaped branches and tulle. 10 1/2 in. high.
103-Y-6218 $12.00 each

15. WEDDING BELLS
Filigree bell clusters in a generous spray of tulle and lace. 10 1/2 in. high.
103-Y-1356 $16.00 each

16. SATIN ELEGANCE
Lace-edged satin heart bursting with "pearls", flowers and tulle bears a pair of wedding rings. 7 in. high.
Ivory
  on ivory base **109-Y-1002 $20.00 each**
White
  on white base **109-Y-1001 $20.00 each**

PETITE ORNAMENTS

ANNIVERSARY ORNAMENTS

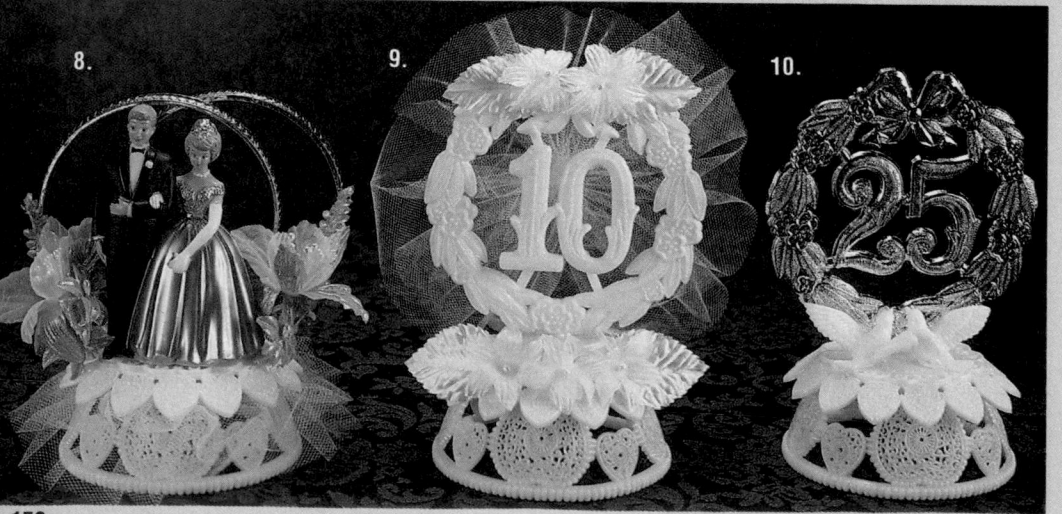

1. PETITE BELLS OF JOY
Eye-catching cluster of white filigree bells enhanced with fabric roses, lace-covered arches and tulle. 7 in. high.
White   106-Y-2658 $12.00 each

2. NATURAL BEAUTY
Singing lovebirds beneath filigree heart trimmed with lily of the valley and a smooth satin bow. 6 in. high.
Peach   106-Y-1104 $10.00 each
Pink   106-Y-1120 $10.00 each
White   106-Y-1163 $10.00 each

3. PETITE DOUBLE RING
Graceful doves land on simple wedding bands on heart base. Adorned with tulle puff. 5 1/2 in. high.
106-Y-4316 $6.00 each

4. LA BELLE PETITE
Tolling bell surrounded by tulle glimmers with iridescence. 5 1/2 in. high.
White   106-Y-248 $9.00 each

5. PETITE SPRING SONG
A dainty song bird duet arched in flowers, "pearls" and tulle. 7 in. high.
White   106-Y-159 $11.00 each
Pink   106-Y-160 $11.00 each
Peach   106-Y-161 $11.00 each

6. 25 OR 50 YEARS OF HAPPINESS
In gold or silver, the number tells the happy story. Accented with blooms and shimmering leaves. 10 in. high.
25TH   102-Y-207 $16.00 each
50TH   102-Y-223 $16.00 each

7. GOLDEN/SILVER JUBILEE
An event that calls for serious celebration. Say it in gold or silver tulle. Couple is on numeral wreath with orchids and ferns. 8 1/2 in. high.
Gold   102-Y-1250 $16.00 each
Silver   102-Y-1225 $16.00 each

8. PETITE DOUBLE RING DEVOTION
Celebrating couple surrounded by rings and the shimmer of pearls and ferns. 5 in. high.
25th Silver 105-Y-4613 $9.00 each
50th Gold   105-Y-4605 $9.00 each

9. PETITE ANNIVERSARY YEARS
The addition of beautiful blooms adds appeal to this versatile favorite. Embossed wreath holds snap-on numbers—5, 10, 15, 20, 40. 5 3/4 in. high.
105-Y-4257 $7.00 each

10. PETITE ANNIVERSARY
Shining numeral wreath is highlighted by two fluttering doves. 5 1/2 in. high.
25th   105-Y-4265 $6.00 each
50th   105-Y-4273 $6.00 each

11. MOONLIT SNOW COUPLE
Plastic. 4³/₄ in. high.

Coat	Couple	Stock No.	Each
White	White	214-Y-5G3	$4.49
Black	White	214-Y-555	$4.49
Grey	White	214-Y-704	$4.49
White	Black	214-Y-302	$4.49
Black	Black	214-Y-301	$4.49
Grey	Black	214-Y-703	$4.49

12. CLASSIC COUPLE
Plastic, 4 ¹/₂ in. high.

Coat	Couple	Stock No.	Each
White	White	202-Y-8121	$4.69
Black	White	202-Y-8110	$4.69
Grey	White	202-Y-300	$4.69

Plastic, 3 ¹/₂ in. high. Petite.

Coat	Couple	Stock No.	Each
White	White	203-Y-8221	$3.99
Black	White	2102-Y-820	$3.99
Grey	White	203-Y-304	$3.99
White	Black	203-Y-301	$3.99
Black	Black	203-Y-302	$3.99
Grey	Black	203-Y-303	$3.99

13. ANNIVERSARY COUPLE
Gold or silver gown. Plastic. 4 ¹/₂ in. high.
25th Silver 203-Y-2828 $3.99 each
50th Gold 203-Y-1821 $3.99 each

14. BRIDESMAIDS
Plastic, 3 ¹/₂ in. high. 2 per package.

White	203-Y-0279	$1.99 pkg. of 2
Pink	203-Y-0281	$1.99 pkg. of 2
Blue	203-Y-0278	$1.99 pkg. of 2
Yellow	203-Y-0280	$1.99 pkg. of 2

15. GROOMSMEN
Plastic, 3 ¹/₂ in. high. 2 per package.

Black Coat	203-Y-0282	$1.99 pkg. of 2
White Coat	203-Y-0283	$1.99 pkg. of 2
All White	203-Y-0277	$1.99 pkg. of 2

16. PARTY PARASOLS
4 in. plastic parasols; 5 in. snap-on handles.
2110-Y-9296 (Pack of 4) $1.69 each

17. LIBERATED BRIDE
Plastic, 4 ¹/₂ in. high.
2113-Y-4188 $3.99 each

18. RELUCTANT GROOM COUPLE
Plastic, 4 ¹/₂ in. high.
1316-Y-9520 $4.99 each

19. PEARL LEAF PUFF
5¹/₂ in. tulle puff with "pearls".
White 211-Y-1125 $4.69 each

20. FLORAL PUFF ACCENT
5 ¹/₂ in. tulle puff with soft flowers and "pearl" sprays.
White 211-Y-1011 $2.99 each
Pink 211-Y-1013 $2.99 each

21. FLOWER BASKET
Plastic basket ready to decorate.
3 x 2 x 2 ³/₄ in.
White 1008-Y-299 99¢ each

22. ARTIFICIAL LEAVES
Green or white cloth; gold or silver foil.
(Add 1005 -Y- prefix before number.)

Color	1⁷/₈"	Per pkg.	1¹/₄"	Per pkg.	#Per pkg.
Gold	6518	$2.59	6712	$2.29	144
Silver	6526	$2.59	6720	$2.29	144
Green	7555	$2.59	7570	$2.29	72
White	7565	$2.59			

23. PEARL LEAVES
2 per package. 2 ¹/₄ in. long.
211-Y-1201 $2.99 per pkg.

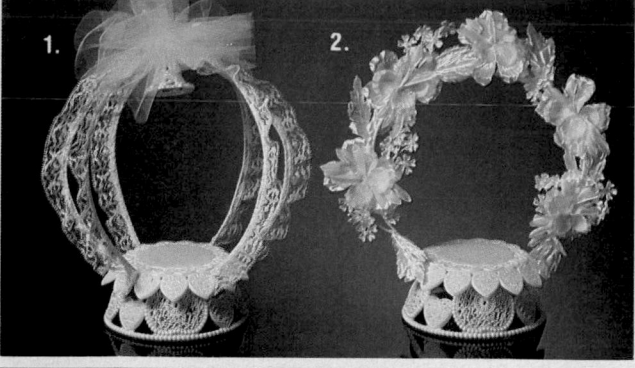

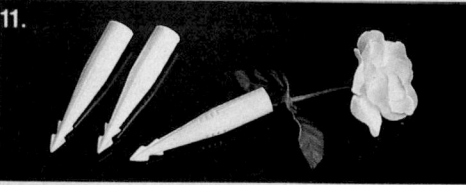

1. CIRCLES OF LACE
10 in. high.
210-Y-1986 $8.99 each

2. FLORAL ARCH
10-in. high.
210-Y-1987 $8.99 each

3. FLORAL BASE
White, 1 1/2 in. high, 4 3/4 in. diameter.
201-Y-1815 $1.99 each

4. CRYSTAL-LOOK BASE
1 3/4 in. high, 4 1/2 in. diameter.
201-Y-1450 $2.99 each

5. PETITE PEDESTAL BASE
3 1/2 in. top; 4 in. diameter base. White.
201-Y-1133 $1.99 each

6. ROMANTIC HEART BASE
White openwork, 2 pcs. 1 1/2 in. high.
4 1/2 in. **201-Y-7332 $2.99 each**
3 1/4 in. **201-Y-7847 $2.69 each**

7. FLORAL SCROLL BASE
Victorian Charm. 4 1/2 X 2 1/2 in. 2 pcs.
White 201-Y-1303 $2.99 each
Ivory 201-Y-305 $2.99 each

8. FILIGREE BELLS

Height	Stock No.	Price	Pack
1 in.	1001-Y-9447	$1.79	12
1 7/8 in.	1001-Y-9422	$1.79	6
2 1/4 in.	1001-Y-9439	$2.29	6
2 5/8 in.	1001-Y-9404	$1.59	3
3 1/2 in.	1001-Y-9411	$1.89	3

9. GLITTERED BELLS

Height	Stock No.	Price	Pack
1 in.	1007-Y-9061	$2.99	12
1 3/8 in.	2110-Y-9075	$1.09	6
1 7/8 in.	1007-Y-9088	$2.49	6
2 1/2 in.	2110-Y-9090	$2.49	6
4 1/4 in.	1007-Y-9110	$2.99	1

10. SMALL WEDDING RINGS
5/8 in. diam.
Silver 1002-Y-1016
Golden 1002-Y-1008
$1.59 pack of 24

11. FLOWER SPIKES
Fill with water, push into cake and add flowers.
3 in. high.
1008-Y-408 $2.49 pack of 12

12. LOVE DOVES
4 x 2 3/4 in.
1002-Y-1806 $2.99 pack of 2

13. SONG BIRD
4 3/4 in. high
1316-Y-1202 $3.99 each

14. PETITE SONG BIRDS
2 1/4 in.
1316-Y-1210 $2.99 pack of 4

15. KISSING LOVE BIRDS
Beak-to-beak romantics. 5 1/2 in. high.
1002-Y-206 $4.99 each

16. SMALL DOVES
2 x 1 1/2 in.
1002-Y-1710 $1.99 pack of 12

17. GLITTERED DOVES
2 x 1 1/2 in. Coated with non-edible glitter.
1006-Y-166 $1.69 pack of 12

18. SERENE SWANS
A graceful and stately pair. 2 1/2 in. high.
1002-Y-11 $1.99 pack of 2

1. NEW! BLACK, SILVER, GOLD PEARL BEADING, WHITE PEARL BEADING

One of the most innovative creations to happen to cake decorating in years. With just one continuous row of lustrous pearls you can transform a beautiful cake into a glorious work of art. Stunning and easy to work with, these pearls will be a must for all serious decorators. The pearls are easy to use as they are molded on one continuous 5 yard strand and can be easily cut to size.

To use: Work with long, continuous strands. Position before icing crusts. Trim after pearls are in position to insure exact measure. Do not trim smaller than 6" lengths. Remove pearls before cutting and serving cake.

Color	Size	Stock No.	Price
White	6 mm	211-Y-1990	$2.99
White	4 mm	211-Y-1989	$2.49
Black	6 mm	211-Y-1984	$3.79
Black	4 mm	211-Y-1982	$3.29
Silver	6 mm	211-Y-1980	$2.99
Silver	4 mm	211-Y-1978	$2.49
Gold	6 mm	211-Y-1988	$2.99
Gold	4 mm	211-Y-1986	$2.49

2. CRYSTAL-LOOK HEARTS
Can be background for many varied settings.
5 1/2 in. 205-Y-1674 $1.99 each
4 1/4 in. 205-Y-1672 $1.79 each

3. CURVED GOTHIC WINDOW
Pretty stand for flowers, couple, more!
5 x 9 in. 2 pcs.
205-Y-3059 $3.99 set

4. GARDEN GATE
Gate swings. 5 1/2 X 5 1/4 in.
205-Y-344 $2.99 each

5. GAZEBO
5 x 9 in. Easy to assemble.
205-Y-8298 $4.69 set

6. GOTHIC ARCH
Plastic pieces simply lock together for easy assembly. 10 1/2 in. high.
205-Y-3109 $4.99 set

7. FORMAL RAILINGS
2 5/8 in. posts, 1 in. pegs, 144 snap-together links.
1107-Y-8326 $2.49 set

8. DOUBLE WEDDING BANDS
3 1/2 in. diameter.
White 201-Y-1008 $1.99 each

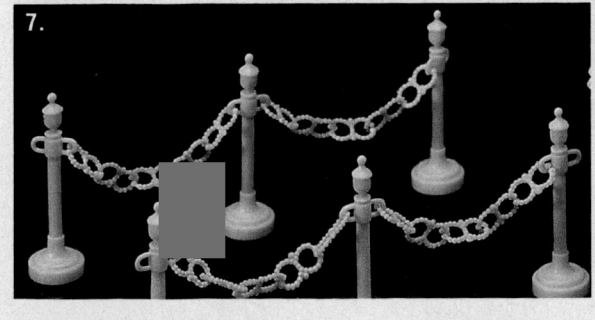

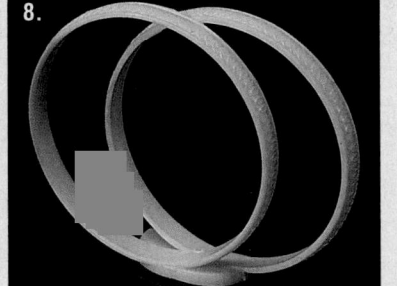

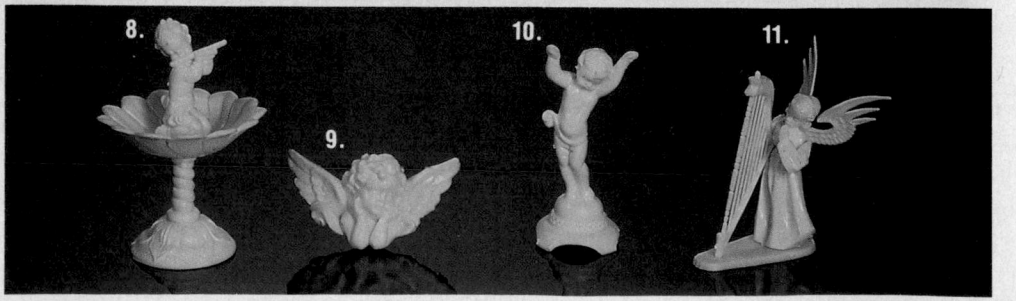

1. ARCHED TIER SET

Quite dramatic when used with Kolor-Flo Fountain. Includes: Six 13 in. arched columns, two super strong 18 in. round Decorator Preferred Separator Plates, and six angelic cherubs to attach to columns with royal icing or glue.
301-Y-1982 $44.99 set
18 in. Decorator Preferred Plate
302-Y-18 $10.99 each
13 in. Pillars
303-Y-9719 $3.99 each
13 in. Pillars
Save $4.95 on pack of six.
301-Y-9809 $18.99 pack of 6

2. HARVEST CHERUB SEPARATOR SET

Includes four 7 in. Harvest Cherub pillars, two 9 in. separator plates (lower plate has 12 in. overall diameter).
301-Y-3517 $11.99 set

3. DANCING CUPID PILLARS

5 1/2 in. high.
303-Y-1210 $7.99 pack of 4

4. CHERUB SNAP-ONS

Accent 5 and 7 in. Grecian pillars. (Pillars not included). 3 1/2 in. high.
305-Y-4104 $1.29 pack of 4

5. FROLICKING CHERUB

Animated character. 5 in. high.
1001-Y-244 $2.79 each

6. ANGEL DUET

Fluttering fancies. A pair per package. 2 1/2 x 2 in.
1001-Y-457 $1.80 pack of 2

7. MUSICAL TRIO

Setting just the right mood. Each 3 in. high.
1001-Y-368 $2.29 pack of 3

8. KNEELING CHERUB FOUNTAIN

Beautiful when accented with tinted piping gel and flowers. 4 in. high.
1001-Y-9380 $1.99 each

9. ANGELINOS

Heavenly addition to wedding, birthday and holiday cakes. 2 x 3 in.
1001-Y-504 $3.29 pack of 6

10. CHERUB CARD HOLDER

What neat place makers, too. (Cards not included). 1 5/8 x 3 3/8 in.
1001-Y-9374 $3.49 pack of 4

11. HEAVENLY HARPIST

Striking the perfect chord. 3 1/2 in. high.
1001-Y-7029 $4.49 pack of 4

1. CRYSTAL BRIDGE AND GRACEFUL STAIRWAY SET
Create a dramatic masterpiece. Includes two stairways (16 3/4 in. long) and one platform (4 3/4 in. X 5 in.). Plastic.
205-Y-2311 $14.99 set
One Stairway Only
205-Y-2315 $7.99 each

2. FILIGREE PLATFORM AND STAIRWAY SET
Bridge the gap between lavish tiers. Includes two stairways (16 3/4 in. long) and one platform (4 3/4 in. x 5 in.). White plastic.
205-Y-2109 $11.99 Set
One Stairway Only
205-Y-1218 $4.99 each

3. THE KOLOR-FLO FOUNTAIN
Cascading waterfall with shimmering lights is the most dramatic way to underscore elegant formal tiers. Water pours from three levels. Top levels can be removed for smaller fountain arrangement. Intricate lighting system with two bulbs for extra brilliance. Plastic fountain bowl is 9 3/4 in. diameter. 110-124v. A.C. motor with 65 in. cord. Pumps water electrically. Directions and replacement part information included.
306-Y-2599 $89.99 each

Replacement Parts

Part	Number	Price
Pump	306-Y-1002	$34.99
Piston	306-Y-1029	$ 2.99
Pump/Bulb Bracket	306-Y-1037	$ 2.79
Lamp Socket	306-Y-1045	$ 4.49
Light Bulb	306-Y-1053	$ 2.49
Cascade/Pump Connector	306-Y-1088	$ 2.29
Floater Switch	306-Y-1096	$11.99
Upper Cascade	306-Y-1118	$ 6.99
Middle Cascade	306-Y-1126	$ 7.99
Lower Cascade	306-Y-1134	$ 8.99
Bowl	306-Y-1142	$12.99
Bottom Base	306-Y-1169	$ 6.99

4. FOUNTAIN CASCADE SET
Dome shapes redirect water over their surface in nonstop streams. Set includes 4 pieces; 2 1/2, 4 1/2, 8 and 11 1/2 in. diameter. (Kolor-Flo Fountain sold separately.)
306-Y-1172 $14.99 set

5. FLOWER HOLDER RING
White plastic. 12 1/2 in. diam. X 2 in. high. Put at base of Kolor-Flo Fountain.
305-Y-435 $4.99 each

6. FILIGREE FOUNTAIN FRAME
Perfect around the Kolor-Flo Fountain. Eight white plastic scallops snap together. 9 in. diameter. 3 1/2 in high.
205-Y-1285 $2.99 each

7. CRYSTAL-LOOK BOWL
Perfect for blooms. 4 1/2 X 1 1/2 in. deep
205-Y-1404 $2.69 each

8. FILIGREE SWIRLS
Variations on a delicate theme. Leaf-framed scrollwork. 4 in. high.
1004-Y-2100 $2.49 pack of 12

9. SCROLLS
Graceful flowing decorations. 2 3/4 x1 1/4 in.
1004-Y-2801 $2.29 pack of 24

10. LACY HEARTS
What delicate beauty. 3 3/4 x 3 1/2 in.
1004-Y-2306 $2.49 pack of 12

11. CURVED TRIANGLE
Dramatic addition. 3 x 3 1/2 in.
1004-Y-3001 $2.49 pack of 12

12. FILIGREE CONTOURS
Lattice and leaves. 3 3/4 x 2 2/3 in.
1004-Y-2003 $2.49 pack of 12

13. IRIDESCENT GRAPES 2" high
1099-Y-200 $3.79 pack of 4

14. IRIDESCENT DOVES 2" wide
1002-Y-509 $3.49 pack of 6

15. FILIGREE GAZEBO 4 pcs. 4 1/4 x 8 1/2 in.
205-Y-4100 $4.69 each

16. FILIGREE HEART FRAMES
7 IN. **205-Y-1501 $2.69 pack of 3**
4 IN. **205-Y-1527 $1.69 pack of 3**

17. SEED PEARL HEART 7 X 6 1/2 in.
205-Y-1006 $3.69 pack of 3

18. FANCY FILIGREE HEART 7 x 6 3/4 in.
1004-Y-2208 $3.79 each

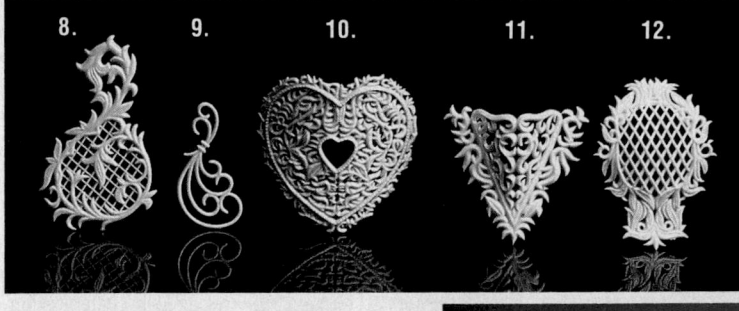

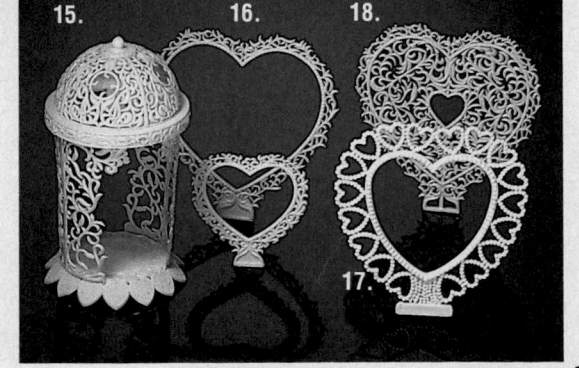

1.

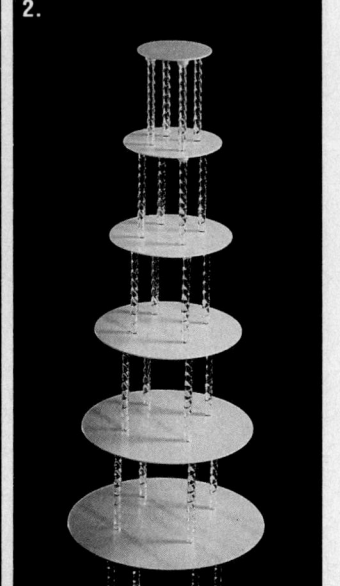

2.

3.

4.

5.

6.

7.

8.

1. FLOATING TIERS CAKE STAND SET

Display three tiers on this graceful white metal cake stand. Fast and easy to use! Set includes stand and 8 in., 12 in., 16 in., smooth-edged separator plates and instructions.

307-Y-825 $62.99 set

Additional plates available (same plates as Crystal-Clear Cake Divider Set).

Plates	Number	Price
8 in.	302-Y-9749	$3.99 each
12 in.	302-Y-9765	$6.99 each
16 in.	302-Y-9780	$10.99 each

2. CRYSTAL-CLEAR CAKE DIVIDER SET

White plastic separator plates; 1/2 in. diameter 7 1/2 in. high; clear plastic twist legs penetrate cake and rest on plate below (dowel rods not needed). Includes 6 in., 8 in., 10 in., 12 in., 14 in., 16 in. plates plus 24 legs. Save 25% on set.

301-Y-9450 $47.99 set

Plates	Number	Price
6 in.	302-Y-9730	$2.99 each
8 in.	302-Y-9749	$3.99 each
10 in.	302-Y-9757	$4.99 each
12 in.	302-Y-9765	$6.99 each
14 in.	302-Y-9773	$8.99 each
16 in.	302-Y-9780	$10.99 each

7 1/2 in. Twist Legs
303-Y-9794 $3.99 pack of 4
9 in. Twist Legs Add more height.
303-Y-977 $3.99 pack of 4

Our new Ruffle Boards™ work beautifully with the two sets above or the spiked pillars on facing page.

3. TALL TIER STAND SET

Five twist-apart columns 6 1/2 in. high with 1 bottom and 1 top bolt; 18 in. footed base plate; 16 in., 14 in., 12 in., 10 in., 8 in. separator plates (interchangeable, except footed base plate). White plastic. Save 25% on set.

304-Y-7915 $45.99 set

Plates	Number	Price
8 in.	302-Y-7894	$3.99 each
10 in.	302-Y-7908	$4.99 each
12 in.	302-Y-7924	$5.99 each
14 in.	302-Y-7940	$8.99 each
16 in.	302-Y-7967	$11.99 each
18 in.	302-Y-7983	$14.99 each
Columns		
6 1/2 IN.	303-Y-7910	$1.59 each
7 3/4 IN.	304-Y-5009	$2.59 each
13 1/2 IN.	303-Y-703	$4.49 each
Top Column Cap Nut	304-Y-7923	79¢ each
Glue-on Plate Legs	304-Y-7930	59¢ each
Bottom Column Bolt	304-Y-7941	99¢ each

4. TALL TIER 4-ARM BASE STAND

Replace Tall Tier Base Plate (See No. 3) with this heavy-duty white plastic support; add separator plates up to 12 in. For proper balance, add up to 3 graduated tiers to center column. Includes base bolt.

304-Y-8245 $11.99 each
Base Bolt Only
304-Y-8253 59¢ each

5. CAKE CORER TUBE

Prepare tiers quickly and neatly for the Tall Tier Stand column. Serrated edge removes cake centers with one push. Ice cake before using. 7 in. long solid center fits into 6 1/2 in. long hollow corer to eject cake bits. Cleans easily.

304-Y-8172 $1.99 each

6. CATHEDRAL CAKE KIT

Transform basic wedding cakes into dramatic masterpieces. Kit includes: 5 easy-to-assemble white church pieces, 4 white plastic cake supports and a church window that can be illuminated from within.

2104-Y-2940 $13.99 kit

7. STAIRSTEPS SET

24 1 in. high stairs with 3 in. candleholders.
1107-Y-8180 $5.49 set

8. SUPER STRONG CAKE STAND

Holds up to 185 pounds of cake! High impact polystyrene and underweb of ribbing make stand super strong. 2 3/4 in. high. 18 in. diameter for larger cakes.

307-Y-1200 $12.99 each

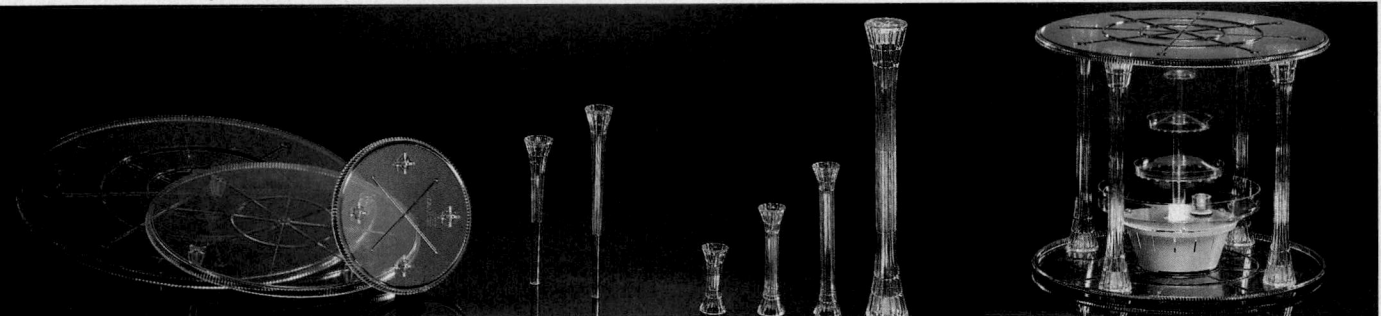

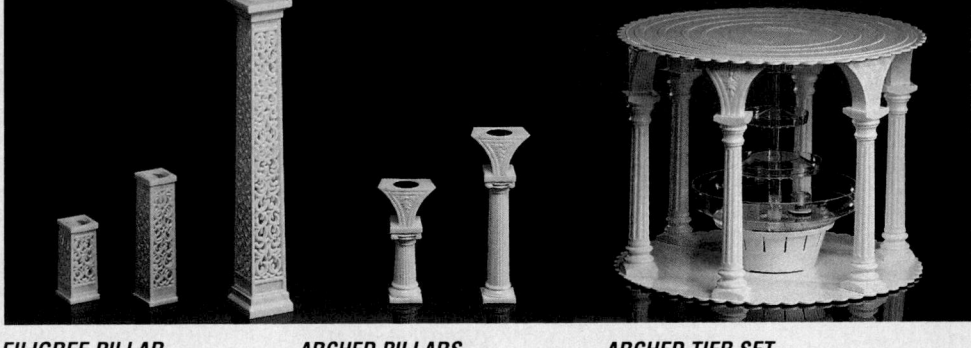

GRECIAN SPIKED PILLARS
Eliminate the need for separator plates on cake tier tops. Push into cake to rest on separator plate or cake circle beneath. Wide diameter bottom for increased stability. For maximum results, double cake boards, or use separator plate when cakes are stacked.
5 in. 303-Y-3708 $1.99 pack of 4
7 in. 303-Y-3710 $2.99 pack of 4
9 in. 303-Y-3712 $3.99 pack of 4

GRECIAN PILLARS
Elegantly scrolled and ribbed.
3 in. 303-Y-3606 $1.99 pk/4
5 in. 303-Y-3703 $2.99 pk/4
7 in. 303-Y-3705 $3.99 pk/4

SWAN PILLARS
Grecian pillars with romantic swan bases add flowering grace to your masterpiece. 4 in. high.
303-Y-7725 $2.99 pack of 4

ROMAN COLUMNS
Handsome pillars may be used with Kolor-Flo Fountain (remove one fountain tier if using 10 1/4 in.).
10¼ in. 303-Y-8135 $2.59 ea
13¾ in. 303-Y-2129 $2.99 ea

SIX-COLUMN TIER SET
Includes six 13 ¾ in. Roman columns and two super strong 18-in. round Decorator Preferred™ Separator Plates. A lovely set to use with the Kolor-Flo Fountain. White plastic.
301-Y-1981 $34.99 set

CRYSTAL-LOOK PLATES
Use with crystal-look pillars.
7 in. 302-Y-2013 $2.99
9 in. 302-Y-2035 $3.99
11 in. 302-Y-2051 $4.99
13 in. 302-Y-2078 $6.99
*17 in. 302-Y-1810 $13.99
*(Use only with 13 ¾ in. crystal pillars.)

CRYSTAL-LOOK SPIKED PILLARS
Push into cake to rest on separator plate or cake circle beneath. Double cake circles for extra support.
7 in. 303-Y-2322 $3.99 pk/4
9 in. 303-Y-2324 $4.99 pk/4

CRYSTAL-LOOK PILLARS
Combine with crystal-look plates and Crystal Bridge and Stairway Set.
3 in. 303-Y-2171 $2.99 pk/4
5 in. 303-Y-2196 $3.99 pk/4
7 in. 303-Y-2197 $4.49 pk/4
*13¾ in. 303-Y-2242 $3.99 ea
*(Use only with 17" crystal plate.)

CRYSTAL-LOOK TIER SET
Teams with the Kolor-Flo Fountain. Plastic. Two 17" plates; four 13 ¾" pillars.
301-Y-1387 $41.99 set

PLATE PEGS
Insure that cake layers and separator plates atop cakes stay in place. These pegs do not add support, so dowel rod cake properly before using. 4 in. long.
399-Y-762 $1.44 set of 12

PLASTIC STUD PLATES
Just glue on to sturdy cardboard cake circles to create separator plate. Real money-savers, especially when cake is to be given away. Fit all white (not crystal) pillars, except 13 in. Arched Pillars.
301-Y-119 $1.79 pack of 8

FILIGREE PILLAR
Airy, **lacy look** open designs on these square, pillars. Just add ribbons or fabric to coordinate with bride's color scheme. 12-in. high.
3 in. 303-Y-8071 $1.99 pk/4
5 in. 303-Y-7717 $2.99 pk/4
12 in. 303-Y-8976 $2.99 ea

ARCHED PILLARS
Grecian-inspired with arched support
4½ in. 303-Y-452 $2.99 pk/4
6½ in. 303-Y-657 $4.99 pk/4

EXPANDABLE PILLARS
(Not shown.)
Column is made up of six individual sections, adjustable from 3 ins. to 10 ins. high!
303-Y-1777 $8.99 pack of 4

ARCHED TIER SET
Quite dramatic when used with Kolor-Flo Fountain. Includes: Six 13 in. arched columns, two super strong 18 in. round Decorator Pre-ferred Separator Plates, and six angelic cherubs to attach to columns with royal icing or glue. (Cherubs not shown above; shown on p. 162)
301-Y-1982 $44.99 set
18 in. Decorator Preferred Plate
302-Y-18 $10.99 each
13 in. Pillars 303-Y-9719 $3.99 each
13 in. Pillars Save $4.95 on pack of six.
301-Y-9809 $18.99 pack

- **Complete Size Selection**
- **Scalloped Edges**
- **Smooth Back**
- **Easy Identification**

SEPARATOR PLATES

No better way to get your baked masterpieces off to a great foundation! Sturdy, yet beautiful, separator plates bring wedding, shower, anniversary, birthday and even Valentine's Day cakes to new decorating heights. Square, heart and hexagon shapes are edged with delicate scallops; oval has a clean, streamlined beauty.

HEART SEPARATOR PLATES

8 in.	302-Y-2112	$2.99 each
11 in.	302-Y-2114	$3.99 each
14 1/2 in.	302-Y-2116	$7.99 each
16 1/2 in.	302-Y-2118	$8.99 each

SQUARE SEPARATOR PLATES

7 in.	302-Y-1004	$2.99 each
9 in.	302-Y-1020	$3.99 each
11 in.	302-Y-1047	$4.99 each
13 in.	302-Y-1063	$5.99 each

OVAL SEPARATOR PLATES

8 1/2 in. x 6 in.	302-Y-2130	$3.99 each
11 1/2 in. x 8 1/2 in.	302-Y-2131	$4.99 each
14 1/2 in. x 10 3/4 in.	302-Y-2132	$5.99 each

HEXAGON SEPARATOR PLATES

7 in.	302-Y-1705	$2.99 each
10 in.	302-Y-1748	$3.99 each
13 in.	302-Y-1764	$5.99 each
16 in.	302-Y-1799	$7.99 each

DISPOSABLE SINGLE PLATE SYSTEM

The Baker's Best® Disposable Separator system features sturdy plates, pillars and adjustable pillar rings. All made of recyclable plastic.

DISPOSABLE PLATES

6 in. Plate	302-Y-4000	$1.49 each
7 in. Plate	302-Y-4001	$1.69 each
8 in. Plate	302-Y-4002	$1.99 each
9 in. Plate	302-Y-4003	$2.49 each
10 in. Plate	302-Y-4004	$2.89 each
12 in. Plate	302-Y-4006	$3.79 each
14 in. Plate	302-Y-4008	$4.39 each

DISPOSABLE PILLARS WITH RINGS

7 in. Pillar w/Rings (4 each)
303-Y-4000 $2.59 pack of 4

9 in. Pillar w/Rings (4 each)
303-Y-4001 $2.69 pack of 4

DOWEL RODS

DOWEL RODS

Essential for supporting stacked cakes and tiers. Complete assembling instructions on page 106.

PLASTIC DOWEL RODS

Heavy-duty hollow plastic provides strong, sanitary support for all tiered cakes. Can be cut with serrated knife to desired length.
12 3/4 in. long x 3/4 in. diameter
399-Y-801 $2.29 pack of 4

WOODEN DOWEL RODS

Cut and sharpen with strong shears and knife.
12 in. long, 1/4 in. wide.
399-Y-1009 $1.99 pack of 12

Guaranteed Non-Breakable

Decorator Preferred.

- **Circles of Strength™ Construction**

The best, strongest separator plates—with features important to cake decorators:

Circles of Strength™ Construction
An exclusive, patented Wilton design distributes the cake weight evenly. Small, round indentations accommodate plastic pegs (if desired). Plastic "knobs" help secure and hold cardboard cake circle to plate.

CLASSIC SEPARATOR SETS
Stately Grecian pillars and scalloped-edged plates create beautiful settings for all tiered cakes. Sets include 2 Decorated Preferred™ Plates, 4 pillars and 4 pegs.

6 in. Plate Set with 3 in. Pillars
2103-Y-639 $5.99 set
8 in. Plate Set with 5 in Pillars
2103-Y-256 $6.99 set
10 in. Plate Set with 5 in. Pillars
2103-Y-108 $8.99 set
12 in. Plate Set with 5 in. Pillars
2103-Y-124 $10.99 set

54-PC. GRECIAN PILLAR AND PLATE SET
(not shown)
A deluxe collection for the serious cake decorator. Features Decorator Preferred™ scalloped-edged separator plates and 5 inch pillars. Includes: 2 each 6, 8, 10, 12 and 14-inch plates; 20 Grecian pillars and 24 pegs.
301-Y-8380 $45.99 set

Guaranteed Non-Breakable
High impact resin composition means maximum strength for durability, dependability and peak performance. Guaranteed non-breakable under normal use.

Traditional Wilton Scalloped Edges
Decorator Preferred plates also have the lovely scalloped-edge design so they are completely compatible with all Wilton plates and pillars.

Easy Identification
Sizes are clearly marked on each plate for fast, easy identification.

Smooth Back
Reverse side of plates have no printing, so there is nothing to hide. Plain back compliments the most elegant decorating.

When the success of your baked masterpiece depends upon its foundation, you'll be glad you've chosen the undisputable best, Wilton.

Size	Item	Price
6 in.	302-Y-6	$1.99 each
7 in.	302-Y-7	$2.19 each
8 in.	302-Y-8	$2.49 each
9 in.	302-Y-9	$2.99 each
10 in.	302-Y-10	$3.49 each
11 in.	302-Y-11	$3.99 each
12 in.	302-Y-12	$4.49 each
13 in.	302-Y-13	$5.19 each
14 in.	302-Y-14	$5.49 each
15 in.	302-Y-15	$6.69 each
16 in.	302-Y-16	$7.49 each
18 in.	302-Y-18	$10.99 each

TIER PAN SETS

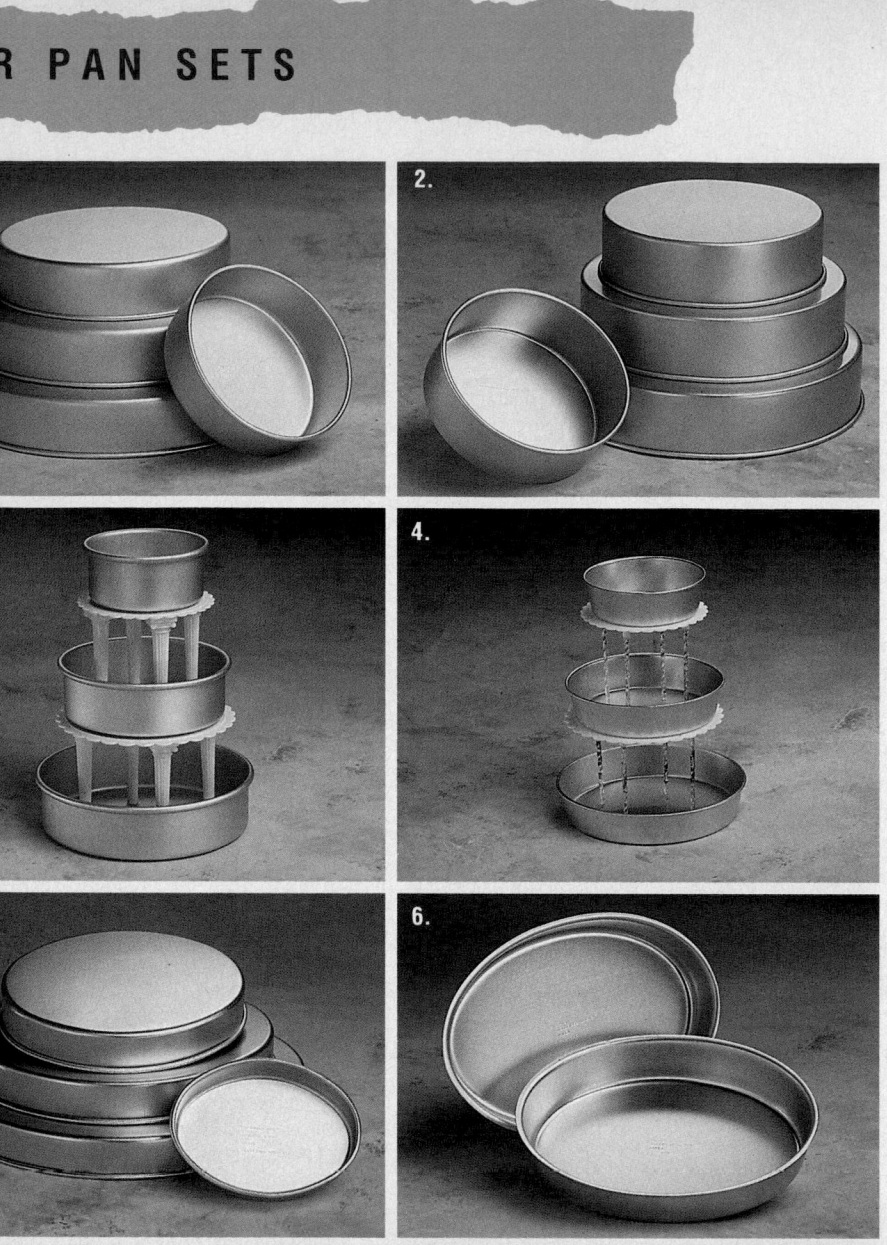

1. CLASSIC ROUND PAN SET
Set includes 6, 8, 10 and 12 in. aluminum pans. 2 in. deep.
2105-Y-2101 $22.99 set

2. 3 IN. DEEP ROUND PAN SET
Set includes 8, 10, 12, 14 in. aluminum pans.
2105-Y-2932 $31.99 set

3. ROUND TIER SET
The perfect choice for engagement parties, anniversaries, religious occasions and more. Set includes 5 x 2 1/2 in., 7 1/8 x 2 1/2 in. and 9 5/16 x 2 5/8 in. aluminum rounds; eight 5 in. Grecian Spiked Pillars; 6 and 8 in. scallop-edged round white plastic separator plates; instructions. Takes 2 cake mixes.
2105-Y-2531 $22.99 set

4. ROUND MINI TIER SET
Takes one cake mix. Set includes 5, 6 and 8 in. round, 1 in. deep aluminum pans; 5, 7 in. separator plates; 8 clear plastic twist legs; decorating instructions.
2105-Y-98042 $11.99 set
ROUND MINI-TIER PLATE SET ONLY
301-Y-9817 $2.99 set

5. 4 PC. OVAL PAN SET
Set includes four 2 in. deep aluminum pans. Sizes are 7 3/4 x 5 5/8 in.; 10 3/4 x 7 7/8 in.; 13 x 9 7/8 in.; 16 x 12 3/8 in.
2105-Y-2130 $23.99 set

6. 2 PC. OVAL PAN SET
Set includes two 9 x 6 3/4 x 1 3/4 in. aluminum pans.
2105-Y-1553 $9.99 set

7. BEVEL PAN SET
Bakes beveled cake edges that can be positioned with layers. Set includes 8, 10, 12 in. tops and 14 and 16 in. base aluminum pans.
517-Y-1200 $25.99 set

8. 4 PC. HEXAGON PAN SET
Set includes 6, 9, 12, 15 in. aluminum pans, 2 in. deep.
2105-Y-3572 $26.99 set

Individual pans available. (not shown)

9 in. x 2 in. 2105-Y-5125 $6.99 each

12 in. x 2 in. 2105-Y-5133 $8.99 each

9. 4 PC. PETAL PAN SET
Set includes 6, 9, 12 and 15 in., 2 in. deep aluminum.
2105-Y-2134 $26.99 set

10. PETAL PANS

9 in. x 2 in. 2105-Y-5109 $6.99 each

12 in. x 2 in. 2105-Y-5117 $8.99 each

OVENCRAFT™
Professional Bakeware

For the professional results you demand, begin with a professional pan-the Ovencraft Pan.

SHEET PANS
Discover endless options with this multi-use pan. 2 ³/₁₆ in. depth.

9 x 13 in.	2105-Y-5616	$11.99 each
11 x 15 in.	2105-Y-5617	$14.99 each
12 x 18 in.	2105-Y-5618	$16.99 each

2 IN. DEEP ROUND PANS
Ideal for two-layer cakes and tier cakes.

6 in.	2105-Y-5601	$4.99 each
8 in.	2105-Y-5602	$5.49 each
9 in.	2105-Y-5619	$5.99 each
10 in.	2105-Y-5603	$6.49 each
12 in.	2105-Y-5604	$8.99 each
14 in.	2105-Y-5605	$11.99 each
16 in.	2105-Y-5606	$14.99 each

3 IN. DEEP ROUND PANS
Bake beautiful, tall cakes.

6 in.	2105-Y-5620	$4.99 each
8 in.	2105-Y-5607	$6.99 each
10 In.	2105-Y-5608	$8.99 each
12 in.	2105-Y-5609	$10.99 each
14 in.	2105-Y-5610	$12.99 each

3 IN. DEEP HALF-ROUND PAN
Use to bake an 18 in. round cake in conventional oven.

18 in.	2105-Y-5622	$12.99 each

SQUARE PANS
Perfectly square corners and 2 ³/₁₆ in. depth produce professional quality cakes.

8 in.	2105-Y-5611	$7.99 each
10 in.	2105-Y-5612	$10.99 each
12 in.	2105-Y-5613	$13.99 each
14 in.	2105-Y-5614	$16.99 each

PROFESSIONAL DURABILITY
▽ Extra thick aluminum provides lifetime performance. Square sheet pans are .060-.065″ thick. (Ordinary bakeware average is .015).
▽ Heavy weight never warps and withstands years of heavy use.
▽ High-quality aluminum evenly distributes heat for superior baking results.

PROFESSIONAL DESIGN
▽ Perfectly straight sides and precise 90° corners on squares and sheet pans bake beautiful straight-sided desserts and cakes.
▽ Welded corners provide lifetime durability.
▽ Designed with extra depth, versus ordinary bakeware, to reduce over-flow of juices and desserts, insuring professional results.
▽ Four-sided lip on square and sheet pans makes lifting and handling much easier.

PROFESSIONAL FINISH
▽ Anodized aluminum finish will not rust, discolor, chip, crack, pit or peel.
▽ Smooth finish is very easy to clean.
▽ Smooth finish releases food quickly and evenly.

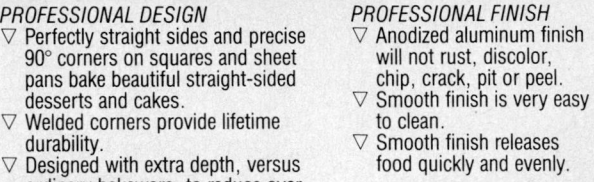

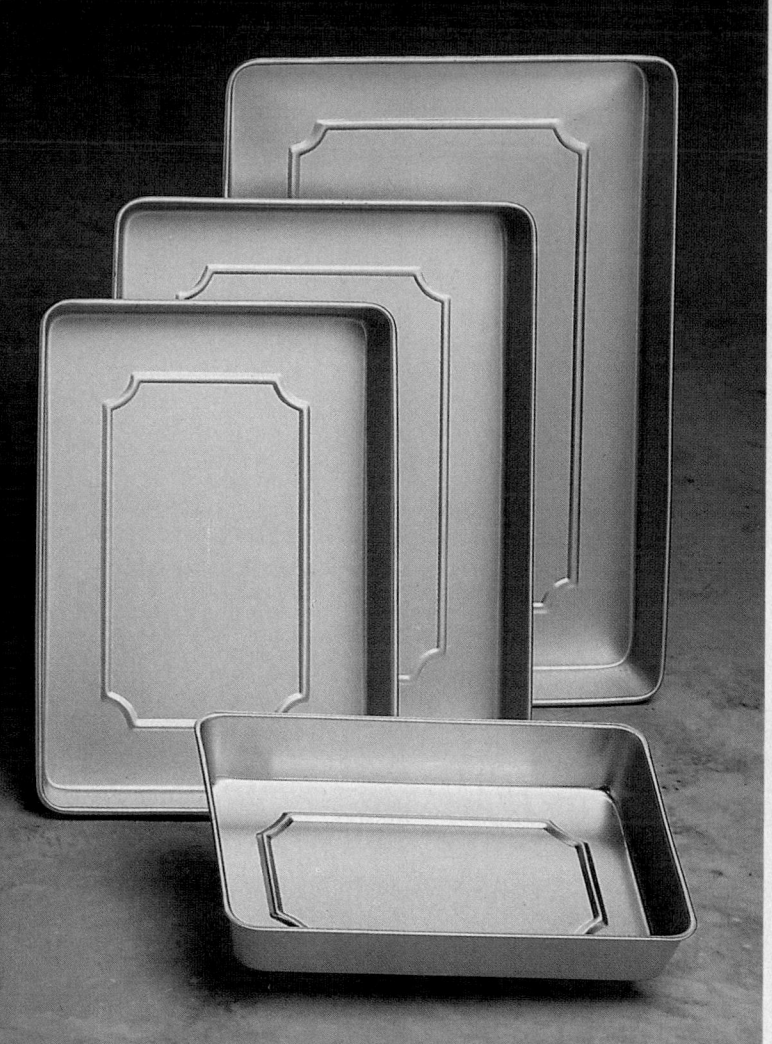

SHEET PANS
2 in. deep.

A priceless collection for any baker or cook. These multi-use pans will be in constant use for everything from special occasion cakes to Sunday dinner. The versatility and high quality of these pans make them invaluable for any kitchen.

Size	Item	Price
7 x 11 in.	2105-Y-2304	$5.99 each
9 x 13 in.	2105-Y-1308	$6.99 each
11 x 15 in.	2105-Y-158	$10.99 each
12 x 18 in.	2105-Y-182	$12.99 each

SQUARE PANS
2 in. deep.

Square . . .the shape that offers an extensive variety of baking and cooking options. Can be used in cake designs from simple to fancy. A great collection to have close at hand.

Size	Item	Price
6 in.	507-Y-2180	$4.99 each
8 in.	2105-Y-8191	$6.49 each
10 in.	2105-Y-8205	$8.49 each
12 in.	2105-Y-8213	$10.99 each
14 in.	2105-Y-8220	$13.99 each
16 in.	2105-Y-8231	$15.99 each

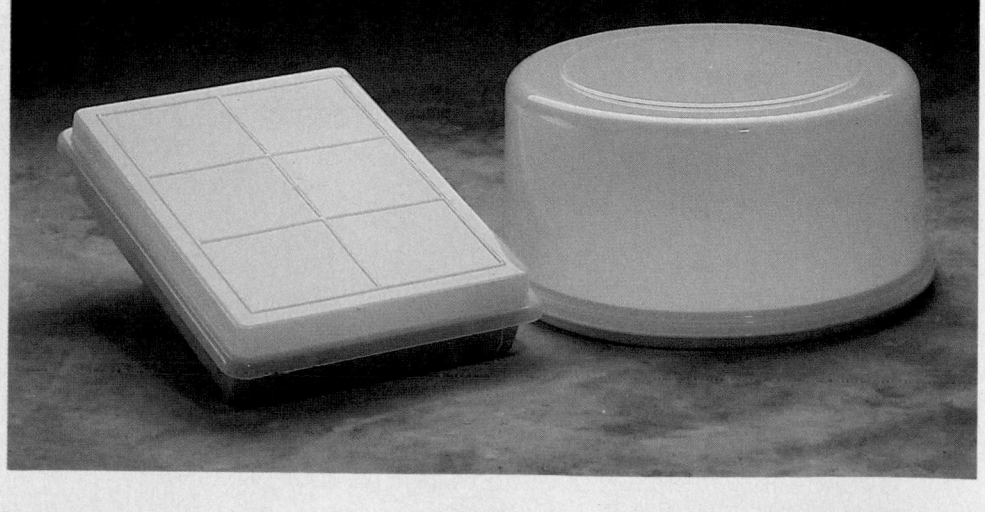

9 X 13 CAKE COVER
Just the protection you need when transporting decorated cakes. Designed for use with the Wilton 9 X 13 in. Performance Pan*, this cover has a raised dome lid which allows you to cover decorated cakes with ease. Keeps cakes and other foods fresh in the pan, even after slicing.
415-Y-903 $4.49 each
*Cake pan not included

CAKE SAVER - 2 PIECE
Designed to carry most elaborately decorated cakes. Generous size accommodates borders and top decorations easily. Use to carry or store all types of cakes, including bundt, angel food, cheese cakes, even pies, as well as layer cakes. Maintains freshness. Wide enough for a 10 in. cake with borders or a 12 in. cake without borders. Includes one 14 in. round base and one 6 in. high cover.
415-Y-905 $10.99 each

PERFORMANCE PANS™

You'll achieve consistent baking results with these professional quality anodized aluminum pans. Not only are they durable, they're dishwasher safe. An unequaled variety of sizes and shapes gives you countless possibilities. Whether you're creating tall-tiered cakes or roasting prime rib, you can depend on Performance Pans™ for the finest results.

ROUND PANS 2 in. deep.			
	6 in.	2105-Y-2185	$4.99 each
Bake everything from	7 in.	2105-Y-2190	$5.29 each
a cake for two to a	8 in.	2105-Y-2193	$5.49 each
wedding cake to serve hundreds.	10 in.	2105-Y-2207	$6.49 each
You'll find it easy	12 in.	2105-Y-2215	$8.99 each
with a varied	14 in.	2105-Y-3947	$11.99 each
collection of round-sized pans.	16 in.	2105-Y-3963	$14.99 each
	9 in. Pan Set	2105-Y-7908	$9.99 set of 2

ROUND PANS 3 in. deep.			
	8 in.	2105-Y-9104	$6.99 each
Bake impressive	10 in.	2105-Y-9945	$8.99 each
high cakes. Perfect for tortes, fruit and pound cakes, and cakes to be covered with fondant icing.			

BAKE-EVEN STRIPS

At last, an innovative way to bake perfectly level, moist cakes. Avoid high-rise centers, cracked tops or crusty edges. Just dampen strips and wrap around the pan before baking. Each band is 1 ¹/₂ in. wide X 30 in. long, with 1 in. overlap.

SMALL SET
Contains 2 bands, enough for two 8 or 9 in. round pans.
415-Y-260 $5.49 set

LARGE SET
Contains 4 bands. enough for one of each of the following: 10, 12, 14 and 16 in. round pans.
415-Y-262 $13.99 set

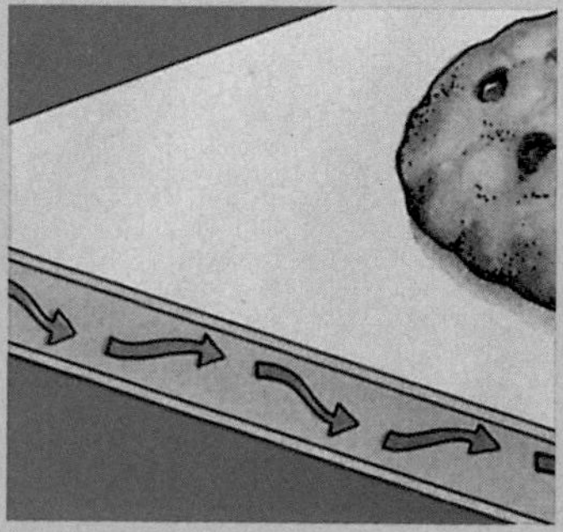

NO HOT SPOTS ...UNIFORM BAKING
Sheets and pans ensure uniform browning with a thick layer of insulating air; on cookie sheets the bottom sheet touches the top sheet only on the perimeter. Results in even baking.

EASY GRIP LIP
The exclusive ribbed edge on the pans is designed for convenience and handling ease. The grip lip on the cookie sheets is on the wide edge, making oven removal safer.

IMMERSIBLE AND DISHWASHER-SAFE
Exclusive patent-pending design allows cookie sheets and pans to be totally immersed and drains the water for immediate use.

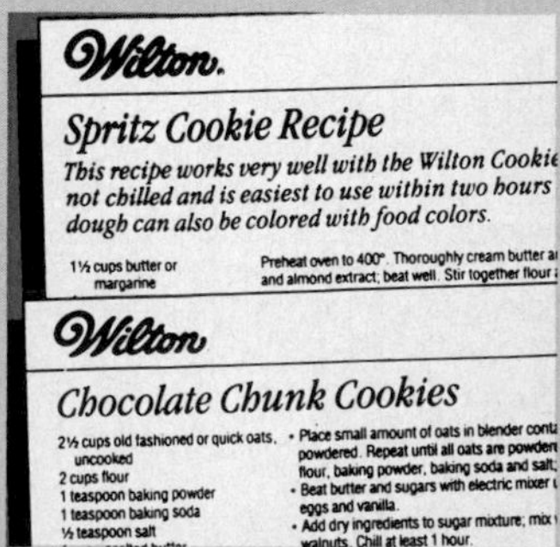

WILTON KITCHEN-DEVELOPED RECIPES
Delicious recipes developed in the Wilton kitchen are included on each label for added baking ideas and pleasure.

Wilton.

Spritz Cookie Recipe
This recipe works very well with the Wilton Cookie not chilled and is easiest to use within two hours dough can also be colored with food colors.

1½ cups butter or margarine

Preheat oven to 400°. Thoroughly cream butter a and almond extract; beat well. Stir together flour a

Wilton

Chocolate Chunk Cookies

2½ cups old fashioned or quick oats, uncooked
2 cups flour
1 teaspoon baking powder
1 teaspoon baking soda
½ teaspoon salt

- Place small amount of oats in blender conta powdered. Repeat until all oats are powdere flour, baking powder, baking soda and salt;
- Beat butter and sugars with electric mixer u eggs and vanilla.
- Add dry ingredients to sugar mixture; mix i walnuts. Chill at least 1 hour.

Paper baking cups sold on page 126.

MINI MUFFIN PAN
Create mini-muffins, fruitcakes, cupcakes, cheesecakes. Aluminum. 7 ³/₄ x 10 x ³/₄ in. deep.
2105-Y-2125 $6.99 each

SIX-CUP MUFFIN PAN
Perfect size for morning muffins, after school treats and desserts. Aluminum. 7 ³/₈ x 10 ³/₄ x 1 in. deep.
2105-Y-5338 $6.99 each

JUMBO MUFFIN PAN
Bake super-size cupcakes and muffins. Aluminum. 13 ¹/₂ x 9 ¹/₄ x 2 in. deep.
2105-Y-1820 $12.99 each

VIENNESE SWIRL PAN
The foundation for elegant continental style desserts. Aluminum. 11¹/₂ diameter x 1⁷/₈ in. deep.
2105-Y-8252 $9.99 each

SHELL PAN
Simple elegance. A pan you'll reach for occasion after occasion. Aluminum. 11 x 12 x 1 ⁷/₈ in. deep.
2105-Y-8250 $9.99 each

NEW! MINI-LOAF PAN
Great for individual-sized nut breads, cakes. 10 ³/₄ x 12 ¹/₄ x 1 ¹/₂ in. deep. Aluminum.
2105-Y-9791 $9.99 each

LOAF PAN
Perfect for sandwich loaves, cakes and breads. Aluminum. 8 ³/₄ x 4 ¹/₄ x 2 ³/₄ in. deep.
2105-Y-3688 $5.99 each

LONG LOAF PAN
Bake classic cakes or angel food delights. Cooling legs provide proper cooling for angel food cakes. Aluminum. 16 x 4 x 4 ¹/₂ in. deep.
2105-Y-1588 $9.99 each

SHORTCAKES 'N TREATS PAN
Decorate these single-serving desserts with in-season fruit and whipped cream. Aluminum. 12 ¹/₂ x 8 x 1 in. deep.
2105-Y-5966 $6.99 each

RING MOLD PANS
Two convenient sizes. Each 3 in. deep. Aluminum.
8 in. 2105-Y-190 $6.49 each
10 ¹/₂ in. 2105-Y-4013 $7.99 each

FANCY RING MOLD PAN
Beautiful bundt-style pan, ideal for pound cakes, mousse, more! 3 inch deep pan. Takes one standard bundt-type mix. Aluminum. 10 in. diameter; 3 in deep.
2105-Y-5008 $9.99 each

PETITE FANCY RING MOLD PAN
Serve impressive desserts in dramatic individual servings. Aluminum. 12 ¹/₂ x 8 x 1 in. deep.
2105-Y-2097 $16.99 each

Double Bottom Set

2 PC. SPRINGFORM PANS
Waffle bottom for stronger support. Release springlock, remove sides and serve. 3 in. deep. Aluminum.
6 in. 2105-Y-4437 $7.99 each
9 in. 2105-Y-5354 $10.99 each

NON-STICK SPRING FORM PANS
Quality non-stick finish on heavy-gauge steel. Waffle-textured surface provides extra strength. 3 in. deep.
6 in. 2105-Y-218 $6.99 each
9 in. 2105-Y-219 $9.99 each
10 in. 0000-Y-2347 $12.79 each
10 in. Double Bottom Set 0000-Y-2385 $22.29 each

2 PC. HEART DESSERT PAN
Create beautiful heart-shaped desserts; removable bottom. Aluminum.
9 3/4 x 9 3/4 x 2 1/2 in. deep.
2105-Y-3217 $12.99 each

2 PC. HEART ANGEL FOOD PAN
Removable bottom for easy transfer. Cooling legs and full 4 inch depth are great for tall desserts. Aluminum.
10 1/2 x 10 1/4 x 4 in. deep.
2105-Y-6509 $12.99 each

2 PC. ANGEL FOOD PAN
2-piece, 10 x 4 1/2 in. deep. Removable inner core sleeve. Aluminum.
2105-Y-2525 $13.99 each

MINI ANGEL FOOD PAN
Create delicate, single serving desserts with easy 6-mold pan.
12 1/4 x 8 x 1 in. deep.
0000-Y-2338 $20.59 each

CONTINENTAL FLAN PAN
Create international recipes with elan. Aluminum. 11 diam. x 1 3/4 in. deep.
2105-Y-2046 $7.99 each

HEART FLAN PAN
Delicately fluted, shaped for fruit, pudding or ice cream creations. Aluminum. 11 x 1 1/8 in. deep.
2105-Y-3218 $7.99 each

HEART RING MOLD PAN
Romantic shape for lovely cakes, gelatins and mousse. Aluminum.
11 x 2 5/8 in. deep.
2105-Y-3219 $12.99 each

HEART PANS
Give your heart away in any fun-loving size. Aluminum. 1 7/8 in. deep.
6 in. 2105-Y-4781 $3.99 each
9 in. 2105-Y-5176 $5.99 each
12 in. 2105-Y-5168 $8.99 each

PIZZA PANS

The Frugal Gourmet

"I've tried the best... this is better!"

Introducing Wilton pizza pans and serving trays. Exclusive patent pending dual action baking design lifts pizza dough from the surface, so that heat circulates and browns the crust. It crisps the crust by eliminating moisture through the vent holes.

 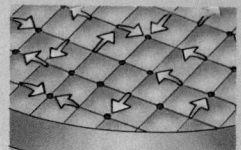

Extra wide rim keeps hot mitts and fingers safely away from pizza. Smooth bottom trays have skid stop rims and keep pizza warm while serving.

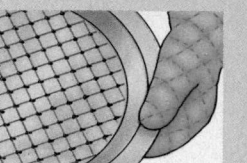 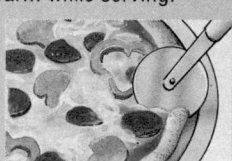

Included with each pan or pan/tray set is a 6-page recipe book developed by the Wilton Kitchen.

14 ¹/₂ in. pan with red tray	2105-Y-3902	$19.99 each
14 ¹/₂ in. pan with black tray	2105-Y-3908	$19.99 each
16 ¹/₂ in. pan with red tray	2105-Y-3904	$24.99 each
16 ¹/₂ in. pan with black tray	2105-Y-3909	$24.99 each
14 ¹/₂ in. pan	2105-Y-3901	$10.99 each
16 ¹/₂ in. pan	2105-Y-3903	$12.99 each

ACCESSORIES

The Wilton pizza accessory collection gives you the ideal way to dish up hot, piping pizza with ease. Each piece is heavy-gauge stainless steel that will not rust or pit. The cutters have a double-sided cutting wheel for a cleaner cut.

2 ¹/₂ in. cutter	2105-Y-3905	$4.99 each
3 ³/₄ in. cutter	2105-Y-3906	$5.99 each
Spatula Server	2105-Y-3907	$6.99 each

MICROWAVE BAKEWARE

A great selection of little pans with the biggest possibilities. Microwave cakes bake up in an instant. Gelatin salads, molded mousse and ice cream desserts take shape and come out great. **$3.49 each.**

Teddy Bear 2106-Y-108	Speedy Bunny 2106-Y-138	Ring 2106-Y-118	Round 2106-Y-100	Heart 2106-Y-106	Square 2106-Y-102	ChristmasTree 2106-Y-122
Big Bird* 2106-Y-116	Flan 2106-Y-112	Fancy Ring 2106-Y-124	Mini Heart 2106-Y-120	Jumbo Muffin 2106-Y-130	Double Mix Rectangle 2106-Y-104	

NEW! SUPER RACE CAR

Spinning out of the turn and headed right for birthday celebrations galore. This fast-paced automobile will travel from party to party all year long. One-mix aluminum pan is 18 1/8 x 7 5/8 x 2 in.
2105-Y-6508 $9.99 each

NEW! LITTLE FIRE TRUCK

This little engine can make any occasion a five-alarm event. Birthdays, school parties, even a retirement party can be fun with this creative pan. One-mix aluminum pan is 16 x 9 1/8 x 2 in.
2105-Y-9110 $9.99 each

LITTLE TRAIN PAN

The new little birthday and all-occasion train packs a cargo-load of fun for party guests and the guest of honor. Lots of laughter on board. One-mix aluminum pan is 8 3/4 x 15 3/4 x 2 in.
2105-Y-6500 $9.99 each

CHOO CHOO TRAIN PAN

Here's the little 3-d engine that could–pulling through again with a trainload of uses. All aboard! Two-part aluminum pan snaps together. Pan is 10 x 6 x 4 in. Takes 6 cups of firm-textured batter.
2105-Y-2861 $10.99 each

18-WHEELER TRUCK PAN

Why not go mobile with tons of warm wishes? It's easy to deliver a special greeting on Dad's Day, moving day and at life's major milestones. One-mix aluminum pan is 8 3/4 x 17 x 2 in.
2105-Y-0018 $9.99 each

NEW! MINI BEAR PAN
These petite bears will have little time to hibernate once kids find out just how much fun they are. Make six individual servings at once. Aluminum pan is 13 1/8 x 12 x 1 3/4 in.
2105-Y-4497 $9.99 each

HUGGABLE TEDDY BEAR PAN
Now here's an old friend who's enjoying more popularity than ever. Maybe it's because he makes everyone feel so good. He'll bring his happy mood to any occasion. Ideas for birthdays and baby showers included. One mix aluminum pan is 13 1/2 x 12 1/4 x 2 in.
2105-Y-4943 $9.99 each

HAPPY CLOWN PAN
Color kids' parties happy. This circus funny man brings on smiles to kids of all ages. His alternate looks can entertain at many occasions. One-mix aluminum pan is 12 x 12 x 2 in.
2105-Y-802 $9.99 each

WONDER MOLD KIT
In every season you'll find use for this shape at the greatest affairs-birthdays, graduations and bridal showers. Use the mold alone or as a part of another design. Alumminum pan (8 in. diam., 5 in. deep) takes 5-6 cups of firm-textured batter. Heat-conducting rod assures even baking. Kit contains pan, rod, stand, 7 in. doll pick and instructions.
2105-Y-565 $11.99 kit

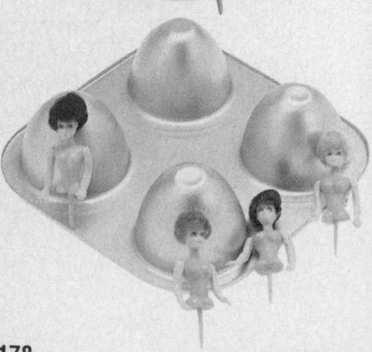

TEEN DOLL PICK
7 in. tall, same as in kit.
2815-Y-101 $2.99 each

PETITE DOLL PAN
Couple this aluminum pan with Small Doll Picks for a quartet of party treats. Alone, it lends itself to all sorts of inventive cake ideas. Great assembled with Wonder Mold kit as a color-coordinated bridal party centerpiece. One cake mix yields 4 to 6 cakes.
508-Y-302 $9.99 each

SMALL DOLL PICKS
4 1/2 in. high.
1511-Y-1019 $5.29 pack of 4

PRECIOUS PONY PAN

A little horseplay is always expected at a kid's party. Create a colt or a filly to prance about with happy birthday wishes. Captivating alternate ways to decorate are included. One-mix aluminum pan is 16 x 11 x 2 in.
2105-Y-2914 $9.99 each

TEDDY BEAR STAND-UP PAN

You'll find this beloved buddy popping up at just about any occasion. Great for birthdays, baby showers, school parties and just warm wishes. Two-piece one-mix aluminum pan is 9 $1/2$ x 8 $1/2$ x 5 in. Core, stand and clips.
2105-Y-2325 $15.99 set

BAKING CORE ONLY*

503-Y-504 $3.59 each
*although slightly smaller than the core included with the pan, this works as well.

ROCKING HORSE PAN

Indulge your hobby for decorating with this perennial favorite. The Wild West carnival or Christmas-time are just a few of the themes to give this lovable toy. It's a winner for birthdays and baby showers. One-mix aluminum pan is 13 $1/2$ x 13 $1/2$ x 2 in.
2105-Y-2388 $9.99 each

PANDA PAN

Here's one of the cutest cakes in captivity! With so many great ways to decorate it, this 3-D Panda is a hit at all sorts of happy events. Two-piece aluminum pan takes 6 $1/2$ cups of firm textured batter. Includes 6 clips, heat conducting core and instructions. Pan is 9 $1/2$ x 8 $5/8$ in. tall
2105-Y-603 $15.99 each

BAKING CORE ONLY

503-Y-504 $3.59 each

PANDA MOLD

Aluminum 2-pc. mold/pan is perfect for baking cakes and molding candy, ice cream, sugar.
About 4 $3/4$ in. high.
518-Y-489 $4.99 each

LITTLE MOUSE PAN

What trick does this little guy have up his sleeve? Nothing but the happiest of birthday wishes for every boy and girl. One-mix aluminum pan is 15 $3/4$ x 9 $1/2$ x 2 in.
2105-Y-2380 $9.99 each

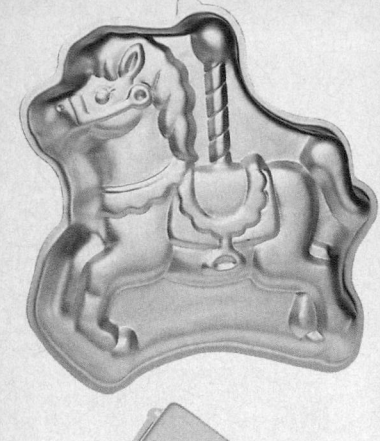

NEW! CAROUSEL HORSE PAN

This galloping horse on a brass pole will find itself the center of attention at baby showers, children's birthdays, and more. One-mix aluminum pan is 14 x 13 x 1 ⁷/₈ in.
2105-Y-6507 $9.99 each

STAR PAN

What better way to honor the celebrity in your life! Brighten birthdays, opening nights, even law enforcement occasions. New possibilities always emerging. One-mix aluminum pan is 12 ³/₄ in. across by 1 ⁷/₈ in. deep.
2105-Y-2512 $9.99 each

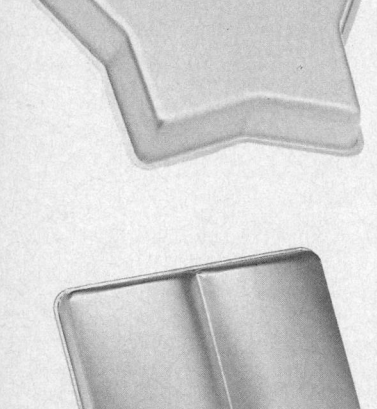

BOOK PAN

Special greetings in black and white, or whatever colors you choose. This open book details every one of life's important chapters-birthdays, baby showers, graduations and much more. Create a colorful greeting card cake, too. Five ways to decorate included. One-mix aluminum pan is 13 x 9 ¹/₂ x 2 in.
2105-Y-972 $9.99 each

TWO-MIX BOOK PAN

Bake a cake of epic proportions. For larger parties, this great volume serves up to 30 guests. The story unfolds as the crowd gathers to celebrate most any occasion. Aluminum pan is 11 ¹/₂ x 15 x 2 ³/₄ in.
2105-Y-2521 $12.99 each

GUITAR PAN SET

From Country & Western to Heavy Metal, music fans will go wild over this cake. Just ice, place plastic trims and pipe simple borders. Strings (not included) can be added for even more musical effect. Includes plastic neck, bridge and pick guard. One-mix aluminum pan is 17 ³/₄ x 8 ¹/₂ x 2 in.
501-Y-904 $9.99 set

GUITAR ACCESSORY KIT ONLY
503-Y-938 $1.59 set

NEW! GOOD TIME CLOCK PAN

No matter what the time, it's always party time with this year 'round pan. Whether its counting down days to graduation, retirement or noting the birth of a baby, this pan is invaluable. One-mix aluminum pan is 13 $\frac{3}{8}$ x 10 $\frac{3}{4}$ x 1 $\frac{7}{8}$ in.
2105-Y-9111 $9.99 each

UP 'N AWAY BALLOON PAN

Get carried away in celebration for all your high-flying events. This cake also successfully transports greetings of "congratulations" and "bon voyage". Four ways to decorate included on label. One-mix aluminum pan is 14 $\frac{1}{2}$ x 10 $\frac{1}{2}$ x 1 $\frac{7}{8}$ in.
2105-Y-1898 $9.99 each

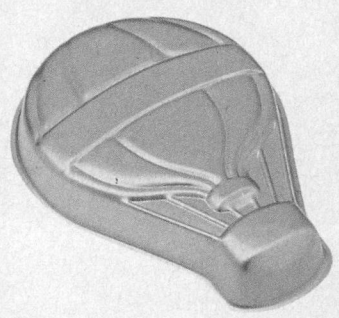

DOUBLE-TIER ROUND PAN

Special effects are simple to achieve. Use just one 2-layer cake mix in one pan to create two classic tiers-6 and 10 inch. Decorate this unique shape quite formally or with creative whimsy. A year-round party pleaser. Aluminum pan is 9 $\frac{3}{4}$ x 3 in.
2105-Y-1400 $9.99 each

T-SHIRT PAN

This universal casual standby will be the most welcome attire at many occasions-birthdays, baby showers and any other celebration you can imagine. One-mix aluminum pan is 13 $\frac{1}{4}$ x 12 $\frac{1}{2}$ x 2 in.
2105-Y-2347 $9.99 each

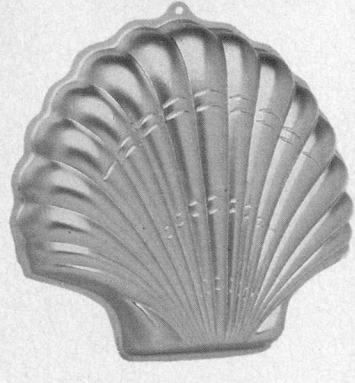

PARTYSAURUS PAN
Back from extinction and ready to party. This continued celebrity of dinosaurs makes our prehistoric party animal a must-have at all sorts of fun fests. One-mix aluminum pan is 16 x 10 x 1 7/8 in.
2105-Y-1280 $9.99 each

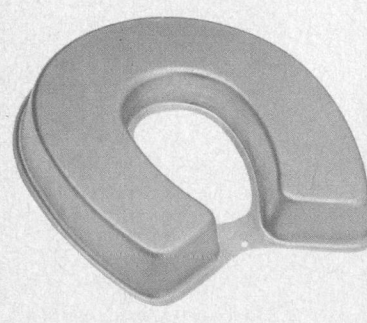

SHELL PAN
Add this sophisticated, streamlined pan to your collection. With the recipe for delicate lemon cake printed on the label, create a delicious dessert topped with gorgeous yellow fondant. A pan you'll use for so many happy times. One-mix aluminum pan is 11 x 12 in.
2105-Y-8250 $9.99 each

HORSESHOE PAN
A horseshoe by any other name still means "good luck." Whether it's a good omen for graduations, bon voyage or a Christmas stocking, it's a style you'll be glad to have. One-mix aluminum pan is 12 x 1 3/4.
2105-Y-3254 $9.99 each

KITTY CAT PAN
The reigning king is basking in the glow of being named the most popular house pet. Why not immortalize him in buttercream? Create sleek or long-haired breeds. One-mix aluminum pan is 9 x 15 x 2 in.
2105-Y-1009 $9.99 each

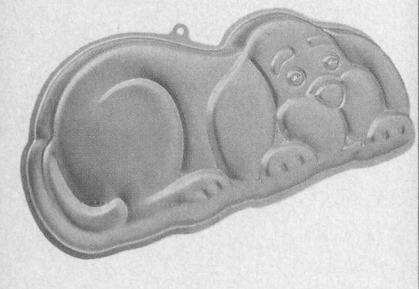

PUPPY DOG PAN
Finally, you can say "yes" when they ask for a puppy. Our frisky four-legged friend would just love a home for birthdays and kids' get-togethers. Make him your party mascot. One-mix aluminum pan is 17 3/4 x 8 7/8 x 1 7/8 in.
2105-Y-2430 $9.99 each

NEW! BOWLING A "STRIKE" PAN

What a great novelty cake idea for that avid bowling fan. Unique ball and pins in action design is sure to strike a happy chord with that bowler in the family. One-mix aluminum pan is 14 3/4 x 11 3/4 x 2 in.
2105-Y-6505 $9.99 each

SPORTS BALL PAN SET

Whether they're fans of all sports or fans of fun, the crowd will get to their feet with this pan. This multi-function ball can go from basketball to soccer and volleyball with ease. Many more uses in store. Set includes two 6-in. diameter half ball aluminum pans and two metal baking stands. Each pan half takes 2 1/2 cups batter.
2105-Y-6506 $9.99 set

BALL PAN BAKE STAND ONLY

503-Y-881 99¢ each

MINI-BALL PAN

Make a grand slam entrance with a tray full of these cakes-for-one. These little treats are perfect in any championship season. Ice mini-balls and push together for a 3-D effect. One cake mix will yield 12 to 15 balls. Aluminum pan is 11 1/2 x 7 1/2 x 1 1/2 in.
2105-Y-1760 $9.99 each

FIRST AND TEN FOOTBALL PAN

Award them the game ball, just like the pros. From little guys to Monday morning quarterbacks, they'll score with this cake. Perfect for Super Bowl parties, homecomings, award dinners and much more. One-mix aluminum pan is 12 x 7 3/4 x 3 in.
2105-Y-6504 $9.99 each

BASEBALL GLOVE PAN

Have an entertaining victory in the palm of your hand. The home team will love this mitt that can be customized with names and team colors. Can also be used for many occasions. One-mix aluminum pan is 12 x 12 1/4 x 1 3/4 in.
2105-Y-1234 $9.99 each

GARFIELD® PAN
Count this mischievous cat to be on his best party behavior for birthdays, holidays and more. Five ways to decorate are included. The plastic face maker is a super decorating timesaver. One-mix aluminum pan is 11 1/2 x 12 1/2 x 2 in.
2105-Y-2447 $9.99 each

GARFIELD: © 1978 United Feature Syndicate, Inc.

BATMAN PAN
It's everyone's favorite crime-fighting caped crusader. Invite him to your next party for a POW! ZAP! BANG! BOOM! good time. One-mix aluminum pan is 13 x 13 1/2 x 2 in.
2105-Y-6501 $9.99 each

© DC Comics Inc. 1989

SUPER HEROES PAN
Double the crime-fighting power in one easy pan. Whomever you choose, he's perfect for many occasions. Set includes one-mix 13 x 13 x 2 in. aluminum pan, SUPERMAN and BATMAN plastic face masks and chest emblems.
2105-Y-8507 $9.99 set
BATMAN MASK & EMBLEM
503-Y-814 $1.99 set
SUPERMAN FACE & EMBLEM
503-Y-857 $1.99 set

TRADEMARKS LICENSED BY DC COMICS, INC. ©1978

SUPER MARIO BROTHERS® PAN
This non-stop character will make sure everyone has a super celebration. One-mix aluminum pan is 14 1/4 x 9 1/2 x 2 in.
2105-Y-2989 $9.99 each

©1989 Nintendo of America, inc.

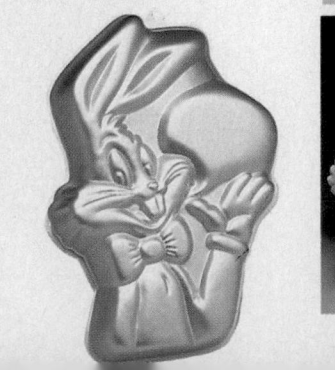

BUGS BUNNY PAN
Lots is up, Doc! This silly wabbit will hop his way into many fun-loving events. On the cartoon balloon, pipe in a special message to suit the situation. One-mix aluminum pan is 14 x 9 x 1 7/8 in.
2105-Y-8253 $9.99 each

Bugs Bunny
Trademark and
©1988 Warner Bros., Inc.

NEW! TEENAGE MUTANT NINJA TURTLE ® HEAD PAN

This big fella is a hit any time! Change his colors to make your favorite fighter. One-mix aluminum pan is 12 ⁵/₈ x 11 ³/₈ x 2 in.
2105-Y-4436 $ 9.99 each

® & © 1990 Mirage Studios, U.S.A. Exclusively licensed by Surge Licensing, Inc.

TEENAGE MUTANT NINJA TURTLES ® PAN

Hey dude, it's those crazy crime-stopping amphibians. Michaelangelo, Leonardo, Donatello and Raphael. Create your favorite creature. Any kid would just love them. One-mix aluminum pan is 15 x 9 ¹/₂ x 2 in.
2105-Y-3075 $9.99 each

® & © 1990 Mirage Studios, U.S.A. Exclusively licensed by Surge Licensing, Inc.

BIG BIRD WITH BANNER PAN

Now lovable Big Bird will print your good wishes right up front for all to see. One-mix aluminum pan is 13 ¹/₈ x 12 x 12 ¹/₄ in.
2105-Y-3654 $9.99 each

Sesame Street Characters
©Jim Henson Productions, Inc.
All rights reserved.

COOKIE MONSTER CAKE PAN

He loves cookies and birthdays, too. This googly-eyed monster makes a great happy birthday surprise. Alternate designs turn his cake into other great ideas. One-mix aluminum pan is 14 ¹/₂ x 11 ¹/₂ x 1 ⁷/₈ in.
2105-Y-4927 $9.99 each

Sesame Street Characters
©Jim Henson Productions, Inc.
All rights reserved.

BART SIMPSON PAN

Everybody's favorite wisecracker will find himself popping up at the most unlikely events. Birthdays, school parties, any occasion! One-mix aluminum pan is 14 ³/₄ x 12 ⁵/₈ x 1 ⁷/₈ in.
2105-Y-9431 $9.99 each

© MATT GROENING
TM & © 1990 Twentieth Century Fox Film Corporation. All rights reserved.

NOTE: LICENSED CHARACTER PANS CANNOT BE SOLD FOR COMMERCIAL USE.

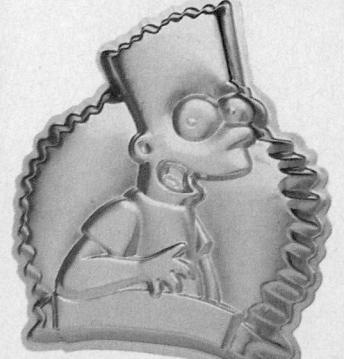

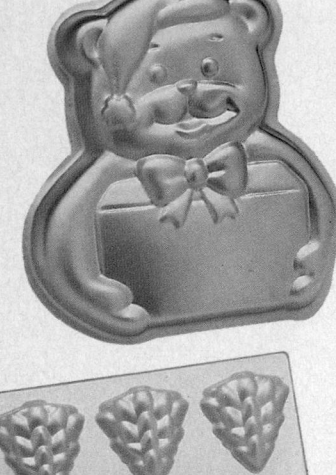

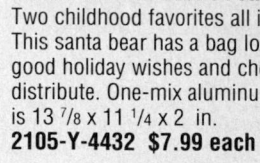

NEW! SANTA BEAR PAN

Two childhood favorites all in one. This santa bear has a bag load of good holiday wishes and cheer to distribute. One-mix aluminum pan is 13 7/8 x 11 1/4 x 2 in.
2105-Y-4432 $7.99 each

MINI CHRISTMAS TREE PAN

Trees, trees and more trees make the holiday merrier. Serve little ones individually or use them to decorate each guest's place setting. Label includes alternate ideas for year 'round versatility. One mix makes approximately 15-18 cakes. Aluminum pan is 13 x 10 1/2 x 1 1/4 in.
2105-Y-1779 $7.99 each

TREELITEFUL PAN

Here's holiday decorating made quick and easy. Just cover with one squeeze, add simple garlands and candy or cookie ornaments. Instructions include several ideas to use throughout the year. One-mix aluminum pan is 15 x 11 x 1 1/2 in.
2105-Y-425 $7.99 each

HOLIDAY HOUSE KIT

Create this enchanted cozy cottage of cake and icing. Can be as simple or elaborate as you wish. One-mix aluminum pan is 8 5/8 x 9 x 3 in.
2105-Y-2282 $9.99 kit

SNOWMAN PAN

This jolly man packs lots of winter fun. Sprinkled with coconut and decorated with candies, this cake makes a tasty Christmas treat. Inventive ideas to adapt for all seasons included on the label. One-mix aluminum pan is 15 1/4 x 10 1/4 in.
2105-Y-803 $7.99 each

MINI GINGERBREAD BOY PAN

Populate your holiday fare with half a dozen of these fun-loving little fellows. The little ones will just love having their own individualized ginger boy at Christmas dinner. One mix makes approximately 12-15 cakes. Aluminum pan is 12 ½ x 11 ¼ x 1 in.
2105-Y-6503 $7.99 each

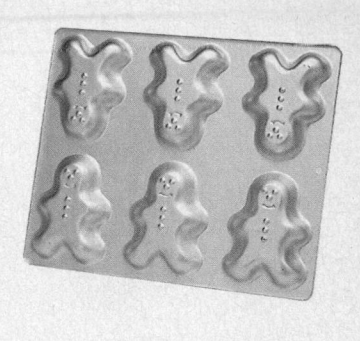

GINGERBREAD BOY PAN

Find this happy-go-lucky guy popping up at all your yuletide get togethers. Simple decorating creates great effects with this easy pan. One-mix aluminum pan is 14 x 10 ½ x 2 in.
2105-Y-2072 $7.99 each

JOLLY SANTA PAN

Send the sweetest season's greetings with the smiling face of old St. Nick. He's great fun for the whole family to decorate! One-mix aluminum pan is 13 ¼ x 11 ½ x 2 in.
2105-Y-1225 $7.99 each

RUDY REINDEER PAN

It's Rudy, our irresistible reindeer. He'll soon be leading the fun at all holiday festivities. One-mix aluminum pan is 10 ¾ x 16 ¾ x 1 ¾ in.
2105-Y-1224 $7.99 each

HEART RING PAN

This delicate heart mold lets you put a little surprise in the center. Fill with fresh fruit, whipped cream, even shaved chocolate. A heart's delight. Two-mix aluminum pan is 11 x 2 5/8 in. deep.
2105-Y-3219 $12.99 each

HEART QUARTET PAN

A bounty of hearts expresses your love in four fold. The unusual shape provides many decorating ideas. Ideal for Valentine's Day, St. Patrick's Day and birthdays. One-mix aluminum pan is 11 x 11 in.
2105-Y-1414 $7.99 each

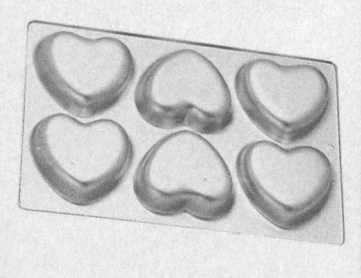

HEART MINI-CAKE PAN

Give away more than your heart for Valentine's Day. Why not give six or twelve! Sweet gestures of love for bridal showers and kids' parties. Each heart of this 8 x 11 1/8 in. aluminum pan is 3 1/2 x 1 1/4 in. deep. One cake mix makes 12 hearts.
2105-Y-11044 $7.99 each

HAPPINESS HEART PAN SET

Let our lovely two-heart layer cake convey your sweet sentiments on any occasion. It takes just one mix to fill both aluminum pans; each 9 x 1 1/2 in. deep.
2105-Y-956 $7.99 set

DOUBLE TIER HEART PAN

Romance is always on the menu with a cake of two pretty heart tiers. It's the perfect show of affection for birthdays, Mother's or Father's Day, wedding showers and much more. Instructions show 4 delightful ways to decorate. One-mix aluminum pan is 11 1/2 x 11 x 2 1/4 in. deep.
2105-Y-1699 $9.99 each

NEW! HEART ANGEL FOOD PAN

Variation on a very delicious theme. The light, fluffy and luscious angel food cake is now in a heart shape. Cooling legs make it easy to properly cool an angel food cake. With removable bottom for easy release. Aluminum pan takes one angel food or chiffon mix. 10 $\frac{5}{8}$ x 10 $\frac{1}{8}$ x 4 in.
2105-Y-6509 $12.99 each

NEW! HEART DESSERT PAN

For those romantic occasions, take it from the heart. Great for cakes, pudding desserts, ice cream and mousse. Aluminum pan is 10 x 9 $\frac{3}{4}$ x 2 $\frac{1}{2}$ in.
2105-Y-3217 $12.99 each

HEART FLAN PAN

What a super idea-fill a flute-edged heart cake with surprises. Choose pudding, ice cream, fruit, even chocolates. It can also be trimmed with icing or whipped cream. One-mix aluminum pan is 11 x 10 $\frac{1}{2}$ in.
2105-Y-3218 $7.99 each

HEART MINI-TIER PAN SET

What a great special effect! Make a petite masterpiece using any one cake mix in three sweetheart tiers. Set includes 5, 7 $\frac{1}{2}$ and 9 in. pans, two scallop-edged white separator plates and six crystal clear twist legs.
2105-Y-409 $11.99 set

SEPARATOR PLATE SET

Includes one 5 $\frac{1}{2}$ in. and one 8 in. Heart Separator Plates with 6 crystal clear twist legs.
301-Y-09728 $2.99 set

HEART PANS

Discover romance in full bloom with three lovely tiers. Just the perfect cake for the most romantic of occasions-anniversaries, bridal showers, birthdays and weddings. The 2-in. deep aluminum pans are sold separately in three essential sizes, 6, 9, 12 in.
6 in. Heart 2105-Y-4781 $3.99 ea.
9 in. Heart 2105-Y-5176 $5.99 ea.
12 in. Heart
2105-Y-5168 $8.99 each

HEART PAN SET

Love is at its grandest in four lovely tiers. Lavishly celebrate showers, weddings and more with the ultimate heart-shaped cake. Set includes 6, 9, 12 and 15 $\frac{1}{2}$ in. diameter aluminum pans.
504-Y-207 $24.99 set

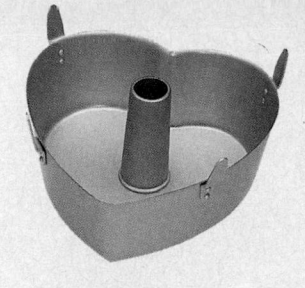

LITTLE DUCKY PAN

This little ducky is the one. He makes Easter so much fun. And that's not all. He's a cute addition to baby showers, kids' birthdays and more. One-mix aluminum pan is 13 x 10 x 0 in.
2105-Y-2029 $7.99 each

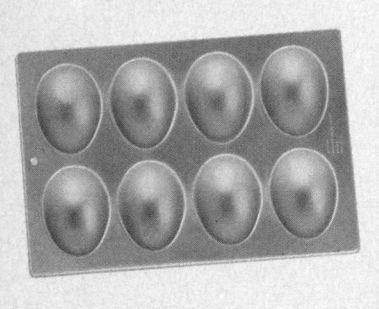

EGG MINI-CAKE PAN

You CAN put all these "eggs" in one beautiful Easter basket. Or use them as colorful place markers at the holiday table. The label includes a variety of versatile decorating ideas. One cake mix yields about 24 cakes. Each oval well is 3 $1/2$ x 2 $3/8$ in.
2105-Y-2118 $7.99 each

EGG PAN SET

Why not decorate the Easter egg to end all Easter eggs. This cake makes a great holiday centerpiece. Two-piece aluminum pan takes just one cake mix. Each half is 8 $3/4$ x 5 $3/8$ in. and includes a ring base for level baking.
2105-Y-700 $10.99 set
EGG PAN RING ONLY
503-Y-954 99¢ each

COTTONTAIL BUNNY PAN

It wouldn't be Easter without him. This fluffy-tailed favorite is such an adorable addition to birthdays and baby showers, too. The label includes a bunny-quick way to decorate. One-mix aluminum pan is 14 x 12 x 2 in.
2105-Y-2015 $7.99 each

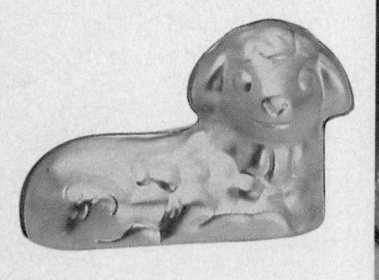

LITTLE LAMB PAN SET

This precious little creature makes a beautiful centerpiece for your Easter table. Two-piece aluminum pan is 10 x 7 in. tall and takes 6 cups of pound cake batter. Baking and decorating instructions included.
2105-Y-2010 $10.99 set

NEW! SPECIAL DELIVERY BUNNY PAN

This little cottontail is hot on the tracks with a basketful of Easter wishes. Alternate decorating ideas included. One-mix aluminum pan is 14 x 11 1/4 x 2 in.
2105-Y-9001 $7.99 each
(Available January, 1992)

GENTLE LAMB PAN

Invite this delicate little lamb to grace your Easter table. You can be assured where good times are this lamb is sure to follow. One-mix aluminum pan is 13 5/16 x 10 1/2 x 1 7/8 in.
2105-Y-2515 $7.99 each

SUNNY BUNNY PAN

This little hare is just hopping to please. His big feet, big ears and big heart make him a most welcomed Easter guest and more. See label for ideas. One-mix aluminum pan is 12 5/8 x 10 1/4 in.
2105-Y-2435 $7.99 each

CROSS PAN

Celebrate a blessed day with a symbol of faith. Bake and decorate this meaningful cake for holidays, christenings and other religious occasions. Instructions include a birthday and family reunion cake. One-mix aluminum pan is 14 1/2 x 11 1/8 x 2 in.
2105-Y-2509 $7.99 each

GREAT EGGS!™ KIT

Create springtime magic! Ornate Easter basket sugar and candy confections. Kit includes 2 egg molds, tips, coupler, brush, 2 candy mold sheets, recipes and instructions.
2104-Y-3615 $9.99 kit

NEW! MINI GHOST PAN
Create gobs of goblins at a time with this newest pan. Children will love customizing these creatures with candies and coconut. Aluminum pan is 13 1/8 x 12 1/8 x 1 1/2 in.
2105-Y-3845 $7.99 each

WICKED WITCH PAN
Invite this not-so-wicked witch to your Halloween bash. This fun-loving lady will bring hardy laughs to the party. Can also turn into other characters. One-mix aluminum pan is 11 3/4 x 13 x 1 3/4 in.
2105-Y-4590 $7.99 each

SCARECROW PAN
Our timid little scarecrow will be happy to join all your autumn celebrations. From Halloween to Thanksgiving, you'll be keeping this little guy busy. Many alternate decorating schemes. One-mix aluminum pan is 15 x 11 1/2 x 1 7/8 in.
2105-Y-801 $7.99 each

BOO GHOST PAN
This giggling ghoul puts his message right up front for your celebration. It's a fun way to add all the extras to a party. Your goblins will love him. One-mix aluminum pan is 14 1/4 x 11 3/4 x 1 7/8 in.
2105-Y-1031 $7.99 each

MINI-PUMPKIN PAN
It's so easy to make little treats for all your favorite goblins. Or create kid-pleasing party cakes year 'round. Even try the fun alternate ideas shown. Each mold of this 12 1/4 x 8 x 1 3/8 in. aluminum pan takes a 1/2 cup of cake batter.
2105-Y-1499 $7.99 each

JACK-O-LANTERN PAN
Carve out this toothless grin for that next Halloween party. It's quick and easy to brighten up your celebration. One-mix aluminum pan is 12 1/4 x 11 5/8 x 2 in.
2105-Y-3068 $7.99 each